Law and the Family in Africa

CHANGE AND CONTINUITY IN AFRICA

MONOGRAPHS UNDER THE AUSPICES OF

THE AFRIKA-STUDIECENTRUM - LEIDEN

MOUTON · THE HAGUE · PARIS

SIMON ROBERTS

Editor

Law and the Family in Africa

MOUTON · THE HAGUE · PARIS

Publications in collaboration with the Afrika-Studiecentrum, Leiden:*

Communications

1. M.L. Daneel: The God of the Matopo Hills. An Essay on the Mwari Cult in Rhodesia. 1970
2. M.L. Daneel: Zionism and Faith-Healing in Rhodesia. Aspects of African Independent Churches. 1970
3. P.M. van Hekken & H.U.E. Thoden van Velzen: Land Scarcity and Rural Inequality in Tanzania. Some Case Studies from Rungwe District. 1972
4. Robert Buijtenhuijs: Mau Mau: Twenty Years After. The Myth and the Survivors. 1973
5. Jan Hoorweg: Protein-Energy Malnutrition and Intellectual Abilities. 1976

Change and Continuity in Africa

1. Robert Buijtenhuijs: Le Mouvement 'Mau-Mau'. Une révolte paysanne et anticoloniale en Afrique noire. 1971
2. M.L. Daneel: Old and New in Southern Shona Independent Churches. Volume I: Background and Rise of the Major Movements. 1971
3. Network Analysis: Studies in Human Interaction. Edited by Jeremy Boissevain and J. Clyde Mitchell. 1973
4. M.L. Daneel: Old and New in Southern Shona Independent Churches. Volume II: Church Growth. Causative Factors and Recruitment Techniques. 1974
5. J.F. Holleman: Issues in African Law. 1974
6. H.L. van der Laan: The Lebanese Traders in Sierra Leone. 1974
7. B.E. Harrell-Bond: Modern Marriage in Sierra Leone. A study of the professional group. 1975
8. Jan Kaayk: Education, Estrangement and Adjustment. A study among pupils and School Leavers in Bukumbi, a Rural Community in Tanzania. 1976
9. Law and the Family in Africa. Edited by Simon Roberts. 1977
10. Jan J. de Wolf: Differentiation and Integration in Western Kenya. A Study of Religious Innovation and Social Change among the Bukusu. 1977

* *The Afrika-Studiecentrum cannot in any way be held responsible for the views or opinions expressed in these books.*

ISBN 90 279 7663 5

Cover design by Jurriaan Schrofer

Printed in the Netherlands

Preface

These essays originated in papers presented at the Seminar 'New Directions in African Family Law' held in Leiden under the auspices of the Afrika-Studiecentrum, 30th September – 4th October, 1974. In the course of that Seminar it was resolved that publication of some of the papers should be attempted, and an Editorial Committee was formed to make a selection and allocate further editorial responsibilities. The members of the Committee were Professor J.H.M. Beattie, The Hon. Mr. Justice Bentsi-Enchill, Mr. G.W. Grootenhuis, Professor J.F. Holleman, Professor A.J. F. Köbben, Professor M.J. Lowy and Mr. R.S. Suttner. The essays published here represent the choice of that Committee, which at the same time invited me to edit them.

This has been a pleasant task, eased by the ready cooperation of the authors and the help generously given by the staff of the Afrika-Studiecentrum. I should particularly mention Miss A. Kuyt who did a great deal; first in connexion with the Seminar, then in helping to prepare this volume. I am also grateful to Mr G.W. Grootenhuis, Secretary-General of the A.S.C., and to Professor J.F. Holleman, for their friendly, wise and unobtrusive guidance. My beloved wife, Marian, read and corrected the proofs and generally helped to see the volume through the press; in this, as in everything else, I could not have managed without her.

There are also two sad matters that must be mentioned. First, shortly after the Seminar, Kwamena Bentsi-Enchill was killed in a motor accident in Ghana. Kwamena had taken an active and important part in the Seminar, and I feel certain he would have written the introduction to this volume had he lived. We remember him as a man of kindness, humour and immense learning; one of the foremost African lawyers of his generation. Those who were with him at the Seminar dedicate this volume to his memory.

Not long after Kwamena's death there was a further blow, when we heard that Raymond Suttner had been imprisoned in South Africa. Raymond had also played a big part at the Seminar; but that was a small matter compared with the very great courage which he subsequently displayed at his trial. Let us hope that the cause for which he spoke on that occasion will soon prevail.

London
1 August 1976

Simon Roberts

Table of contents

Introduction 1

SIMON ROBERTS
London School of Economics

Due in large measure to the accidents of colonial development, most contemporary African states are composed of a variety of indigenous ethnic groups with differing cultures and social organisation. Subsisting beside these groups, and drawn from within them, there are also elites subscribing to values and pursuing life-styles associated with the former colonial presence or assumed in pursuance of some independently adopted ideology. Both of these kinds of pluralism are reflected in, and have implications for, the legal order: the 'legal' institutions of one ethnic group may differ from those of another; and beyond all of them lies the national legal system, introduced during the colonial period and subsequently retained in a modified form. Further, within a given ethnic group discrete sub-systems, with attendant dispute settlement agencies, may be located.[1] Phillips in his *Survey of African Marriage and Family Life* (1953), noted some of the problems inherent in these forms of legal pluralism and identified this as an area demanding intensive research. But even though the next two decades produced at least three major works of African legal anthropology – by Gluckman (1955), Bohannan (1957), and Gulliver (1963) – and numerous writings by lawyers on different aspects of 'family law', rather narrow facets of legal pluralism were adequately considered and the seemingly complementary skills of the respective disciplines were never combined in this research. For this reason the shared interest in problems of pluralism revealed by anthropologists and lawyers at the Seminar 'New Directions in African Family Law' was specially welcome.

Introducing a selection of the papers delivered at that Seminar, I shall try to place them in the context of earlier approaches to pluralism and draw out their implications for future research in this field.

Phillips and Mair confirmed, as Llewellyn and Hoebel (1941) had strikingly demonstrated, that anthropologists and lawyers could work fruitfully together; but in studying marriage and the family in Africa during the 1950's and 1960's members of the respective disciplines worked apart and pursued very different interests. Insofar as anthropologists were concerned with 'law', as distinct from other institutions of social control, they looked at it in the overall context of the social groupings within which it was located. Their basic research strategy was the sustained observation of the regularities of everyday life, and of instances of dispute where these occurred, within a given community. If they were interested in 'rules', it was in how these were invoked and utilized in the context of a dispute by those immediately involved and by third parties. Almost invariably observation was confined to a single ethnic group, or a section of such group. The implication of this focus for the study of legal pluralism was that anthropologists tended to explore the relationship of different dispute settlement agencies *within* a single society, rather than relationships *between* these and adjacent agencies of the national legal system. Thus, for example, in *Social Control in an African Society* (1963), Gulliver principally examined Arusha dispute settlement procedures located in the lineage, the age-set, and the parish. While he recognised the importance of the courts at the lower end of the national legal system, to which Arusha could take disputes where indigenous agencies failed, these were peripheral to his study.

In sharp contrast, lawyers typically did their research within the national legal system, taking legislation and the legal rules derived from decisions of the higher level courts as the subject of investigation. Where they did do research in small-scale indigenous societies, as did the personnel of the Restatement of African Law Project, the objective remained the discovery and systematic organisation of 'rules of customary law', and little attempt was made to set these 'legal' data in context or to acquire a profound understanding of indigenous institutions and procedures. Typically, fieldwork was conducted swiftly and material derived for the most part from rule-centred questioning of informants. Thus, undifferentiated normative data were transformed into legal rules and organized in preconceived legal categories derived from the common law or civil law background of the researcher; where marriage-type relationships were discovered, they were assumed to share key characteristics of civil and common law forms. Consistent with all this, lawyers approached problems of legal pluralism in Africa using the techniques developed under the private international laws of modern western states. Noting differences between the socially approved norms of different ethnic groups, and between the norms of such groups and the national legal system, they sought to resolve the conflicts inherent in this situation by formulating 'choice of law rules' identifying the system of law to be applicable in a given case. This approach contemplated the co-existence of two similar legal systems, whose rules operated in the same way, and made no allowance for the possibly different characters of the systems involved. A solution of this kind, under which a straight choice between different systems is made by referring to a further set of rules provided by statute, has obvious advantages from the point of view of a High Court judge; but it was typically formulated and discussed without reference to the situation on the ground, ignoring the fact that in practice litigants saw themselves free to make their own choice between two systems, and to manipulate different elements of each system as best they could. Because legal draftsmen were remote from the lower levels of the system, where conflicts actually originated, the abstract choice of law rules formulated for inclusion in legislation generally had an air of unreality.

The reasons underlying this wasteful failure to co-operate and the separate pursuit of such contrasting programmes of research have been fully explored elsewhere (e.g., by Twining 1973), but basically they lay in vast differences of training and objective. The anthropologist was primarily interested in *other peoples*' institutions and procedures and was made aware at an early stage that his understanding of these institutions and procedures was liable to distortion by preconceptions acquired in his own society. The background of the lawyer was entirely different. He was trained within, and expected to work as an official of, a specialised sub-system of his own society. Nothing in his training encouraged him to distance himself from this sub-system, and he communicated with fellow lawyers through a specialised language which lay members of his own society found hard to penetrate. Such a background put great difficulties in the way of co-operation with anthropologists, let alone the detached observation of alien systems of social control.

While this work carried out by anthropologists and lawyers in their respective areas of interest undoubtedly touched upon important and complementary aspects of legal pluralism, other facets were neglected. Even taken together, the two bodies of research provided an inadequate data-base upon which policy could be formulated or law reform contemplated. For example, little research was undertaken into the extent to which family structure and marital role behaviour might undergo change in the different sectors of a given society, or as to the way in which changes observed in one sector might be related to those in another. There was also almost no systematic observation of the effects of changes in the national legal system introduced through legislative action. Equally, little was known about how processes of dispute settlement actually worked in those border areas where different legal systems interacted with one another. What strategies did litigants develop when faced with a choice of agency? How far did the courts of the national legal system, particularly at the lower levels, succeed in adapting their procedures to the needs of the communities within which they were located? Did problems arise out of the fact that litigant and judge might hold differing values? Beyond all of these questions lay the need to formulate appropriate methodologies for their investigation.

At the Leiden Seminar there were clear signs that the historical differences in research focus between anthropologist and lawyer were breaking down and that members of both disciplines were showing interest in hitherto inadequately investigated aspects of legal pluralism. As already noted, during the 1950's and 1960's, anthropological interest in legal pluralism was largely confined to investigating the relationship of different dispute settlement agencies *within* a single small-scale society. At the Seminar it was most noticeable that this centre of attention had altered, and that the main focus was upon the relationship *between* institutions of these small indigenous societies and those of the larger nation within which they found themselves. Attention was directed particularly towards dispute settlement agencies operating on the periphery of two systems such as the Local Courts (and their Franco-phonic counterparts). The papers of Lowy, the van Rouveroys, Canter, and Van Binsbergen reflect this interest. Among a minority of the lawyers there was also a significant movement away from the formal analysis of legal rules in favour of an investigation of judicial values. The papers of Kasunmu and Sawyerr illustrate this. A further sign of developing community of interest between anthropologists and lawyers can be found in papers by Pauwels and Roberts which reject the use of concepts drawn from western jurisprudence as aids to comprehension and description of marriage-type relationships in indigenous African societies. But beyond this many of the papers delivered at the Seminar, and much of the discussion that surrounded them, conformed to the traditional lawyerly preoccupation with formal analysis of rules abstracted from decisions of the superior courts.

Any assessment of the relationship between parallel systems of 'family law' must necessarily be preceded by and founded upon an understanding of family structure and the nature of marriage-type relationships prevailing within the different sectors of the society to which the co-existing systems of law are respectively applicable. The acquisition of such an understanding takes on particular importance under conditions of rapid social and economic change. Much too often in the past, particularly among lawyers, critical evaluation of legal rules has proceeded on the assumption, based on evidence of an impressionistic and anecdotal nature, that patterns of marital behaviour observed in the urban areas will be reproduced after a lapse of time in the rural sector. An equally important area of study concerns the relationship between legislative regulation and changes in family structure. While during the last two decades there has been an increasing flow of legislation in the area of family law in many African states, studies of the impact which such legislation has had in rural areas have been rare. The papers of Bleek and Bond/Rijnsdorp are concerned with these questions.

Bleek compares the family structure and marital role behaviour observable among elite groups in Ghana with those of a rural Kwahu grouping, and sets out to test the assumption that '... the new patterns of living adopted by the wealthier residents of the towns are likely to diffuse down to the urban poor and out to the villages'.[2] On the basis of surveys and direct observation he found that certain features of marital behaviour noted among the urban elites were not noticeable in the rural community he observed, and concluded that they were unlikely to be so in the near future. This finding is in itself of great interest, but Bleek's paper does reveal a number of methodological difficulties potentially present in this important area of research. First, the notion of 'diffusion' seems at once too vague and at the same time suggestive of too simple a process to be of much heuristic value where changes taking place within complex institutions like marriage are being observed. There also seems to be an assumption here that the effects of social and economic change will necessarily manifest themselves *in the same way* in both the urban and the rural sector. It is not clear that this need be so. Further, even if matching changes were shown to be present in both sectors, this would not in itself prove that the changes in the rural sector were to do with a process of 'diffusion'. You do not prove the case merely by establishing the 'fit'. This difficulty does not face Bleek directly, as he finds no evidence that a process of diffusion has taken place, but he does not give any indication as to how it could have been dealt with had the need arisen.

Bond and Rijnsdorp take as their starting point the legislative introduction in Sierra Leone of a system of permits granting residential rights to strangers in a given locality. They then go on to demonstrate how the availability of these permits has been exploited by persons indulging in novel, or at least hitherto socially disapproved, forms of cohabitation. It is perhaps necessary to stress that Bond and Rijnsdorp do not show that the piece of legislation *caused* these novel forms of mating. Rather it was exploited by those anxious to avoid certain consequences of these relationships and to accommodate them to prevailing ideas about the movement and residential care of women. What seems of particular significance in this context is that this legislation was put to uses quite outside the contemplation of those framing it. Despite Aubert's early work, studies of the operation of legislation on other than a formal legal level remain rare and this area presents important opportunities for research in both urban and rural settings.

In discussing processes of 'change' both Bleek and Bond/Rijnsdorp face one basic methodological difficulty which neither paper entirely overcomes. Where you try to show that change has or has not taken place in any area, the argument can only be convincing if there is adequate data from an earlier period against which contemporary material can be assessed. In other words, there must be a clear answer to the question: 'Change from what?' Although this is a simple point to state, in practice it seems to involve very serious problems. A single scholar is seldom in the field long enough to observe over time the whole course of the transition in which he is interested. Nor can he be sure of reliable information from other sources as to an earlier state of affairs, because it is probable that nobody then was interested in recording it; or if they were, changes in theoretical orientation and research method make data from the two periods hard to match. As Bleek freely states, an adequate base-line of this kind is absent in his study, and he is obliged to conjecture about an earlier state of Kwahu social organisation. Bond and Rijnsdorp face this difficulty too. While they have acquired data on contemporary mating habits in Sierra Leone from direct observation of people's everyday lives, their need to preface this with a picture of an earlier situation has to be met through idealized statements about approved forms of conduct. These two forms of data are not directly comparable, and the use of normative statements about the past cannot safely be juxtaposed to accounts of actual events in the present. Too many studies of 'law' in small-scale societies slip to and fro between these two dimensions almost unconsciously; great efforts must be made to avoid this fundamental methodological pitfall.

Several of the papers published here contain a reminder that there are other methodological difficulties to be faced in understanding and describing the marriage-type relationships found in different societies. In discussing such relationships both anthropologists and lawyers have relied heavily on concepts drawn from western jurisprudence. Sometimes this borrowing has been explicit, as in the case of Leach's (1955) advocacy of the 'bundle of rights' approach to marriage. In an African context, Kuper (1970) has expressly adopted this method of analysis in his study of the Kgalagari marriage. More often, however, this reliance is not expressly acknowledged, and may not even take place on a conscious level. This can have very serious repercussions because 'marriage' as contemplated under English law and the law of most other modern western societies has some marked characteristics which can certainly not be treated as universal. For example, it is formed on an identifiable occasion, when all the rights potentially associated with it are acquired; it acquires validity through the ceremonial procedures associated with its formation; and it is clearly distinguished in terms of social approval and in terms of legal consequences from less approved forms of mating. Thus, if marriage is approached from this standpoint there are involved assumptions as to the way in which marriage-type relationships come into being, as to the nature and importance of ceremonial procedures associated with formation, as to the manner in which 'rights' are created and transferred in association with formation, and as to a distinction between approved and disapproved forms of mating and their relationship to one another. The unconscious adoption of these starting-points involves bypassing a vital question as to whether mating relationships in a society under investigation can accurately be seen through the categories of western jurisprudence. Several papers delivered at the Seminar and published here draw attention to these problems.

Repeatedly, lawyers particularly, have come back to such questions as: 'At what point in time does marriage come into being in society X?' 'What ceremonial procedures are essential to its formation?' Yet there is now a growing body of data indicating that these questions are inappropriate. First, in many African societies 'marriage' does not come into being on some clearly defined occasion, but is formed slowly over time (e.g., Evans-Pritchard 1951; Kuper 1970). The papers of Bleek and Roberts demonstrate that this is also the case with the Kwahu and Kgatla respectively. This characteristic in itself makes marriage formation in these societies difficult to analyse in western categories. Secondly, as Roberts shows, the formation of marriage is not necessarily linked essentially to any ceremonial procedure and may take place in the absence of formalities, notwithstanding the fact that informants may make normative statements linking formation with given ceremonial observance. In this context Pauwels' insistence that the concept of 'nullity' has very specialized origins in western ecclesiastical jurisprudence, and is not necessarily found at all in African societies, is of importance.

There is also a tendency to overlook the fact that the distinction between 'marriage' and less approved forms of mating, strongly entrenched in our own system, need not be duplicated elsewhere. The papers of Lowy, Bleek, Bond/Rijnsdorp, and Roberts suggest that it is unsafe to assume that in all societies a rigid distinction is drawn between approved and disapproved forms of mating. Even where such a distinction is important, there may be a continuum running from most approved to least approved with a very hazy area in the middle of the band. In this context an observation made by both Lowy and Bond/Rijnsdorp is of great interest. They note that under certain circumstances in Ghana and Sierra Leone *neither* party to a mating relationship need have any interest in having it treated as marriage, and sometimes this status will be seen as disadvantageous by both. All of this comes back to the simple point that great care must be taken by the researcher not to invest the form of mating he observes with inappropriate and possibly seriously distorting elements of his own values.

Against this background the major interest of the Seminar was in the way that disputes are handled in the context of plural legal systems. Here two distinct but complementary lines of research were followed, both illustrated in the papers published here. First, there is what Lowy terms 'the litigant's perspective', under which the main focus of research is upon the way litigants handle instances of dispute in which they become involved. It embraces both wider strategic questions (such as the choice of remedy agent) and narrower tactical issues (such as the handling of argument before a particular agent). Contrasted with this approach is one under which the centre of attention is the dispute settlement agency itself. Here the research is concerned with the performance of different agencies in a plural context, and such matters as the compatibility of values held by judicial personnel with those current in the community that the court is designed to serve.

It is implicit in what has already been said that dispute settlement processes have been examined almost invariably from the standpoint of the legal specialist and that the litigant's perspective has generally been neglected. This neglect has particularly serious implications where an element of choice is present through the availability to the litigant of agencies located in different legal systems. The significance which this element of choice has, and the purposes to which it may be put in litigation, can only be understood if the processes are considered from the angle of disputants using the system. This point is brought home in Lowy's paper, 'Establishing paternity and demanding child support in a Ghanaian town'. There he considers how litigants view different dispute settlement agencies available to them in the handling of paternity cases, assesses factors governing choice between them, and describes strategies followed before different agencies. The agencies he observes (supernatural agencies, 'traditional' informal agencies of conciliation *(Afiesem)*, the Reconciliation Committee, and the Magistrate's Court) cover a wide spectrum and include those located at the lower levels of the national legal system. A significant observation concerns the heavy psychological costs associated with attendance at the Magistrate's Court with its formal procedures reminiscent of those of the common law. Van Binsbergen's paper, 'Law in the context of Nkoya society', shares the same approach with its examination of the different dispute settlement agencies available to members of a rural Nkoya community in Zambia. A comparison of the business handled by the Local Court (the lowest level agency in the national legal system) with that of indigenous Nkoya agencies indicates that different types of dispute are taken to each and that distinct purposes underlie this differential use. Although they do not dwell upon this conclusion themselves, it is equally clear from the van Rouveroys' paper, 'To claim or not to claim', that the Anufom people of Northern Togo resort to indigenous agencies and the lower level courts of the national legal system with quite different objectives. These studies, the emphasis of which owes much to Turner's work among the Ndembu (1957) and Gulliver's among the Arusha (1963), assume great importance where the relationship of parallel agencies located in plural systems has to be examined. Perhaps the most serious problem revealed by the papers published here is the difficulty of obtaining data of equal depth and richness in respect of each of the agencies involved.

Complementary to this approach is one under which the behaviour and values of third parties involved in resolving the dispute is the main subject of investigation. In the papers presented at the Seminar, research of this type was focused principally on two questions: 'how far were agencies at the lower levels of a national legal system proving successful in handling family disputes in the communities they served?'; and 'How did the alien values of members of the higher judiciary affect their handling of family disputes with 'customary law' elements?'. Canter is concerned with the first of these two questions in his paper dealing with the treatment of family disputes by a single Local Court in Zambia. Taking all the family disputes heard by the Court within a given period, he finds that (with very limited exceptions) the Court refrains from making any order which does not enjoy the support and approval of kinsmen of the parties immediately concerned; in particular, he notes that a divorce is not granted unless this solution is positively supported by the kinsmen. On the basis of these observations he concludes that this newly established agency has succeeded (through sensitivity to indigenous values and procedures) in adapting itself well to the needs of the local community. While this study is convincing to a point, and its findings certainly reassuring, the conclusion that the Court has succeeded in meeting the needs of the local community may represent an over-simplification. First, the Court seems to do no more than affix a rubber-stamp to what has been resolved at a lower level. The achievement is wholly negative in the sense that it does no more than bolster up the lower level agencies, contributing nothing to problems they have been unable to resolve. These very limited objectives perhaps go some way towards explaining how this Court manages to combine acceptability in the local community concerned with retention of the ceremonial and procedural features of an English court of law ('Out of the box.' 'Do you plead guilty or not guilty?' etc.). The 'success' of the Court (given the retention of these features) is curious at first sight, and it may well be that its legitimacy would have been brought more closely into question had it adopted a more positive and independent role. Perhaps also Canter concentrates his attention on too narrow a segment of each dispute for us to obtain a clear picture of the Court's function. Focussing exclusively on case histories as revealed in the proceedings of the Local Court, he does not fix the Court in the context of the overall life of the community it serves. We do not know what prompts people to go to it, and what kind of disputes are dealt with at home. In this respect Canter and Van Binsbergen dwell on complementary and equally necessary parts of the same picture. The van Rouveroys' paper addresses a similar dimension when it reveals the very different ways in which an indigenous Anufo agency and the lowest level court in the Togo legal system tackle the same type of marriage dispute. In many of the former British and French African territories, the dispute settlement agencies on the periphery of the national legal system and of small indigenous communities have undergone modification since independence, and many more studies of the parallel operation of these agencies are necessary.

No less important is the performance of the superior courts at the apex of the hierarchy. Although this is an area which lawyers have studied extensively, most attention has been given to the formal 'choice of law' rules derived from judgments in disputes perceived by the court to contain a 'customary law' element. The papers of Sawyerr and Kasunmu constitute a valuable departure from this tradition. Sawyerr, studying decisions of the higher judiciary in East Africa during the colonial period in matters involving a conflict of law, concludes that most such decisions were sharply affected by the predominantly western, Christian values of the judges concerned. It is certainly possible to sympathise with Sawyerr's critical stance in the light of these findings, as many of the decisions were grossly at variance with the values adhered to in the communities to which the litigants concerned belonged. But the finding is not surprising. As has been noted, English-trained lawyers are creatures of a very specialized sub-system of English society, totally unequipped in their training and canons of conduct to distance themselves from their own values. Kasunmu raises a point similar to Sawyerr's when he observes that contemporary Nigerian judges fail to achieve 'specifically Nigerian solutions' in dealing with maintenance claims in matrimonial proceedings. Again this failure should not surprise us as these judges are typically men with a firm common law background, who broadly subscribe to western values both in the court room and outside in their personal life-styles. Typically also many of the litigants who come before these judges in matrimonial proceedings will be members of the same urban elite, with values remote from those adhered to in a rural Nigerian community. But this fact does not reduce the difficulty of the problem which Kasunmu raises. In contemporary Nigeria, as elsewhere in Africa, there is constant physical movement between the urban and rural areas and kinship ties link the member of an urban elite to the rural peasant. Thus, for example, where the senior civil servant is called upon to pay maintenance on the divorce of his wife, the court must take into account the possibility of burdens imposed upon him as a consequence of his membership of some rural grouping, in the same way that it must consider the wife's links with kinsmen in the rural sector. The two sectors constitute interacting fields, rather than discrete compartments. We shall return to the problems which this poses for the legal system in some concluding remarks.

Alongside these diverse interests, a majority of the lawyers presenting papers at the Seminar adopted a more conventional approach to legal pluralism, confining themselves to the formal analysis of substantive law. Of those published here, Achike examines the formation and dissolution of marriage under the various legal systems in Nigeria, Daniels considers different notions of legitimacy in the same state, and Poulter explores choice of law problems in Lesotho. While this approach to legal pluralism constitutes a necessary part of the day-to-day running of a legal system, and is in a sense complementary to those already considered, it has two drawbacks in the context of an inter-disciplinary Seminar. First, although the level of analysis is not wholly internal, in that the discussion and criticism of rules is to some extent linked to social objectives, the values upon which the criticism is based are generally not explicit and the social context in which the rules operate is seldom itself the subject of more than perfunctory investigation. Secondly, because the mode of analysis is parochial, in that it '... identifies, organises and criticises the rules by means of criteria proper to the legal system' (Abel 1972), it cannot provide a viable basis for communication with those (such as anthropologists) who are not fellow specialists within the system. Before a satisfactory dialogue can be possible, more lawyers must be prepared to supplement this mode of analysis with others more suitable to the purposes of inter-disciplinary contact.

Given these widely different research goals embraced within the general field of legal pluralism, the problem of formulating an adequate methodology for each should be referred to. Such reference is made imperative by virtue of the fact that on several occasions prior to the Seminar the very extensive use currently made in legal anthropology of case histories of disputes had received criticism (e.g., Gluckman 1973; Holleman 1973), and these doubts were raised again in the course of the Seminar. The arguments that can surround the merits of different research strategies are interminable, and there is no room to enter into them here. Nevertheless some short and (hopefully) clarificatory remarks will be attempted. First, we should all be able to agree with Gluckman (1973) that any properly rounded investigation of the ways members of a society contrive to live a relatively ordered life and handle conflict where it arises must involve the co-ordinated treatment of at least three dimensions: the regularities observable in everyday life; stated normative prescriptions ('rules'); and instances of dispute. Beyond that, any argument as to the suitability of a particular methodology can only be valuable in the light of a specific research goal (i.e., 'Given what I am trying to study, what is the best way of going about it?').

All of the papers published here, except those of Bleek and Bond, rely heavily on case histories of disputes. Such reliance would have been inappropriate in these two papers which were necessarily dependent on careful observation of the regularities of everyday life in the communities concerned. All the remaining papers had to do with some aspect of the dispute settlement process; hence the use of case histories seems justified. But it is worth noting at this point the very varied uses made of case data in the different papers published here. These uses include: the ascertainment of rules in the narrow 'legal' sense (Achike, Daniels, Poulter); the understanding of indigenous categories and modes of argument (Pauwels, Roberts); the investigation of judicial values (Kasunmu, Sawyerr); judicial behaviour (Canter, van Rouveroy) and litigant strategies (Lowy); and the observation of on-going social processes within a group insofar as these are affected by conflict (Van Binsbergen). There may, of course, be argument as to whether the depth and range of case data used in each instance is exactly appropriate, and the overall picture obtained will undoubtedly depend on the particular 'slice' of the dispute severed for observation. As van Binsbergen points out in his conclusion, the results will be very different depending on whether '... one concentrates on formal court cases as the unit of study' or on the ongoing social process '... taking as one's unit of study such social conflicts as arise, and tracing the social processes through which these conflicts are brought to an end' (at p. 67). For the most part the case data used in the various papers seem adequate for the purposes to which the different authors put them. Whether or not that is so, it is important to keep criticism of research goals, and criticism of the methods used in attaining those goals, distinct.

As these papers show, one reason why case histories of disputes are so often utilized in research is the versatility of the information which they yield. Perhaps it is sometimes forgotten that careful observation of disputes can provide much important material that is not solely related to conflict at all. In many societies it is only in the context of a dispute that people express themselves explicitly about the values of their society and its socially accepted norms as they see them. Thus, utterances in the course of litigation may provide valuable insights into values and meanings underlying the regularities observable in everyday life. Certainly, as Nader and Yngvesson recently pointed out (1973), there are some very important questions which case histories of disputes cannot help us to answer. Among these are such questions as: 'Why do people obey laws?'; 'How are people socialized?' It may well be that we should pay more attention to these questions.

Despite the title given to the Leiden Seminar by its organizers, little discussion directly about law reform or legal development took place, nor was this subject explicitly dealt with in the papers presented. The

Seminar turned out to be 'about' research, and the papers included here provide a fair guide to the kinds of research presently being underaken in this field. Nonetheless two general conclusions of importance for law reformers were implicit in the papers and discussions at the Seminar. First, given the plural nature of any contemporary African state – plural in each of the senses identified at the beginning of this introduction – no one legal system is at any given moment going to hold total legitimacy for all members of the state, and the over-arching national legal system must be accommodated to this fact. Just as important as this, in many situations (perhaps in most as time goes on) no one system will provide a total solution even in respect of the individual transaction or instance of conflict. 'Mixed' elements, in other words, will increasingly be present in matters relating to marriage and the family. The implication here is that the traditional 'choice of law' approach, under which in a given situation one system of law is mechanically selected as being applicable rather than the remainder, must be given greater flexibility. In dispute settlement this flexibility must go both to the *selection* of criteria invoked, and to the manner in which these criteria are *used*. On the latter point, judges in the higher level courts have assumed for too long that 'rules of customary law' can be applied in the manner characteristic of 'rules' under common law and civil law systems.

The second general conclusion has to do with the fact that law reform is something talked about and carried through by members of an urban elite, lawyers in particular. A lesson repeatedly brought home in the course of the Seminar was that lawyers typically have a rather limited and one-sided view, both of the 'problems' to be dealt with and of the possible consequences of legislative action. Here the value of the anthropologist's field of vision, directed at the lower levels and often corrected to the 'litigant's perspective', must receive wider recognition.[3]

NOTES

1. I am aware that the use of the term 'pluralism' in this further sense does not accord with the more restricted meaning sometimes given to the word elsewhere (e.g. by Smith and Kuper, *Pluralism in Africa*).
2. Caldwell, *Population growth and family change in Africa: the new urban elite in Ghana*, p. 184.
3. An earlier draft of this Introduction was read by J.L. Comaroff, G.W. Grootenhuis, J.F. Holleman, and W. Van Binsbergen. I have drawn freely on their critical suggestions and ideas, but they are in no way responsible for the defects of the ultimate result.

Establishing paternity and demanding child support in a Ghanaian town* 2

MICHAEL J. LOWY
University of Pittsburgh

Families are perpetuated by the socially approved accumulation of new members. If personal and family interests completely overlapped, and material and non-material resources were equally distributed amongst families in society, strategies for insuring the establishment of paternity and continued maintenance of children would be insignificant. However, in Koforidua as elsewhere, parents in dispute use available remedy agents to pursue their divergent interests.

In the first section of this paper I will point out the socio-cultural contexts in which paternity and child maintenance disputes arise. Next I will briefly describe the important features of the available conflict management agents, and the frequency with which these family law cases come to their attention. In the third section two extended cases which I witnessed during a one month observation period of the Koforidua Magistrates Court Grade Two are considered in detail. The discussion section highlights the potential social consequences of litigants' incentives and constraints in the management of paternity and child support cases.

* The data was collected during thirteen month's residence in Koforidua in 1968–1969. Methods and research design are discussed in some detail in Lowy (1974). The research was supported by a National Institute of Mental Health Predoctoral Fellowship and Dissertation Field Grant. The work was carried out under the auspices of the Faculty of Law, University of Ghana. Some of this paper was written during my tenure as a Fellow in Law and Modernization at the Yale Law School 1973–1974. I would like to thank Wolf Bleek and Simon Roberts for their editorial suggestions.

THE CONTEXT OF PATERNITY DISPUTES

The commercial and administrative town of Koforidua had a population of about 40,000 in 1968–1969. Approximately seventy percent of adults (aged 15 or more) have known the joys and sorrows of a long term heterosexual union. Although the percentage of parents in the population could not be accurately determined, at the time of the census more than sixty percent of all households included a parent and offspring. Considering the shifting composition of these units, it seems reasonable to assume that close to seventy percent of the adult population have produced offspring. Despite the diversity of the population ethnically, educationally, and occupationally, they share a number of basic expectations associated with the birth and future care of children.[1] These expectations which reflect variable interests form the basis of disputes. However, the incidence of these conflicts which involve a third party in their management is far from random. In fact, male civil servants, including the police and armed forces are present as defendants in these cases almost five times more often then their proportion in the population. Along with businessmen and lorry drivers, who taken together represent most defendants, they form part of a growing section of Ghanaian society. Among the characteristics of this segment are relative mobility, good education, and the receipt of reliable fixed income. The urban residence of these men, whose life style is often highly valued, places children in their custody at a socioeconomic advantage. These men are also vulnerable to threatened attachment of salary and public scrutiny of their integrity.

Before examining case material involving these defendants we must briefly consider the basic features of marriage and mating relations among ethnic groups in Koforidua. Despite the many social forces which favour individualism, and although individuals exercise final choice in mate selection, arranged marriage is not uncommon and the marriage relationship is cast in the idiom of an alliance between two families. Friends often encourage a marriage to a member of their family. In the face of increasing heterogeneity and mobility of the population, elders still try to investigate the family background of their children's prospective mates. Inter-ethnic marriage presents more than the usual strains on the husband-wife tie, but is not categorically discouraged. Although some patterns ideally produce children able to inherit from both parents or neither, in the former case the children may inherit from the family with which it has maintained the closest ties, and in the latter the husband may make a pre-marriage declaration to support the children and alienate enough self-acquired property to remove the spectre of disenfranchisement.

Finances of spouses are generally kept separate; although a wife often demands an initial lump sum to be used for trading, she may be expected to feed her children from the proceeds. Men are expected to help support their wives and contribute toward their own children's maintenance. The presence of a child by a previous mate adds strain to a new marriage relationship. Men are expected to assume responsibility for their own children's education. Besides other gifts, they give each school-aged offspring a 'Christmas Box', money for fees and/or school uniforms. The extent of a father's support of his offspring's education beyond Middle School is an indication of his sound economic position and the affection he feels toward his wife and her family. He is also subject to similar demands from his sisters in favor of their children. Matrilineal Akans find it difficult to deny this demand.

Men aspire to plural marriage. As the Magistrate of Koforidua's Magistrates Court Grade II put it, 'if you go to marry two, you must speak with two mouths'. The status of co-wife is referred to by the same word used to describe female jealousy (*Kora*). Gifts and attention must be shared equally if peace is to prevail. Men try to maintain such wives in different towns or in different compounds in the same town. These arrangements are costly and therefore, infrequent.

If a young man sees a woman he thinks might make a good wife, he seeks out an intermediary, a friend or close relative of the girl. He will announce his intentions and send her a gift through the mutual aquaintance. If the woman accepts the gift, the two might begin to meet. If the man wants to marry her, he will announce his intentions to an elder who will see the girl's parents and arrange a time for the boy to perform the 'knocking' ceremony.[2] The man's father should help him pay the 'head rum' at this time, which may include one large bottle of schnapps and one to two pounds (two to four dollars).[3] After these payments the boy is officially 'known' to the girl's family and can co-habit with her without paying damages. However, if further ceremonies (*Ayefo*) are not performed for the girl's family (i.e., mother, mother's brother, etc.), then subsequent gifts which the man may give to the woman do not return to him upon divorce. It is becoming more common in Koforidua for women and their families to avoid receiving these additional marriage payments. The increasing cost has also made the completion of the ceremony prohibitively expensive. In this way, a woman can expect financial support from the man for herself and children, and upon separation, which is frequent and anticipated, she may keep all gifts received from him since the man has never *truly* married her, i.e., concluded the payments to her family. Prestige which may have accrued from making these payments in the past is often no longer of primary importance. Many women are married just through knocking fee; others are lived with in *Mpena* ('friendship', i.e., regular cohabitation without paying the knocking fee). However, it should be pointed out that any long term 'marriage-like' relationship from which children have been born is treated like true marriage by the magistrate in court.[4]

If the couple agree, the man may perform *Ayefo* which includes *Akonta Seken* (brother-in-law's cutlass), a payment to the wife's brother. Adult men remember when such payments were forty cents. Eighty cents is now considered appropriate. One informant said 'two to forty dollars' was appropriate. A younger man, hearing that statement, was quick to add that the payment to the brother-in-law is usually not that high but is a measure of the love a man has for the woman. Another payment of eighty cents to four dollars should be given to the wife's mother. Besides these payments, the man should provide the woman's family with schnapps (gin), one leaf of tobacco *(Tawaboh)*, one enamel pan of salt, and a money gift in addition. In order to complete a customary marriage a man must contemplate a minumum cash outlay of about twenty dollars.

If the man and woman begin to co-habit and the woman becomes pregnant before her parents are formally informed of the relationship, the man is liable for an additional payment – *Onyame Dwane* – for 'stealing' the girl. Present adults remember when this customary pacification necessitated the slaughter of a sheep. Nowadays estimates of reasonable fees range from $ 8.00 to twice that amount. If the man accepts the paternity of the child and he maintains the girl during the pregnancy, the payment for 'stealing' may be overlooked by the girl's father. Despite social class diversity the following example reflects the flexibility of non-elite marriage ceremonies in Koforidua:

One Sunday morning in December, 1968, I was asked to accompany a friend to *Bo Opun* (knock the door). He had been living with the woman for over one year, and she was pregnant. The night before the ceremony he said he had bought one full bottle of schnapps and was giving one guinea ($ 2.10) for 'knocking' or 'head rum'. He complained that the girl's father might ask $ 20.00 for *Onyame Dwane*. Mr. A., the 'groom', thought her father would accept three or four guineas if he begged. On Thursday we went to ask the seventy-six-year-old best friend of Mr. A. 's deceased grandfather to accompany him to perform the custom. The old man, Opanin K., agreed.

The morning of the ceremony before 8:00 a.m., Mr. A., his deceased father's brother, another friend, and I brought the bottle of schnapps and money to the old man. Together, dressed in fine cloths, we approached the 'bride's' compound. She and her mother greeted us at the entrance and placed chairs under a comfortable shade tree. Five more chairs were placed to complete a semi-circle. The girl and her mother retired to the kitchen area with other women and took no part in the ceremony. The girl's father, his nephew, two sons, and a friend faced us. The 'linguist' (representative) for the girl's parents was the nephew. We were greeted and asked our business. Opanin K., who was a friend of the girl's father, said we had come for his daughter. He produced the bottle of schnapps which had been wrapped in paper and put one guinea on top of it. The linguist accepted it. The father then asked about the damages for stealing the girl. He wanted $ 8.00 compensation. The old man begged that it was too much. The girl's father *Dashed* us one guinea. Three guineas ($ 6.30) were then given to the linguist. We all thanked the father and the family. They thanked us with drink. We shared half of the bottle of schnapps. We rose together and left – Mr. A.'s wife followed. The entire performance lasted twenty-five minutes.

Fathers in Koforidua are likely to be satisfied if the men who impregnate their daughters perform a ceremony similar to the one just described. For example, one relatively wealthy informant was pursuing a Court case against a man who impregnated his daughter and was not maintaining her during pregnancy. The defendant had never come to perform the ceremony. I asked the girl's father: 'Would you have been satisfied if the boy just paid "knocking fee?"'

Answer: I would have been satisfied ... the men no longer have money ... but there are more women walking about. If they come 'knock' we thank God. Even today my son took a girl to Ashanti.

Question: What do you mean?

Answer: He went to the girl's father's house and told him he wanted the girl to see his house in Ashanti, and they just left ... no fee, no schnapps, nothing! Fathers nowadays are just happy if you look after the girl. The women are too many. Even one of my friends wants me to marry his daughter ... he said if the girl agrees I could just take her ... (however) if you don't support her she will leave at once.

When pregnancy results from a relationship of cohabitation, the genitor is notified and is expected to acknowledge paternity. Initiation of disputes at this point is exceptional. Most men are quite pleased to learn of their impending fatherhood. For those who are not, immediate denial of paternity is often avoided since the pregnancy may be terminated, the potential for naming another genitor exists, and expenses for pre-natal care have not yet begun to mount. Physical or mental health problems during pregnancy lead to the use of hospitals and shrines. These expenses and the growing demand for hospital delivery[5] are likewise the ultimate financial responsibility of the genitor. Men finding themselves responsible for unwanted pregnancies arising from casual relationships suspect women of exaggerating health problems at this time in order to elicit financial aid – a symbol of acknowledged paternity. The symbolic nature of maintenance payments can work the other way, as when women who bear children by men from patrilineal tribes refuse to accept maintenance until the man has customarily married them or named the child. (see below).

Soon after the birth of a healthy baby the genitor is expected to name his child at a ritual 'outdooring' *(abadinto)*. Marital status and social class more than ethnicity account for the variations in such ceremonies. If the man has not previously married the woman or informed her family of their relationship, a more lavish 'outdooring' can 'cool the anger' of the woman's family. If he fails, or refuses paternity at this time, the woman or her family is likely to initiate a case *(Asem)* for *Kwasia Buo* (fooling). The outdooring provides an opportunity to accomplish a number of important tasks. The child's spiritual and physical health is believed to be associated with the public recognition, acceptance, and naming by its father. The genitor is given a chance to provide the mother with the necessary items of child care: soap, towels, pans, and toilet articles. In addition, he is expected to furnish the woman with cloth for her first public appearance after the birth. The expected cash contribution is used by the woman's family for the expenses they incurred on their daughter during her pregnancy, and excess is said to go for the future benefit of the child. The symbolic value attached to the cash contributions is very important. The amount of money reflects the genitor's pleasure with the woman, the birth of their child, and the woman's family. The following examples recorded at 'outdoorings' demonstrate the basic similarities of the event among divergent ethnic groups.

(i) The third child of a wealthy Ashanti carpenter and cocoa farmer was named by his paternal grandfather. After giving them his advice, he invited the thirty adults present to offer theirs. The following proscriptions for happy marriage were offered by two elder men in the wife's family:

1) If there is ever any case with the wife, settle it in the room and don't let it get outside for all to see and hear;

2) Since women are moody and unpredictable and troublesome, the man has to overlook the problems;

3) If trouble arises which cannot be settled with the wife alone, he should go to her father, just as she should go to the husband's father if any difficulty arises;

4) Husbands never like to be called 'foolish' by their wives, because they do not like the truth told to them. A man is foolish to take on the troubles of a wife

He has to provide for her and worry about her.

A female friend of the wife advised the husband:

1) Women can only have one husband, but men like to take more than one wife.

2) Before they take more wives, they should be sure the first wife is happy and pay her compensation.

After the speeches, relatives and friends began giving cash gifts which were recorded in a book. The audience, by now over fifty, listened as each person's name and donation was read aloud. The husband gave ten guineas (£ 10 10s., i.e., thirty dollars).

(ii) A similar procedure was followed at an Ewe 'outdooring' at which a hospital labourer presented his daughter with four dollars and forty cents. Male friends, including an Ashanti co-worker and approximately fifteen members of his ethnic association, donated one dollar and five cents. Each female present donated twenty cents. The approximate total of thirty dollars was more than double the outlay for drinks served to the guests.

(iii) The presents were lavish at a ceremony for the first child (a girl) born to a Yoruba university student and his wife, the daughter of an Ashanti subchief. The husband's father's brother described the presentation in this way:

> Immediately after the prayers, the relatives of the man presented to the girl who was their daughter-in-law thirty-five pieces of dumas cloth, toilettes of different kinds and sizes – powder, pomade, lavender soap, twelve different sizes of towels, pillows, bed sheets, pillow cases, blankets, buckets, basins, trinkets for both the child and the woman, a mat, and an amount of $ 42.00.

The money came mostly from the man's paternal grandfather and eldest paternal uncle. After the ceremony, the student's friends came to eat and dance to 'soul music'.

Judging from case records examined at the Welfare Department's Reconcilliation Committee (which administers the Maintenance of Children Act 1965) a woman and her family may spend a great deal of time and effort to convince a man to accept economic responsibility for his child. Ambiguous situations persist for many years, while men employ delaying tactics: waiting until the end of cocoa harvest, finishing their education or returning from a long trip. Renewed demands for accepting paternity and support often closely follow a request for educational advancement from a child, subsequent plans for marriage of either party, or financial crisis. In addition to the situations already noted, claims for paternity and child support frequently occur in two other contexts: during an action for divorce, to insure a father's continued support; and at the time of the genitor's death when the children's interest in his estate is denied or curtailed by the legal successor.

The factors reponsible for growing tension in the marriage relationship in Ghana have already been identified (McCall 1956; Lystad 1958) – the economic burden of children, the increasing reluctance of women to take the traditional role under the husband's authority and, among Akans, the growing reluctance of uncles and fathers to accept responsibilities for 'training' of children.

In Koforidua, casual sexual encounters begin shortly after puberty. Mature women regard pregnancy as a desired state, and are eager to prove their child-bearing capabilities to avoid abuse from other women, such as charges of witchcraft. Strong informal pressure by family and friends is placed upon a woman pursuing higher education to stop and produce children.[6] Accompanying this emphasis on child-bearing for women, in recent years (at least since the end of World War I and with increasing force since the end of World War II) has been the increased mobility and independence of women through trading. Women have learned that the income from trading can remove them from the authority of men – fathers and husbands – and provide them with the security and sociability of other women. Women increasingly prefer to trade and 'see the world', instead of tilling their husband's farms in the bush. There is evidence to support the contention that many women are as much against the idea of marriage as men.

Men are interested in 'keeping' (living) with women of proven procreative ability, but are reluctant to support another man's child. 'Educated', and upwardly socially mobile men are likewise disinterested in marriage. There are few benefits and many liabilities. The positive aspects of marriage are found in *Mpena* (friendship) without the liabilities. A friend can be counted upon to cook and occasionally supply financial assistance while a man is 'fighting' for a secure economic future. In addition, *Mpena* provide the sexual and psychological satisfaction which comes from a marriage. The woman in this relationship is constantly seeking 'gifts' from her friend – in *Mpena*, unlike marriage, all gifts are non-refundable should there be a split. In marriage, if a divorce occurs and the woman is at fault, all gifts which a man has made her throughout the life of the marriage must be returned. A frequent pattern is for a woman to help support a man through his education or until he achieves a good position in life and, at the end of that time, to expect the man to marry her and give her and her children economic security. Needless to say, in the highly mobile and fluid situation of town life for the socially upwardly mobile man, this ideal is seldom realized. Transfers, promotions, and trading have increased the frequency and duration of separation between partners.[7]

In this type of social situation, the *Mpena* relationship is suited to both men and women. However, someone must support the children of such unions. This increasingly more expensive duty falls upon the woman's father, brother, or mother's brother – if he can be made to accept it. The genitor of the child may complain that this state of affairs is made necessary because the older men and the families are asking too much *Nsa* (drink) for their daughters in marriage. They prefer to be casual friends or just pay the knocking fee. Older men rebutt this point of view (see page 20). The young men are, of course, constantly pressed by their sisters and sisters' children for money. Also, they reason, it is useless to spend money on a woman in marriage if the expectation is that divorce is likely. According to cases reported at the Department of Social Welfare, women's desire to leave the farm and go to trade is one of the primary reasons for divorce. Men equate trading with casual prostitution. In the following section, I will briefly describe remedy agents which can be used by litigants pursuing their interests in paternity and child maintenance cases.

DESCRIPTION OF REMEDY AGENTS[8]

Four categories of remedy agents are used to manage interpersonal conflict: Court, Quasi-judicial, Home, and Supernatural. The description of each remedy agent will include its source of power and jurisdiction, accessibility or likelihood of public exposure in its use, economic and psychological cost, and its effectiveness.

Court

The Koforidua Magisterial District (1960 population of 54,000) as well as the law administered in it are established by statute. The court can hear cases involving contract, tort, ownership, possession, or occupation of land where the amount of claim does not exceed $ 360.00. Additionally it has jurisdiction over civil matters between landlord and tenant, as well as family law matters such as divorce, and succession to property where the applicable law is customary. During the 21 months preceding observation, less than one percent of the civil cases heard concerned paternity or child maintenance.

The agency's location is well known and accessible to the general public so that litigants anticipate public scrutiny. Court personnel are available 8:00 a.m. to 5:00 p.m., Monday to Friday, and hear cases from 9:30 a.m. to 3:00 p.m. A civil case is initiated through the court registrar, after paying fees based upon the amount of claim and the number and location of witnesses.

The staff of the court are usually younger and more well educated than the parties to disputes. Their ethnically heterogeneous composition, scanty knowledge of several widely spoken languages, and their formal dress and manners provide a psychic cost to many litigants both difficult to measure and impossible to ignore. The differences between lawyers, prosecutors, and magistrate and the litigants are even more striking. The swift airing of their case (average time 12 minutes), the magistrate's overt concern with efficiency, the restrictions upon non-legally relevant discussion, the deference demanded and shown to the court personnel, and the intimidating arrangement of court room space and written records all combine to impose heavy psychological costs upon the user of this agency.

The effectiveness of a remedy agent in managing a dispute can be measured in many ways. Three measures applicable to short range post-hearing results are: appeal, compliance with the decision, and the continued willingness of the parties to greet one another publicly. Only one civil case in a sample of 198 was appealed, and only twenty-two percent of 46 parties intensively investigated said they were paid in full or complied with the order of the court. Seventeen percent of the 46 parties said they would greet the other, or continue the relationship out of which the case arose.

Quasi-judicial

Under the provisions of the Maintenance of Children Act, 1965, the Reconciliation Committee can hear cases,

> ... where a father neglects to provide reasonable maintenance for his infant child or when a man alleged to be the father denies that he is the father of the child, the mother of the child may apply to ... persuade the father to make reasonable provision for the maintenance of the child ...

This reasonable provision cannot exceed $ 10 per month. A father may also petition the Committee to give him custody of the child. An order may not extend after a child has reached the age of seventeen or has died. Payments may be extended until age twenty-one if the child is continuing a course of study.

In the first two complete years of operation (1965, 1966) 112 complaints were made from Koforidua; seventy-four percent for non-maintenance, three percent by women asking for a man to be declared the father of their child, nine percent by men asking for the custody of their child, and fourteen percent miscellaneous.

The hearing room is situated at the offices of the Department of Social Welfare and Community Development away from the commercial heart of the town. The record storage room where hearings are conducted is relatively private. The Welfare Department can receive complaints from 9:00 a.m. to about 4:00 p.m., with a rest break between 12:00 to 2:00. Hearings are held on Fridays beginning at 10:00 a.m. although the officer in charge has set an informal limit of eight cases per day, no more than four were heard during the period of observation. There is no fee for filing complaints, and funds are allocated to pay the transportation of any witnesses called.

After receiving a complaint, the officer in charge of the case prepares an invitation to attend the hearing. About seventy-five percent of the complaints reach the hearing stage. If a party fails to attend the hearing, the officer cannot force the complainant to take court action. However, he can send an explanatory letter to the man's employer and/or help the complainant prepare a court summons and, if necessary, act as witness.

The non-professional members of the Reconciliation Committee are chosen from among prominent men and women in town, and serve without pay. Three civil service officers handled maintenance cases, two men and one woman. Their social characteristics were very similar to the members of the court staff. The non-professional members were older, wealthier, and less well educated than the civil servants. Unlike the court, grievances are more completely aired (average hearing, 50 minutes). Spatial arrangements are less intimidating and signs of respect for authority in dress and manners are generally absent.

Hearings are frequently conducted in Twi, and none of the participants are sworn. Questioning is quiet and unhurried and the decision is overtly achieved through consensus of the parties. During the hearing members of the Committee constantly stress the welfare of the child. They want each child to have the opportunity for 'advancement', preferably in a large town in custody of the parent who can provide the best education.

At the conclusion of the few hearings at the Welfare Department that I witnessed, the parties seemed relaxed and in good spirits. Since intensive interviews of litigants were not conducted, my assessment of the effectiveness of the agency is measured by the percentage of those who complied with the orders of the Committee, and the number of appeals taken from the decision or enforcement of non-compliance with the order.

Out of seventy-eight cases heard in 1966, over seventy percent of the male defendants were ordered to pay a debt or maintenance allowance. Reconciliation or the continuation of the family relationship was achieved in only two percent of cases. Ten percent of the support orders were paid for at least six months, twenty-five percent were never paid, and sixteen percent were part paid and stopped before the six month period ended. Only four percent of the cases were the subject of an appeal to the Magistrates Court.

Afiesem (household cases)

The jurisdiction of *Afiesem* is not regulated by statute. However, this method of settlement is recognized under legislation as a legitimate alternative in all civil suits and in non-felony criminal cases. Once the defendant has tacitly accepted a decision by attending and hearing the agreement announced, it can be enforced. In such instances those who were present and received a part of the hearing fee are morally obliged to support the complainant in court.

Household cases usually concern family matters, inheritance, divorce, land boundaries, assault, and insult. The landlords in 102 of 178 compounds surveyed have settled disputes for their tenants. Of the forty-three cases settled in the past year almost thirty-five percent were family matters.

Elders of a major Christian church in Koforidua and headmen of tribal and hometown unions reported that divorce and husband-wife problems are the most frequent disputes brought to their attention for management. Similar replies were given by heads of corporations, voluntary associations, and Government agencies.

Afiesem are private. During nine cases I observed at four different sub-chiefs' compounds, the average attendance was fifteen. The usual time for a hearing is around 6:00 a.m. or 7:00 p.m., after the morning or evening bath. Saturdays are good days to settle cases, since many people who do not farm, neither work nor attend church.

The aggrieved party pays a 'complaint' or 'messenger' fee, and then waits to be informed of the reponse of the other person and the date and time of the hearing. These fees are non-refundable if the person called does not attend the hearing. The lowest complaint fee reported was forty cents but it varies with the prominence of the person hearing the complaint. Members of ethnic associations, church groups, and corportations who hold *Afiesem* receive gifts of eggs, vegetables, or drinks as complaint fees. Besides witnesses, supporters, and the litigants, *Afiesem* include an individual who hears the case (*Odiasem* – literally the person who eats the case – also called 'the President'), one or more *Okyeame* (linguists), and the *Beguafo* (counsellors or *Panyinfo* [elders]). These individuals constitute the 'panel'. When the *Afiesem* is regularly held, the panel membership tends to remain constant.

Afiesem personnel are older than the litigants and are usually elderly (over 50). The social characteristics of the disputants closely approximate the personnel of the *Afiesem.* It is not unusual for one or both of the litigants to be a relative of a panel member.

The use of space is not intimidating. The two parties sit with their supporters and are encompassed by a circle of the participants. Gestures of respect and everyday clothes are conspicuous. The time spent on a case allows rather complete airing of grievances. Two hours is the average of fifteen cases I witnessed. Adjournments are infrequent; the issue is called to be settled that day. A land case may require the panel members to visit a disputed boundary or property. These cases may be settled at the property the same day or at the following meeting.

Afiesem may be settled in an attenuated manner, the president 'stamps on the case' and gives a quick decision. These cases can be settled in about 40 minutes. The procedures followed at hearings vary with the individual called upon to act as president. Notes are generally not taken. Parties and panel members speak in the language that is most comfortable. Witnesses are generally asked to leave the room and are called to tell what they know after the party who has called them to witness has finished. A general period of discussion follows the cross questioning of witnesses and parties. Participants are usually quite enthusiastic and shout each other down. The president and other panel members use questioning to steer the discussion onto issues which stand a good chance of clarification and agreement. The relative faults of the parties are identified and a tentative solution is suggested by the president. This initial proposal is generally rejected and counter-suggestions are offered. Besides the immediate implementation of monetary settlements, one or both parties are required to provide some token of the settlement; money, matches, or alcoholic beverage to be divided among the assembly. Then the plaintiff and the defendant are advised not to continue their quarrel nor boast of winning the case. The litigants may be asked to swear an oath that the dispute is settled.

Afiesem seem effective since awards, damages, and fees are generally paid immediately. The frequency of appeals to other agents, either before or after a decision is announced, could not be determined on a large sample of cases. However, of the seventy-four court cases selected for intensive interviewing, twenty-four percent had previously been heard by another agency – most were *Afiesem*. Twelve percent of cases at the Welfare Department were previously heard at *Afiesem*.

Supernatural

The practice of using the supernatural in the settlement of disputes has been under legislative attack since the early days of the colonial period. For many years the operation of shrines, and other supernatural methods of detection and attack were either outlawed or the operators made liable to civil suits for defamation if they could not substantiate their allegations. However in the 1960 Criminal Code, the entire class of supernatural offences was omitted. These agencies are now primarily used to determine who amongst a group of suspects is a thief, witch, or sorcerer. In connection with family law cases, sorcery is reportedly used by men to kill children when paternity is being denied. However, I was unable to ascertain even in general terms the frequency of such use.

The effectiveness of supernatural agencies is high amongst those who have a strong belief in their efficacy. During the period of fieldwork, several court cases were instituted in order to have curses removed. Much to the plaintiff's discomfort the court considered itself impotent to order such curses removed. Nothing more will be said concerning these agencies since I was unable to document adequately their use in matters of paternity and child maintenance disputes.

Disputes over paternity prior to the birth of the child are infrequently brought to the attention of the court. Cases of seduction, in which such matters arise, if carried through to their conclusion almost always result in 'success' for the female plaintiff and her family. However such short term benefits which may accrue from the payment of damages for the female's lost educational opportunities (often requested if the plaintiff is a 'school girl') and the expenses associated with the pregnancy and delivery undoubtedly lead to long term, persistent difficulty in child maintenance. However, the attitude of the court towards a man's defence in such situations places the defendant under considerable pressure to settle the matter 'at home'. In exchange for short term economic relief and avoiding public embarrassment, the defendant is prepared to offer the valued spiritual and emotional support to the child, mother, and in-laws, and at least the potential for long term child support based upon amicable relations. For example, one defendant's defense that he was only one of several sexual partners of the woman met with the magistrate's scorn: 'Here is a spoon-take your portion out!' In addition, most court personnel and other informants were convinced that women who name the father of their child always tell the truth.[9]

Decisions by women to trade short term economic benefit for potential long term economic and emotional advantages are equally important in child maintenance cases arising after the acceptance of paternity and naming have taken place. With this background to the remedy agents in Koforidua, we can now examine the incentives and constraints operating on litigants in two conflicts.

Case 1: The policeman's 'friend'

Plaintiff: Mrs. B., a 24-year-old illiterate Ashanti woman. She is a member of an Apostolic Church, belongs to the Kona clan and is unemployed. Although living five miles north of Koforidua in Asokore all her life, she belongs to no other voluntary organization besides the Church.

Defendant: Mr. A., a 23-year-old Ashanti man, has been an escort policeman for two years. He lives in the police barracks outside Koforidua. Before becoming a policeman he lived in Asokore and completed Form 4 of Middle School. He belongs to the Agona clan, is a Roman Catholic, but belongs to no other voluntary organizations.

This case came to Court in January, 1969. The defendant was absent. After rhetorically asking if the man had been served, the Magistrate said, 'Let it wait for awhile'. The case was again called in April, 1969. Since the defendant was still absent, a bench warrant was issued for his arrest.

From the docket, I learned that the case, which first entered Court in November, 1968, was actually a claim for $ 21.00 (including costs) for a breach of promise to marry and failure to support a child for five months. The claim read, ... defendant had sexual connection with plaintiff, and she brought forth a male child. When plaintiff was pregnant, defendant promised to marry her. Defendant, since five months ago, has not given subsistence to the plaintiff. Plaintiff therefore claims $ 20.00, being five months subsistence.

In December, 1968, the Magistrate delivered his judgment against the defendant and ordered him to pay the plaintiff $ 22.10.

The case in January, 1969, was a summons to show cause issued against the defendant since he had not complied with the earlier Court order.

Plaintiff's account-March, 1969:

The defendant is my husband for 2½ years. It was at that time that I conceived. His father was informed by my father, and he said he would come to perform the custom during the cocoa season. They never came. My husband maintained me until I brought forth. He named the child. He then stopped maintaining me for five months, and my father maintained the child. During this time, I went to him when he got his pay, but he said he had nothing. I left my child with him. He brought the child to his father, who later brought it to my mother. My mother accepted the child, but I didn't want to touch it, because the father had brought no money. Two months after this, just before Christmas, my father and a letter writer helped me prepare the summons. I had gone to his superior officer to advise him, but the officer could do nothing. I didn't go to Social Welfare, because I wanted mine first, the child's would come later. The defendant never begged me. I didn't call a lawyer because I had no money.

Defendant's account-April, 1969:

The plaintiff is a friend. We have been friends for three years. She was conceived about three years ago. The girl's parents came to tell my father I conceived their daughter. I maintained her until she brought forth, and for eight months after that. When I conceived her, I was working in the workers' brigade, but I quit. For more than eight months I was unemployed, but I started with the police just before she brought forth. My fathers' younger brother named the child. After I supported her for eight months, I had to leave on an operation for six months, so I could not give her money. The girl's parents went to my commander while I was gone to say that I had not supported the child for six months. I was then summoned to Court, I told the Magistrate I don't love the girl because of how the parents have treated me. I was afraid they will treat me worse if I have to leave in the future. The Magistrate made me shake hands with the girl and her father. The father asked for $ 10 ($ 20.00) chop money and said we should go home to settle the matter. I agreed, but I wanted my father to be present. He has gone to bush, and up till now has not returned. I travelled for three months again, and I have just returned to find the S.S.C. I never promised to marry her. I knew it was me, so I didn't refuse the pregnancy. I am guilty, but I have no money. At Court, I will beg for leave to get my father, so we may settle the case.

Further investigation revealed that while Mr. A. was unemployed Mrs. B. had helped him financially. Now that he has achieved a secure position and can help her and their child, he neglects them. As a policeman, he is vulnerable to censure from his superior officers. Mrs. B. has used this pressure. He accepted paternity by naming the child, but Mrs. B. is *Mpena*, and he has many more responsibilities and demands upon his salary. Since his father did not come to perform the custom originally, the defendant is convinced that it is his father's duty to pay the maintenance debt. The defendant and his father are making fools of the plaintiff and her father. Mrs. B. feels cheated but her father thinks the decision to send the young man to Court and ask him publicly to support his daughter and grandchild is shameful. He does not want to get a reputation for being a litigant and advised his daughter to take out the summons only after Mr. A. told her, 'You can take me anywhere' (i.e., he refused *Afiesem*). His harsh words were provoked by the attempt to put pressure on him through his commanding officer. Mrs. B.'s father was also aware that the threat of a case in Court might be a speedy way to encourage the defendant to settle at arbitration. He was looking beyond the amount claimed. If the matter could be settled peacefully at home, it might be better to settle for less money immediately and expect the defendant to take responsibility for the future.

Mr. A. felt that his *Mpena's* father's reaction was too swift and too severe. He was trying to force his own father to help him meet the burdens of his child. Mr. A.'s father is avoiding his responsibilities. It is his duty to find his son a wife and give a 'gift' to help him start a family. Mr. A.'s strategy is used in many types of disputes. He has refused to accept individual responsibility and deliberately placed himself in 'trouble' in order to get the 'proper' persons to live up to their responsibilities. Effective links exist between the parties through which a private resolution of this case can be achieved. The plaintiff did not call the defendant to an arbitration, since she felt he would not come. The defendant is trying to avoid his responsibilities is order to force his own father to accept responsibility towards his offspring. The plaintiff's attempts at forcing the defendant's father to accept responsibility failed. Her attempts at forcing the defendant by leaving the child and by informing his senior officer have failed. She feels the Court is the only place to be able to force him to support her and the child. Mrs. B.'s father, although reluctant to take Court action, is quite happy to accept arbitration of the dispute. Once this was rejected, a S.S.C. was issued. This was designed not to force the defendant to pay the $ 22.00, but to have him and his own father consent to arbitration, during which pressure can be put on Mr. A. to act as a proper husband and both of them to relieve Mrs. B.'s father of his financial burden toward his daughter and her child.

Case 2: The soldier's 'divorce'

Plaintiff: Mrs. M., a 33-year-old female Ashanti from Effiduase of the Bretuo clan, is a farmer and a member of the Methodist Church.

Defendant: Mr. K., a 48-year-old male Ashanti from Asokore currently stationed in the Army at Burma Camp, Accra, is Ekona clan and also Methodist.

The case came to my attention one day in January, 1969, the first time it appeared in Court. The claim had been filed earlier that morning. The plaintiff was claiming $ 200.00 damages ($ 204.00 including costs) as follows: Plaintiff as mother of X (same surname as defendant) and the customary wife of the defendant claims why defendant the real father of X of eight years, should not be responsible for his proper care.

Both parties were present at the hearing where the defendant pleaded not liable. The interaction was as follows:

Magistrate: You married customarily. You haven't provided for eight years. You haven't looked after him. Come and look after him. Do you have witnesses? *Plaintiff:* I have four. *Defendant:* I have one.

The Magistrate then called the boy and asked him to point out his father. The boy pointed out the defendant.

Magistrate: When did this start? *Defendant:* I am a soldier at Accra. *Magistrate:* Why don't you try to settle this case and stay peacefully. Do you want the case to be settled? *Defendant:* I want you to go on with the case.

The Magistrate tried to get them to adjourn the case until the next day. The defendant said he had to go on maneuvers for a month.

Magistrate: Can you stay until we close so that I can settle the case privately for you? Can you get your witnesses? *Defendant:* They are not here. *She is not my wife ... Magistrate:* It is a hard case, and we will waste time. Why don't you take it home? But I think you think you are being cheated. Are you worried? You all sit down and consider things.

Later on the plaintiff came in and informed the Court that she agreed to wait for one month. The Magistrate set the case for March, and said.

I wanted to settle it, but your witnesses are not here, so there is nothing I can do. Adjourned for them to subpoena their witnesses.

When the case was called again in March, a man stepped forward to request that the case be settled at home.

Man: They are both my grandchildren. I was not in when the case came, and I, therefore, beg for settlement. *Magistrate:* Do your agree? *Defendant:* Yes. *Magistrate* (laughing): You as a soldier. You prefer that ... that will be on your own detriment ... that will be up to you if you are found guilty. *Plaintiff:* I agree, he is my grandfather.

The arbitration of the case was held in Asokore two hours later, at the house of the plaintiff's grandfather. Twelve individuals had gathered to hear the case (excluding the plaintiff and defendant) – the plaintiff's relatives, including her mother's brothers (2), brother, mother's father, father's brother (who was also the defendant's mother's brother), and another man whose relationship to plaintiff was unclear. The defendant was present with a friend from the Army and his own father. Also present was an Ashanti sub-chief and a police constable who was not related to either party.

The sub-chief started off the proceedings by asking about the summons since he was not at the Court. The defendant passed around the summons, and the plaintiff stated that there are three issues:

... He does not want to make himself as a husband. He dislikes seeing me as a wife. He does not maintain our only son. There is a proverb: *(sE yEnnya bɪribi amma Y' ase a yen nyae mmy no krono)* (If we have nothing for our 'in-law' [Note: affinal relative] we should not rather steal from her.) He took £ 5 ($ 10.00) from me and did not give it back to me.

After the *Okyeame* repeated the three allegations the defendant answered:

She came to me in Accra. I gave her the £ 3 ($ 6.00) she gave me. It was alleged that the £ 3 ($ 6.00) belonged to the mother. I gave her £ 3 ($ 6.00) and £ 2 10s ($ 5.00) lorry fare or maintenance for my son. She threw the money away ... I gathered up the money and told her that I did not invite her to Accra ... She went to ... my uncle and begged through them for me to give back the money ... I had by then use (d) it. I, however, gave her the $ 2 10s ($ 5.00) and said if I got the £ 3 ($ 6.00), I will send it to her. *Okyeame:* What about the child? *Defendant:* It is untrue that I do not maintain him. If I do not maintain the child, my wife's family would not have sought help from some elders to beg me to marry (i.e., stay married to) her. When the mother visits me, I give her money.

At this point, the plaintiff and her mother called the defendant a liar, and there began a heated exchange. As the argument ebbed, the elders, including the subchief, the individuals who withdrew the case from Court, the *Okyeame*, the defendant's friend and one more went for consultation. After eight minutes they returned with the following decision:

Aberewa[10] says that the child is for both the father and the mother, but it is customarily the father who cares for the child. We have, therefore, agreed that the child be sent to live with the father in Accra. Secondly, we have also found it better to let the husband compensate the wife with £ 5 ($ 10.00) as cloth and divorce her because we have known that you do not want to marry her. In addition, you must bear the Court expense of $ 3 5s. ($ 6.50).

In response to this decision, the plaintiff agreed to forego the monetary settlement entirely. She also stated that before she would agree to send the boy to Accra, she had to consult with her mother's mother, who was currently looking after the boy. After the plaintiff explained her feelings of love for the defendant and their child and began to explain the incident in Accra again, the gathering begged her to remain silent and let the case end. She then mentioned one old debt for 7s (70c.) and said that, although she had forgiven the defendant all other 'monies' she wanted that. The chairman asked for £ 1 4s ($ 2.40) as *Aseda.*[11] After begging, the Chairman accepted 13s and 4s from plaintiff and defendant for sanctioning the divorce. No compensation was taken from the defendant, but he did pay the alleged £ 3 ($ 6.00) debt. The total cost to the defendant was £ 3 ($ 6.00) debt, 13s ($ 1.30) *Aseda* and 4s (40c) for divorce, a total of $ 7.70. This amount was paid in the presence of those gathered.

This is a clear example of how the Court is used to force settlement of maintenance cases at home: the man's desire for divorce is used to make him take custody of his child. The plaintiff's claim in Court of $ 204.00 was certainly unrealistic, considering the fact that she settled for $ 6.00 at the arbitration. In court, the man denied that the plaintiff was his wife. Yet, the issue was never raised at home. The underlying issues in the case emerge clearly at *Afiesem:* (1) The plaintiff wanted to remain married to the defendant and to have him support her and her child. (2) The defendant is in the Army and is in a vulnerable position. He wants to divorce the woman. In exchange for sanctioning the divorce without compensation, he is prepared to take responsibility for the upbringing of the child and admit his fault in the case.

DISCUSSION

In this section I will discuss the potential social consequences of paternity and child maintenance disputes in the context of litigants goals and their use of the available remedy agents in Koforidua.

The court, Welfare Department, and *Afiesem* handle different amounts of paternity and child maintenance cases because litigants use them in different ways, to achieve different goals. Non-economic concerns which emerge from the case materials include: the spiritual protection of the child, the good name and reputation of family and self, and the desire for remarriage. Economic concerns include long and short term expectation of gain directed towards, self, child, and family.

The use of remedy agents singly and in combinations offers the litigant different expectations of achieving these goals. In estimating potential success, the litigant considers the morality, as well as the effectiveness of the source of the power to enforce a decision. The amount of money needed to initiate the dispute is measured against the chance of losing and the total amount which can be lost. Psychological cost is assessed with regard to the degree of public exposure and the likelihood of settlement associated with different procedural styles.

Using these criteria, litigants rank *Afiesem*, Welfare Department, and court, along a series of continua: from the most moral, private, least disruptive to social relations, least coercive, least expensive; to least moral, most public, most disruptive to social relations, most coercive, and most expensive. Generally speaking *Afiesem* are the most often used agency since plaintiffs have the best chance to achieve long term economic advantage based upon the restoration of amicable, albeit altered social relationships. The court, on the other hand, is less often used since it provides the winner with the best chance of achieving short term monetary gain based upon the alteration of social relationships.

The pattern of the allocation of litigants goals to specific dispute contexts is socio-culturally determined. For example, non-economic goals predominant in disputes concerning paternity and naming. Both male and female plaintiffs use *Afiesem* and the Welfare Department to help manage these problems, since they are most suited to their goals. However, the goals of litigants in cases involving the maintenance of grown children at the time of the genitor's death are usually clustered around short term economic gain for self and family. Plaintiffs can best achieve this goal by a court produced and enforced decision.

Despite this division of legal labour in Koforidua we should not lose sight of the potential such a multiplicity of conflict management agencies has for bluffing. Although vexatious litigation and a plurality of legal systems have been criticised as inimicable to economic development, it is quite possible that in family law matters such as paternity and child maintenance, the threatened use of less moral agencies provides a basis for long range improvement by increasing the distribution of the fruits of economic development.[12]

These considerations formed important aspects of litigants strategies in the two cases described in this paper. If Ghanaian society of the future involves the expansion of an educated group of male civil servants, the choice of remedy agent to manage these disputes takes on considerable importance. For example, female plaintiffs in divorce actions may opt to maximize their children's long term economic benefits and their own good name and reputation. If the defendant is an upwardly mobile male pursuing short term economic gain, the two strategies can combine to produce benefits to both parties. In exchange for avoiding a short term economic settlement to his former wife, the male defendant may accept custody of his child which may provide the latter with increased educational opportunities. If the macro-socio-economic variables which support these goals continue to re-enforce them, such as socio-economic advancement being tied to increased formal education, it appears that the magistrates court will be used to bluff high status male defendants into settling problems of paternity and child maintenance in the Welfare Department and especially *Afiesem*. Only in these settings can both parties' goals be realized. It should be obvious that such choices will tend to keep claims of paternity and demands for child support fairly well insulated from legislation and case law applied in the Magistrates Court. However, it may be this very insulation which will create a desirable distribution of educational opportunity.

As noted above such macro-sociological statements ultimately rest upon world wide socio-economic conditions. The utility of the approach adopted in this paper lies in raising our expectations above the 'common sense' level when faced with changed external conditions.[13]

I accept the notion that litigants' goals, the rules they manipulate to reach them and the meanings they attach to both tend to diminish, or at least make problematic the role of the intervener in the process of dispute management.[14] However, by adopting this position I have not meant to imply that the cases I described represented disputes in which norms were not at issue. Rather I intended to leave to inquiry the degree to which the litigants amongst themselves and each in relationship to the third party shared the perception of the rules in dispute. The creativity of interveners in such situations of legal pluralism has already been described.[15] I do not deny the occurrence of such synthesis, yet it is also likely that the genesis of new principles will not take place. Exploring cases of disputed paternity and child support from the litigant's perspective rather than the intervener's highlights the complex interplay between legislation, case law, and parties' goals without assuming their identity.

NOTES

1. The population over 15 include: Ashanti – thirty-two percent; Other Akans – twenty-three percent; Non-Akans – forty-five percent. In all, 57 distinct ethnic groups were elicited on the census. However, even this picture obscures the strategic fluctuation which takes place in ethnic identity. See Sanjek (n.d.). Twenty-five percent identify with the Islamic faith, fifty-six percent with an established Christian church, twelve percent with separatist Christian churches, and seven percent placed their faith in traditional supernaturals. Thirty-six percent of adults had received primary education, fourteen percent in a Muslim school forty percent had attended middle school, four percent secondary school, five percent had the opportunity to receive training at a technical, vocational, nursing, or training college. Less than one percent were University graduates. Occupations were equally diverse, more than 100 being mentioned. Only five percent represented themselves as primarily farmers. Thirty-four percent were traders, six percent civil servant or clerk, six percent labourer, fifteen percent apprentice or student, sixteen percent craftsmen, five percent were in business or the professions, and almost eight percent considered themselves to be housewives. Of those reported 'married' on a census of slightly less than ten percent of the population, ninety percent reportedly were in customary unions, five percent under Islamic law, three percent were married in church, and less than one percent responded that their marriage involved only their mutual 'consent'. I suspect that many customary marriages are not complete, and that a larger percentage are living in consensual unions.
2. Women use intermediaries in similar ways to express their desires towards men. Ideally, any dispute arising from a marriage will be brought to this person for management.
3. Ghanaian currency has been converted to 1968 dollar equivalents. During the period of fieldwork, a labourer could expect to earn about seventy cents per day. The per capita income (which does not accurately measure the distribution of income) was one hundred and seventy-nine dollars in 1962.
4. Examples of this process are presented in Lowy 1971: 206–21.
5. Seventy-six percent of the 1,237 children reported in the 1968 Birth Register were delivered in a hospital rather than home.

6. For a discussion of methods and attitudes towards birth control in one Kwahu lineage, see Bleek (1974a).
7. See Oppong (1974) for a discussion of marriage involving civil servants in Accra.
8. An expanded version of this section will appear in Lowy (n.d.).
9. There is a complementary belief held by many people that a man would not refuse to accept responsibility for his child and name him, since failure to do so might make the child sick (excessive pulsation of blood in the fontanelle of an infant's skull is a diagnostic feature of such neglect). Also, it is believed such a child would closely resemble the genitor making him an object of scorn.
10. Literally 'The old lady'. Panel members who retire to a private place to consider a solution to a dispute euphemistically refer to this process as 'asking the old lady'.
11. This is a thanks or judgement fee divided among the assembled group.
12. One of three fundamental measures of economic development recommended by Seers (1970).
13. For a lucid example of this approach, see Salisbury and Salisbury (1972).
14. This term has been suggested by Abel (1974) to replace the often used 'remedy agent'. Dispute management likewise is more general than resolution or settlement.
15. Collier (1973); Tanner (1970).

Law in the context of Nkoya society 3

WIM M.J. VAN BINSBERGEN
University of Leiden

1. INTRODUCTION

Much successful research into African law appears to have been guided by the following two premises: that law as a social process primarily takes shape within the highly formalized setting of the court of law; and that this process focuses on the examination of such conflicts as are of prime importance to the members of the society concerned. These certainly are the assumptions underlying most of the contributions to the 1974 Leiden seminar, out of which the present volume has emerged. Likewise, these assumptions underlie the Central African legal-anthropological studies initiated by the late Professor Max Gluckman's Barotse research (Gluckman 1943, 1967a, 1972) and carried on elsewhere by Gluckman's one-time associates (e.g., Epstein 1951, 1953, 1954a, 1954b; Werbner 1969; Gluckman 1969).

Indeed, Gluckman's Barotse studies rank among the few classics of legal anthropology, and form the indispensable starting point for anyone who, as I did, engages in a study of social control among a so-called Barotse subject tribe, the Nkoya, some three decades after Gluckman's first Barotse fieldwork. With a wealth of descriptive detail, great insight into the wider social background, and inspiring theoretical and methodological sophistication, Gluckman traced the Barotse judicial process as manifested in the proceedings of the formal courts of law that were defined within the relatively autonomous Barotse administration of the 1940's. He laid bare the notions underlying Barotse law, the principles of their functioning (whose built-in contradictions he revealed and explained) and their connections with the general Barotse ideological and political system focussing on kinship and the land. Having emphasized the plural nature of Barotse society (Gluckman 1941) he paid considerable attention to the local incorporation of the non-Barotse tribes' custom within the Barotse state and legal system (Gluckman 1967; 204, 234, 244f).

Yet, my own research findings among the rural Nkoya, in the first analysis, seem to run counter to whatever could be anticipated on the basis of Gluckman's approach. In the society I studied formal Local Courts (the immediate heirs to the chief's courts Gluckman described) did exist all right, but they were peripheral rather than central to the judicial process, and to the conflict-regulatory process in general, and such conflicts as most deeply concerned and aroused local communities, were hardly subject to formal litigation in these courts.

In this chapter I shall first argue these rather sweeping statements concerning the Nkoya legal system. I shall qualify them in the light of the actual, if limited, occurrence of Local Court cases under specific conditions. After an attempt to interpret the Nkoya legal situation against the dynamics of their village society, I shall conclude by briefly comparing the Nkoya to the Central Lozi and other Central African groups, and by pointing out the methodological implications of the present approach.[1]

2. THE NKOYA: THE LOCAL COURT

Nkoya (Brelsford n.d.: 15f; Clay 1945; McCulloch 1951; Van Binsbergen 1975, 1976 a, b) is today the name of various groups of people who inhabit the light forests of the plateau of Central Western Zambia. They speak, with dialectical variations, a common Central-Bantu language known as Nkoya, and largely share a common culture, in which hunting, chieftainship, bilateral kinship, sorcery, and the village dead are some of the major themes.

With the general expansion of long-distance trade and slavery in the area during the last few centuries, immigrants of Northern origin brought about a sharp increase of political scale, superimposing a new and more elaborate chief-centred political system upon the older pattern of minor hunting chiefs presiding over local elders. Among the neighbouring Luyi (later called Lozi) (Mainga 1973) a similar process, but stimulated by the eminently favourable ecology of the Zambezi flood plain, and intensified by the Kololo invasion from South Africa, led to a political expansion which in the second half of the nineteenth century brought most of the Nkoya under Lozi political influence. Although Lozi political control over the Nkoya was in many parts limited, the Nkoya came to be considered one of the Lozi subject tribes, and it is as such that they entered colonial rule at the turn of the century. Since colonial rule based its legitimacy on a treaty with the Lozi king, the white administration boosted the Lozi political claims and favoured the development of a system where Lozi representatives (*indunas*) would take up residence with the major Nkoya chiefs and share in their political and judicial functions (Stokes 1966). Until then the inchoate, shifting political structure of the Nkoya had centred on the open competition for major and minor chiefly titles, most of which would exist for only a few generations between their emergence (as the proper name of a 'big man', leader of a powerful following), and their sinking into disuse. Lozi and colonial rule supplanted this system by a theoretically clear-cut hierarchy of village headmen, minor chiefs, *indunas*, and senior Nkoya chiefs, under the ultimate authority of the Lozi 'Paramount Chief'. The senior chiefs and *indunas* were entrusted with courts of law over which they exerted a strong personal control.

When Barotseland became incorporated into the newly-independent Republic of Zambia, most of the formal judicial and executive functions of the chiefs were taken away from them.

Jurisdiction areas of the Local Courts continue to coincide, by and large, with the areas of the senior chiefs and *indunas*, but between the chief and the Local Court little more than this nominal relation exists today. Thus, in in Chief Kathembe's[2] area (on which we shall concentrate in this chapter), we find the following situation. The court, which used to be at the palace, is now located at a distance of 30km, in the Kapondwe area that has a high incidence of recent non-Nkoya immigrants, and that only after a post-independence redefinition of chiefs' areas fell to Kathembe. The chief appoints only one member of the Local Court, in consultation with the local minor chiefs, headmen and elders, and subject to the approval of the Court and of Legal Affairs. Once appointed this member is in no way answerable to the chief, and he is paid, and trained, by Government. The Local Court's membership is partly Lozi, proceedings are predominantly in Lozi[3], and a jurisprudence is used which consists of the Lozi legal tradition, adapted to local and to modern conditions.

This paper explores why only a small selection of all the conflicts and grievances occurring in Kathembe's area finds its way to the Local Court of Kapondwe. A few minor reasons can already be indicated here. Geographical distance is an obvious constraint in a rural society where motor transport is hardly available for local traffic. Moreover, against the background of a long history of Nkoya-Lozi antagonism (Van Binsbergen

1975) there is some distrust of the application of the law by Lozi Court members. But these are minor factors. Much wider geographical distances are covered in the normal routine of subsistence, ceremony, and recreation. And against occasional allegations of anti-Nkoya attitudes, stand statements supporting the Local Court in its present form. There are no allegations that the Local Court upholds a law that is at variance with 'Nkoya law'. For even if the population is aware of minor discrepancies between Court and village practice (cf. note 8), a century of increasing incorporation into the state systems of the Lozi kingdom, Northern Rhodesia, and the Republic of Zambia (both in the rural area and in the course of labour migration) has led the Nkoya at least to recognize, and subscribe to, a comprehensive legal order beyond the limits of Nkoya rural society. Nkoya villagers consider the task of protection against open violence and crime in the narrower sense to lie ultimately with this comprehensive legal order; they show no reluctance to deliver trouble-makers and criminals from their own ranks to the outside agents of this order. However, the major problem of Nkoya village life is not posed by the odd thug, but by the everyday struggle to maintain a liveable social order in which multiplex, face-to-face relationships and precarious economic conditions are the main elements. The allocation of personnel, goods, services, rights, and status presents a continuous, many-faceted problem always prone to precipitate acute crisis. This may be true for any society; it is all the more true for contemporary Nkoya rural society, whose economy balances around the minimum subsistence level and moreover has to accommodate claims for assistance from (temporarily) urban members. In these fundamental social processes one would suppose the Local Court to be very frequently resorted to – but it is not.

It is the main point of my argument that the Local Court remains at the fringe of Nkoya rural society, largely because it represents a mode of conflict regulation which, given the structure of interaction and the participants' conceptions of the social and moral order, has only a very limited applicability there – whilst internal alternatives to the Local Court are well developed and effective.

3. VILLAGE LIFE AND INTRA-VILLAGE CONFLICT RESOLUTION

A central theme in Nkoya social structure is the tendency for multiplex social relations between co-residing kinsmen (members of a village) to develop into insoluble conflict, leading, through a phase of intense sorcery accusations, to fission, with individuals or small factions moving to other villages or starting a new village on their own. Fissiparous tendencies are built into the very structure of Nkoya society. On the one hand this society fosters the model of the happy, stable village of more or less close kinsmen, headed by the successor to a chiefly title. On the other hand, precisely because Nkoya society regards succession to a chiefly title, and having a village of one's own, as the ideal culmination of a man's career, every male follower is induced to compete for leadership and to pursue the value of individual autonomy that counteracts the values of authority and respect. Succession among the Nkoya is largely a matter of achievement. A new incumbent is chosen out of a large pool of people (bilateral kinsmen of previous incumbents) who live dispersed in several villages over a vast geographical area. In principle, therefore, every talented man has the chance to acquire, in the end, a senior title and his own village. But this means that men from their late thirties on are in constant competition with their age-mates and their seniors over succession to titles which ordinarily can only become available upon the previous incumbent's death: a set-up conducive to ill-will, sorcery, sorcery accusations, – to such an extent as to make natural death an unlikely occurrence, in the eyes of the Nkoya villagers.

Apart from this long-term perspective there is the day-to-day concern for health, food, respect, and security. With respect to these fundamental concerns, anthropologists have tended to conceive of kinship as allocating to Ego *specific* rights and duties vis-à-vis his kinsmen in a specific geneological position. Peculiar to the Nkoya bilateral system is that, as far as everyday interaction between kinsmen is concerned, these rights are highly *unspecific;* they are to some extent determined by age, sex, co-residence, but they are hardly implied or dictated by precise genealogical relation or by the kinship terms people use to each other.

No single statement could better sum up the Nkoya kinship system than the adage:

Mwana wa hakati ka jifumo (the child is in the middle of the womb).

Here we have in a nutshell the basic principle of bilateral descent: *jifumo*, womb, stands for line of descent through either the father or mother. A person's patrikin and matrikin have essentially the same rights over him, just as he has similar rights over both clusters of kinsmen. No single individual or group has complete, exclusive rights over a person. And, while patrikin and matrikin are free to compete over the realization of whatever claims of domestic, economic, political and religious support they may foster in relation to Ego (and these claims are usually secured through co-residence), Ego retains the right to choose between them in his own interest. Whatever the specific content (in terms of transactions of goods and services) a particular kinship relation between two Nkoya will have, depends on the dynamics of the concrete situation in which these two find themselves. A general morality (enforced to a degree by the village dead, fear of sorcery, and by the dynamics of status allocation) prescribes unconditional support between kinsmen particularly if living in the same village. But no specific and formally-sanctioned norms indicate what constitute reasonable claims and reasonable refusals. Interaction between kinsmen is based not so much on norms and rights, but on general expectations, and here disappointment and resentment are rife.

Example A illustrates the general problem with reference to inheritance. When someone is to inherit from his deceased kinsman, other relatives do have expectations about what portion of the inheritance will be shared out amongst them. They may even present these expectations as based on 'the law' (*milao*). However, these expectations are not fixed rules in the sense that formal redressive action could be undertaken on the basis of them. Should someone fail altogether to honour the expectations, then there is no effective judicial or other mechanism to make him part with the inheritance. The relatives are left with their resentment, and are likely to turn to sorcery for revenge.

A. The Greedy Successor. Headman Shipande had amassed considerable wealth, including a gun, a sewing machine, and a wireless set. When he died, his cousin Kabesha, who for several decades had stayed at the distant court of Chief Kathembe, managed to get himself elected successor. But instead of taking up residence among the previous Shipande's following (as a headman should do), he collected the entire inheritance and returned to his place. So, in addition to leaving the village without a leader, he did not share out part of the inheritance (normally he would only have retained the gun, as a central symbol of male and chiefly identity); and by taking all this wealth, he deprived his kinsmen even of the possibility of using or borrowing it. The kinsmen resented this action very much. No one wondered however, how Kabesha managed to escape their wrath; he is regarded as a powerful sorcerer. His nephew joined him in his distant village, and started to use the inherited goods. When a few years later several of this nephew's young children died in quick succession, extensive divination pointed out that the wronged kinsmen had, by means of sorcery, allegedly directed the spirit of the deceased Shipande to Kabesha's village, where, unable to attack the old wizard himself, the aroused spirit had, allegedly, turned against the children of the village. Public opinon rather favoured the wronged kinsmen, and, unscandalised, agreed that there was nothing else they could have done – least of all take the matter to court.

If crucial interaction in Nkoya society focuses on kinship; if kinship roles merely stipulate expectations which generally lack effective formal sanction within and without the judicial sphere; if resentment and sorcery are the common results of this situation, and ultimately lead to the breaking-up of relationship between co-residents; what conflict-regulatory processes, then make Nkoya society possible at all?

Fission and inter-village migration constitute powerful mechanisms to get over a crisis and make a fresh start. Most people have moved to another village at least once in their lifetime, many have moved much more often, and in a majority of cases an insoluble conflict was at the bottom of the change in village affiliation. A person staying in a village (e.g., his father's) and feeling that he does not get his due, will contemplate what other possible refuges he may have: the villages of his mother's brothers, of his classificatory fathers, actual and assumed grandparents, his joking partners (*ba-thukulu:* putative grandchildren) failing these, his own new village, and (as a temporary option) settlement in town. One moves away from a disappointing relative and, if possible, towards a more promising one. Often moves of the latter type are encouraged by senior kinsmen who try to attract junior kinsmen (their main political following) from elsewhere; in this process of recruitment expectations are kindled which, after the move, are often not met: characters may turn out to be incompatible, whilst other, already co-residing, junior kinsmen try to prevent their common leader from bestowing undue favours upon the newcomer. Thus, the solution of one crisis tends to breed the next.

A second major conflict-regulatory factor may be looked for in the religious sphere. Writing about Ndembu Lunda society, which is both historically and structurally closely related to the Nkoya, Turner (1957, 1961, 1962, 1968) has presented the view that such profound conflicts as originate in the field of close kinship and co-residence, can be effectively expressed and partly resolved in the ritual sphere: divination, village shrine ritual, and cults of affliction. Very similar institutions exist among the Nkoya (Van Binsbergen 1972, 1976 a, c, in press) but their contribution to conflict management should not be overestimated. These religious institutions may express general structural tensions in the society, they may even reveal (cf. A) the concrete participants and events of a specific non-religious conflict, but they only lead to redressive action implying a restoration of disrupted social relations if decisive conditions deriving from the social process outside the ritual sphere already make such a restoration desirable and feasible. An example of this is B, which brings out some local-political factors working towards conflict resolution through ritual mechanisms.

B. The Son who ran amuck. Dickson, a man in his early twenties, was in love with a Lozi girl from the Kapondwe area, some 20 km. away from his village. His relatives, among whom his father Shelonga is prominent, wanted him to give up the girl: they did not favour a marital tie with Lozi people, whom they alleged to ask too high bride prices and to lack respect for Nkoya affines; moreover, Dickson's relatives feared the high damages that would be due in the case of elopement or a premarital affair. They refused to assist Dickson financially, and he had no money of his own. Tensions mounted and the result was that Dickson ran amuck after an evening of drinking. He set fire to his own house and threw his father's bicycle as well as his elder brother's wireless set in the flames – the inconceivable waste of long years of thriftiness. Shelonga, also in his cups, ritually cursed his son and kicked him out of the village. Dickson exiled himself to Lusaka, where he was admitted to a Nkoya urban yard in Kalingalinga compound, of which his cousin is the leader. After the better part of a year he finally managed to secure a job. Throughout his stay in town he kept in frequent contact with his elder brother and his sister in Lusaka, who through letters communicate regularly with the village home. When the elder brother visited the village shortly after Dickson had found work, their mother dug up a few tubers from the redflowered shrub that constitutes the village shrine. Taken from the sacred spot that represents the village, its unity, ancestors, and continuity, the tubers symbolize that Dickson is still considerd attached to the very life of the village, in other words that the curse ('you are no longer my son') may be lifted. When Dickson receives the tubers he is quick to take the hint. No sooner is he allowed to take a long weekend from his job than he takes the bus home in order to reconcile his father to him and – to elope with the Lozi girl! In the village a small ritual is performed at the shrine: the curse is revoked, and a prayer is said to the ancestors ('We were misled, we quarrelled, but now we have regained our mutual understanding'). Still the family is not prepared to give in as far as his Lozi love is concerned, and Dickson is again angry about this, but this time he controls himself well.

In this intra-family conflict, resolution was possible, and even imperative, for a complex of reasons. Shelonga is highly respected throughout the chieftancy, because of his wisdom and integrity. His political position however is precarious. About twenty years ago he left his distant valley, as a result of intra-family conflict. He took refuge in Mukuata's village, where his mother had come from. Since his migration, throughout a complex, conflict-ridden local-political process, Shelonga had always refused (partly under pressure from his sons, who feared for their father's life) to succeed to the several very senior chiefly titles that circulate in his family. As a result he now finds himself as the reluctant *de facto* headman of a small village, with his only daughter and three of his four surviving sons in town, and surrounded by villages whose headmen are closely related to him but most of whom consider him as a major rival in the competition for titles and honour. In the past Dickson had already given a heavy blow to

Shelonga's prestige: at another drinking session he had become violent and insulting and Shelonga had been reproached in the neighbourhood court for failure to control his child. So a second time Shelonga had to act firmly. But on the other hand he could, both as a leader and as a politically insecure person, not afford to let the size of his effective following diminish. Another contributory factor in the resolution of the conflict lies in the fact that, despite such momentary disruptions as described in this case, the Shelonga family in general displays exceptionally high harmony and integration as manifested, e.g., by the lasting marriage of Shelonga and his wife, the pride and concern that the sons take in their father, and the firm support between the children when in town. His siblings in town pressed for a reconciliation between Dickson and his father, whereas on the other hand Dickson's relations with the cousin with whom he had put up deteriorated to a state where Dickson was eager to restore the good relations with his original village.

Example B shows how religious institutions focussing on the village shrine can underpin a process of intra-familial reconciliation and seal its ultimate completion, provided that non-religious social conditions towards resolution are present. More often however, among the Nkoya, if a conflict spills over into the religious sphere, this means that the development of the conflict is accelerated, and that whatever potential for reconciliation may have existed, is now lost forever. The conflict will leave the sphere of everyday inter-personal interaction and the exchange of goods and non-religious services, and, more or less under a symbolic disguise, will live on mainly in the ritual sphere. The outcome of example A was a typical one: after divination had pointed out (no doubt as a result of the diviner's knowledge of prevailing social relationships) the conflict allegedly responsible for the children's deaths, no attempt was made to approach the wronged kinsmen and to arrive at some settlement (e.g., sharing out the disputed inheritance); while concerned about the well-being of those children and adults that had survived the spirit's attack, all attention of Kabesha subsequently concentrated on the ritual means of allaying the spirit. Once conflict has entered the sphere of sorcery, little is left but ritual which amounts to accepting the rupture as irreparable.

The third major form of conflict regulation (which, contrary to the two discussed so far, goes on continuously in every Nkoya village) is the informal action by which most minor clashes are prevented from developing to an ultimate stage of fission and sorcery. The petty frictions and irritations that spring from living closely together and from sharing crucial economic, political and religious tasks are the subject of constant scrutiny and concern especially of those who are held responsible for the integrity, general welfare, and honour of the village: the village headman (who may leave part of his tasks to a younger assistant), and any other elder people of either sex. Seeds of disruption are quickly detected and brought to the fore in informal impromptu gatherings of those involved. They concern trivialities; children who make noise and upset the village; young, inexperienced wives who are late in sending their prepared meals to the men's shelter; a mother-in-law who leaves too much of the heavy job of pounding to her daughters-in-law; a man who cannot hold his drink. The successful headman is the one who manages to deal with these petty issues in such a way as to avoid their becoming laden with such long-standing grievances as individuals or factions associated with either party in the petty conflict may have.

In this form of conflict settlement emphasis is not on justice and formal rules of behaviour. It is 'discussing' *(ku-ambola)*, not a 'court case' *(mulandu)*. The headman is hardly concerned with assessing who was right or wrong and does not press for admission of guilt. Rather he applies all his psychological skills and wisdom to appeal to the parties' obligations vis-à-vis the integrity and solidarity of the village. He emphasizes that village unity (*ku-jiuva:* understanding) is primarily in their own and their children's interest. The appeal is usually strengthened by reference to the disasters that struck members of certain villages that had not managed to preserve their unity; and this will not be a tale of the distant past, but the accounts of the misfortunes of well-known close kinsmen of those present. The headman has a practical, informal authority in these situations insofar as he represents the unity of the village. He is the one who, on occasion of his installation at the village shrine, has ritually inherited the name and social person of the village founder; and although he is not considered to have control over the actions of the now deceased former members of the village (he cannot invoke the dead in order to add supernatural sanctions to his authority), people believe that the dead have power to interfere and take revenge on those living members whose actions threaten village unity. The headman is the main link between the living and the dead[4] and when he has managed to quench a more serious-looking intra-village conflict, he informs the dead of the outcome through a short prayer and offering of mealie-meal at the village shrine.

This standard pattern of conflict resolution, which is frequently resorted to in the everyday life of the village, brings out important structural characteristics of the Nkoya system of conflict regulation, including their legal system. Conflict is primarily regarded, not as a matter of right or wrong against abstract, unalterable criteria of formalized rules of behaviour – but as a direct threat to group unity. Nkoya consider such unity essential for both collective and individual well-being. Without unity, the village members will not be able to co-operate in their crucial tasks; the village would be hit by shame, ancestral revenge, sorcery, and (as the minimal subsistence barrier is so very near) by hunger, disease, and death. It is not the optimistic conviction of the actual existence of village unity, but on the contrary the awareness of continually being of the edge of disruption, that makes the village deeply afraid of open expressions of conflict – they may well turn out to be the straw that breaks the camel's back. Meanwhile, no doubt, it is in the direct, personal political interest of those in authority (elders, the headman) to pose as the advocates of such a lofty goal as village unity; underneath their admonitions a measure of cynical manipulation of their fellow-villagers might be discerned, but this does not greatly diminish the generally integrative effect of their pleas for unity.

The principal aim of conflict resolution in an intra-familial context is not to define and administer specific rights and obligations as attached to particular kinship roles but to take away the sting from whatever animosity has arisen. Such conflict resolution cannot afford to go into the depths of latent fissiparous tendencies, old grievances, fundamental incompatibility of characters, as will usually exist within the family group. On the contrary, for as long as possible, in the face of mounting tensions, those responsible for conflict management have to present, artificially, each incident of observable conflict as a small matter, ephemeral and without consequence. The standard approach is to hush up matters, to emphasize that a full discussion would be a waste of time; no formal setting is given to the discussion, the reconstruction of the events leading to a petty conflict is intentionally kept scanty and the analysis superficial, and often the matter is abandoned in the most inconclusive manner. The parties may not be entirely satisfied, but the general appeal to their responsibilities towards group unity keeps them from saying so openly. Each has a strong personal interest in keeping peace within the family group: both for reasons of future assistance and for the avoidance of sorcery.

But this central concern of avoiding open conflict is often overrun by the equally important values of individual autonomy and honour; and then expressions of animosity, sometimes violence, do occur. Against the plea for unity and understanding stands the management of self-respect and honour, expressed by the aggressive assertion: *Ami mulume!*, 'I am a man!'. Usually, one has sufficient opportunity to assert one's honour in the course of the public, if informal, attention given to an incident. If one drops the matter publicly this can easily be presented not as an admission of weakness and guilt, but as a magnanimous yielding to group interests. But as soon as either party stubbornly refuses to drop the issue for unity's sake, the headman and village elders are virtually at a loss. Not only do they openly fail as leaders but, more important, there will be no way out except through sorcery and fission.

Informal settlement of intra-familial conflict is not only a contribution to village unity, but also a test of it. Under certain conditions a member of the village may cause a small matter to escalate often beyond repair, ignoring the values that suppress conflict. These crises often take place in a context of drinking, or immediately after the death of a member of the village. In the latter case many people will be frantic with fear of sorcery, and the authority of the headman is at its lowest, for he has obviously failed to protect his followers, and at the same time (in view of the connections between power, age and sorcery in Central-African societies: (Van Binsbergen 1976 b, c; Parkin 1969), he himself is tacitly suspected of having caused the death. Example C illustrates however, how in such a crisis *ku-ambola* can produce positive results.

C. The sick child. A few years previously Yona, now in his early thirties, had left his village in the valley of Kashanda. Returning from work in town he found his father's village considerably dwindled, his wife and children neglected, and his baby son very ill. So he left after a row and settled in Malasha village among his distant uterine kin. The child recovered there, but never became very healthy. Shortly after two adult members of Malasha village had died in quick succession, Yona's children fell ill, formost the problem child of old. In a *ku-ambola* session with the headman and other adult male residents. Yona complains that this village, too, has become a bad place (the implication is: full of unidentified sorcerers). He points out that if the health of the children does not improve soon, he will move again to another village. He knows, as admitted on a different occasion, that he would have no other place to go but back to his agnatic kin, where he would hardly be welcome. The elders of Malasha village appreciate his fears: they too are in a state of frenzy over the recent deaths. On the other hand, Yona's remonstration implies that he takes them to task for failure to protect the village; moreover Nkoya believe that those occupying, or aspiring to, high status may turn to sorcery to enhance their powers. In the situation, Yona needs scarcely say explicitly that he suspects his elder fellow villagers of being responsible for the evil influences themselves – the hint is clear, and covertly arouses, and distresses, the village elders. Yet, with the recent losses and the general despair in the village, they are very keen on retaining Yona's support. Therefore, the situation is not allowed to escalate, no offence is taken publicly, and Yona is not offered an easy exit out of the village. Quietly he is reminded: 'You came here while your son was ill, now that he is ill again you may go and take him elsewhere if you wish, but do realize that it is just your child being of a sickly constitution, and don't come to us accusing us of committing sorcery against him'. This skillfully neutralizes Yona's argument. That the village is severely tried during these weeks, nobody denies; it is in fact an issue debated night and day. However, the *ku-ambola* has now manipulated Yona into a situation where he can no longer with justification set himself off against the rest of the village; he would himself become liable to accusations if he did. He stayed on.

The values of village unity mean that one cannot simply move from one place and settle in another without good reasons. One cannot overtly refer to one's desire to become autonomous; and (in view of the lack of specificity in the stipulation of kinship role behaviour) one's objection to the treatment in the present village of residence is often too vague and too general to convince widely. Thus, to force the issue, petty occasions have to be blown up into a socially-acceptable pretext for leaving.

The success or failure of informal intra-familial conflict resolution reveals the degrees of structural stability of the village at that moment. If a party is intent on leaving, has an alternative place to go to, and/or is already considered expendable in his present village, then conflict settlement is likely to be unsuccessful, and the conflict will be allowed to escalate. In the opposite case, settlement will be accepted. On this basis a complex model of village stability could be constructed, taking into account such parameters as: age and sex of the village members, kinship relation to the headman, availability of residential alternatives, ecological pressure within the village, etc. This, however, falls beyond the scope of the present paper.

4. LITIGATION IN THE NEIGHBOURHOOD COURT: 'RESPECT CASES'

Against this background of the suppression of expressions of antagonism, a few social situations have to be isolated where the rights and obligations attached to certain roles are sufficiently well-defined to be susceptible to formal litigation – which may then reinforce, instead of threaten, group unity.

One class of such situations revolves around the management of honour and respect *(shishemo)* in the interaction between individuals and between groups. Consanguineal and affinal kinsmen of various categories, members of different generations, of either sex, of different local groups, common village members vis-à-vis headmen and chiefs, a chief vis-à-vis his headmen and his people – they are all subject to complex and well-defined rules of etiquette involving manner of address, of greeting, bodily postures and spatial arrangements, taboos on names and subjects (e.g., sexual matters), the proper way to voice a difference of opinion in front of members of that category, etc. Violation of these rules is taken very seriously not only by the direct victims of the insult, but also by close relatives of the offender and by outsiders. Unless the culprit can be pardoned for lack of age and experience (a child, a newly-married woman), he is sure to have a case *(mulandu)* on his hands. His close kinsmen, though highly embarrassed, will not be eager to let the matter drop. For here is, at last, a situation in which evident conflict can be resolved along clear institutional lines; instead of the ambiguities of personal friction in the intra-familial context, here is a touchstone of behaviour provided by fixed, impersonal, explicit rules. The respect case will lead to a clear verdict which will definitely end the matter. Once the case is publicly dealt with, those wronged are rehabilitated and reinforced in the respect to which they are due in the light of unchallenged principles; and the culprits are isolated and exposed as erring individuals. Once they have acknowledged their mistake, there is little fear left that the wronged party will pursue the matter by means of sorcery.

The close kinsmen of the offender therefore participate in, and may even push, the case for a number of reasons. They want to dissociate themselves, as a group, from the insult – thus publicly advertising (no matter what they feel privately) that no smouldering inter-group conflict lay at the bottom of the incident. They also want to protect their offending kinsmen, as well as themselves, from the sorcery the injured are sure to direct against them if the latter should not be placated. And finally, the kinsmen are in favour of their straying relative being taught a lesson since they themselves will benefit from an improvement of his social behaviour.

The main difference between such respect cases and the type of intra-family conflict discussed above (where formal legal action is impossible) seems to be this. In the respect cases both parties act not so much as individuals on the basis of their personal concerns and inclinations, but primarily as representatives of abstract, broad, general categories of society – young versus old, male versus female, parent-in-law versus child-in-law of the opposite sex, chief versus subjects, etc. The public interaction between these societal categories is subject to unchallenged explicit rules irrespective of the quality of the personal relationships that may exist between particular individual members belonging to these categories. An offence against these rules is not just an individual concern of the individual member in whose person the category is offended –

it is an assault on the total societal and moral order, and therefore of importance to allmembers of society. By contrast, in the case of intra-familial conflict we have to do with relationships whose form, contents, gratifications, and disappointments are almost entirely determined not by norms and rights but by such chance factors as the compatibility of character, the possibility of benefiting from each other in the pursuit of individual goals, etc. A closely related, and equally important, difference is that in respect cases the conflict revolves primarily around the management of such invisible, abstract, highly symbolic values as honour and respect, whereas the transactions between kinsmen in the village, such as tend to lead to crisis and intra-familial conflict regulation, primarily revolve around indispensible, down-to-earth, material items: money, food, assistance in concrete tasks, property. This suggests the possibility of a fascinating semantic analysis – but, again, not within the present paper.

In theory close kinsmen can litigate against each other in the idiom of respect cases, provided each represents a distinct general societal category. But, whereas this possibility is sometimes hinted at in the course of a quarrel, it is seldom put into effect. And even if a formal procedure is started, the case is usually hushed up much in the way of other intra-family conflict.

Example D illustrates the main aspects of respect cases.

D. The offensive youth. Chief Mukuata, the most senior of the 'original owners of the land' and therefore second only to Chief Kathembe, died suddenly at the end of a week in which a plot to oust him from his title had been exposed and had been generally discussed. The situation was likely to precipitate into violence, and so Mukuata was quickly buried next morning near the village in which he died: Malasha village, where his son lived and where Mukuata had happened to be mourning his recently deceased daughter-in-law. A chief should, however, be buried inside his own house, in the village that bears his name. After the burial some twenty closely related and senior mourners remained in Malasha village, including several chiefs and senior headmen from distant places. In the afternoon Shaimon, a classificatory sister's son of Mukuata from Mukuata village, and Kalembwe, a joking partner of the deceased chief from an adjoining valley arrived at Malusha village. They rode their bicycles to the middle of the village (very rude behaviour among the Nkoya), upset vessels with water and beer, threw around heavy logs of fire-wood and shook the roof of the mens' shelter under which the male mourners were assembled, all the time shouting insults: 'You old men, all of you, you killed Mukuata, you are sorcerers, and you even admitted to the fact by burying him not in his own house but in the bush. Is Mukuata not a great chief? You are sorcerers intent on killing his name', etc. Part of this behaviour was acceptable as expression of extreme grief, but to call a person a sorcerer publicly is a very great insult and especially to include all the great men from distant parts in this insult was inconceivable. Only with great difficulty did the local elders who had organised the burial manage to refrain from answering back. One who started to reply was quickly called away by an old woman. Bloodshed was in the air. However, those present lived up to their role of wise, senior men and ostensibly ignoring the provocations they began to discuss the necessity of building a respect case against Shaimon and Kalembwe. The case was heard next morning. Kalembwe, himself in his fifties and a headman, and more politically-minded than his companion, had retired from the scene at an early stage. He absented himself from the proceedings next morning, but sent a messenger offering his apologies for his behaviour of the previous day. These were accepted. The case against Shaimon however was heard, in Malasha village, with the offended high-ranking mourners constituting part of the neighbourhood court. The defendant showed not the least repentance, repeated his accusations and challenged his close kinsmen to refute them. Discussions the previous day had already indicated that public opinion, while disapproving of Shaimon's unskillful presentation strongly agreed with his protests against the improper burial. The court was greatly embarrassed: as hosts to the mourning chiefs from elsewhere they could not allow their guests to be insulted; but on the other hand, Shaimon was their close kinsman, and although he should not accuse them and their guests of sorcery, he was right in taking them to task for the improper burial of Mukuata. After extensive deliberations, when the boy adopted a more reconciliatory attitude, the most senior guest, Chief Shindovu (classificatory father to the deceased chief, and occupying in the distant valley of Kalombe a position similar to Mukuata's) saved the situation by the weak pretext that the youth had been intoxicated by drink and could not be held responsible for his statements. This suggestion was eagerly adopted by the local elders, and the case was dismissed without further steps being taken against Shaimon.

Litigation before the neighbourhood court can indeed be termed 'formal' by comparison with the utterly informal procedures of *ku-ambola*. A neighbourhood court case *(milandu)* has a fixed procedure which can be summarized as follows.

When there is public breach of respect rules, the more senior amongst those present raise the question of whether the incident could make an admissible case. This preliminary discussion will include close kinsmen of the injured party, of the offensive party, and outsiders. If they agree that the matter should be pursued further, they usually give it into the hands of one of the most senior headmen in the cluster of villages (a valley) where the incident took place. The proper person to be entrusted with the case is the 'subchief' (*mutwe ya ba mwene*, 'the chief's head') one of the senior local headmen whom the chief, in consultation with local headmen and elders, has appointed to represent him in each of the several valleys that make up a chief's area. The subchief's prerogatives are confined to the judicial field and (in contrast to the chief) neither government recognition nor payment are attached to his office. The sub-chief has by no means the monopoly over formal conflict regulation in his valley: any widely respected headman can organize and preside over cases in his neighbourhood. But a subchief is prone to claim a monopoly over the referral of cases to the official Local Court in Kapondwe, whenever such is deemed necessary (see below). When a case is entrusted to a senior person, he quickly informs other headmen and elders in the same, and occasionally adjoining valley, and a meeting is scheduled for the next day or so. Not infrequently such meetings are abortive, because either plaintiff or defendant or important witnesses or a sufficient number of headmen and elders, fail to turn up. If all necessary people are present, the case is heard. There is no fixed chairmanship: everybody in turn contributes questions and points of view, interrogates the parties and their witnesses, and helps to arrive at a consensual agreement. There is no entourage of ritual, and no oaths are taken. The verdict at which the neighbourhood court arrives can be acquittal, apology, or the payment of a fine to the wronged party. No payment goes to the court, the chief or the community in general.

By virtue of its own powers the neighbourhood court has no proper sanctions to enforce a verdict – it has, in particular, no power to use physical coercion. There are, however, many reasons why people accept the verdict, evenif this involves payment of a considerable sum of money. People are very keen to quench the conflict and thus to avoid sorcery. In addition, in those cases that could also be heard in the official Local Court (see below), the fines imposed by the neighbourhood court are considerably lower than those to be expected in the Local Court. So for defendants likely to be found guilty, it is advantageous to settle 'out of court', i.e., before the neighbourhood court. Moreover, ignoring the neighbourhood court's verdict carries unmistakable sanctions in terms of social credit as well as alleged susceptibility to sorcery and to ancestral revenge. More important than all these rather pragmatic calculations however is the fact that for the Nkoya villagers the headmen and elders in the neighbourhood court are not make-shift judges without proper authority (as they might appear from the point of view of a bureaucratic, centralized national legal system), but the very embodiment of moral judgement and authority. They are the heirs to great chiefly titles established in previous generations. Acceptance of their rulings is reinforced by deeply internalized values. This is not to say that these values are not increasingly challenged by the penetration, into the rural area, of modern organisational forms greatly at variance with the Nkoya gerontocratic model, and by the concomittant intensification of the rural inter-generation conflict. I have dealt with this complex problem, however, elsewhere (Van Binsbergen 1976 b). Finally, of course, the most comprehensive factor making for the effective functioning of the neighbourhood court is the fact that its structure is embedded in the total extra-judicial social process of Nkoya rural society. Patterns of authority, power, status, resources, which determine the social process in the neighbourhood, also determine the personnel and, to a large extent, the outcome, in the neighbourhood court. This does not exactly amount to a model situation of judicial independence – such as would be desirable, and possible, in a highly diversified industrial society. The Nkoya neighbourhood court displays far-reaching manipulation of the judicial process for the sake of extra-judicial processes, but this is precisely what endows this judicial institution with great relevance and efficiency in keeping Nkoya rural society more or less together.

5. MARRIAGE LAW IN NEIGHBOURHOOD COURT AND LOCAL COURT

Given the structure of Nkoya society, personal relationships and transactions between its members can become the object of formal litigation if between those involved rights and obligations have been stipulated to a sufficient degree of specificity and definition. Common, everyday transactions between kinsmen do not satisfy this condition and therefore are not subject to litigation. Etiquette however, provides one class of situations where this condition is met. The major other class of such situations concerns sex and marriage.

I will not try to give a full picture of Nkoya marriage law as it exists today, nor sketch the very considerable changes this institution turned out to have undergone over the past hundred years: the increase of geographical distance over which marriages are contracted; the decrease of kin-endogamy and village-endogamy; the increasing juxtaposition between bride-givers and bride-takers (complementary roles which tend to merge in the case of endogamy); and the introduction of bridewealth. A full discussion will involve a rather technical kinship-theoretical and quantitative analysis (Van Binsbergen 1974, forthcoming). For the purposes of the present paper, let it suffice to say that, while common everyday interaction and such conflicts as spring from it, are still mainly interpreted by contemporary rural Nkoya by reference to the fundamental bilateral orientation ('the child is in the middle') – the same people tend to adopt a rather different perspective when they discuss the legal position of adult women, and of minors, in the context of sex and marriage. In the latter case, emphasis is increasingly put on the question of custody, with all the close-to-exclusive rights implied in this term. In fact, the allocation of custody of women and children among their male consanguineal and affinal kinsmen, and the custodians' claims to marital payments and fines in relation, respectively, to transfer of and infringement upon their custody, have become the central issues in Nkoya family law today.

Nkoya now consider a child to be, primarily, in custody of his father's family if the father has paid bridewealth for the child's mother. If so, then the father is free to take the child wherever he wants, irrespective of dissolution of his marriage with the child's mother, through death or divorce. At the same time, the father is considered responsible for the care of the child, and he must compensate any other persons (e.g., the child's maternal relatives, or a subsequent husband of the child's mother[5]) who have temporarily acted for him. As long as no bride-price has been paid for a woman, her services as a woman and her powers of procreation are considered to be in the full control of her consanguineal relatives. Theoretically a distinction should be made here between her agnates (who control her if in the past they paid bridewealth for her mother) and her uterine kin, who control her in the alternative case; but in practice control over an unmarried woman is exercised by the senior kinsmen (agnatic, uterine, or both in case of overlap) in whose village she happens to dwell at that moment. In other words, the exercise of custody rights over an unmarried woman reflects not so much fixed rules but, pragmatically, her actual network involvement at a particular moment.

Custody is not unrelated to a notion of ownership. One is 'owner of a woman' *(mwine ya mbeleki)* much in the same way as one is 'owner' of a village, a title, a patch of cleared land, a gun. To any student of Central African ideas about property, and such connected themes as honour, masculinity, autonomy, and respect, it will be clear however that such an assertion hardly does justice to the complex underlying conceptual reality (cf. Gluckman 1972: 141f; Van Velsen 1964: 140f, 185f). Particularly, village, title, land, woman, and (to a certain extent) gun have the following connotations in common, which help to amend an all too naïve conception of 'ownership'. They represent central attributes of accomplished masculinity and as such have very strong symbolic implications. They impose upon the 'owner' *(mwine)* heavy moral obligations which are subject to constant scrutiny (occasionally leading to effective formal sanctioning by means of respect cases) from the total surrounding community: it is trust, in the legal sense, much more than ownership. And finally, the actual transfer of the implied rights from one individual to the next involves distinct procedural and ritual conditions, and, particularly, rules out purchase as a means of access.

All the same, usurping a custodian's control over a woman is considered 'stealing' and answerable under that heading. Thus, there is a fundamental identity between adultery (i.e., infringing upon a husband's rights) and premarital or extra-marital affairs with an unmarried woman (i.e., infringing upon the rights of the consanguineal kinsmen acting as custodians). There is the difference, though, that the latter is not supposed to enter into sexual relations with the woman concerned, whereas the husband is. While there is a great deal of extra-marital sex going on in the village (mainly in exchange for cash), sexual offence, if publicly known, is never considered lightly: it affects a woman's good name; large sums of money can be gained in litigation over such cases; even more important, public failure to control that of which one has the custody causes a fall in prestige, which can only be restored by successfully suing the offender.

The very high fines usually imposed for sexual offences have nothing to do with a transfer of custody over a woman. Therefore, a man who is known to have entered into an extra-marital relation with a woman, and who subsequently wishes to obtain paternal rights over the children that were born out of this union, normally faces the payment of both a fine and a regular bride-price. As long as a man is legally married to a woman (i.e., he has paid, or started to pay, the bride-price and has not yet gone through the legal procedure of formally divorcing her), he can sue any other man who usurps his rights. Emphasis here is upon sexual rights, but essentially the same applies to other domestic tasks such as cooking food, washing clothes, helping out at a funerary party, etc. Hence the necessity of formal divorce: without divorce any husband, even after a *de facto* breakdown of his marriage, could successfully sue any other man who tries to take his place.

Because of the recent development of a considerable body of well-defined rules and obligations, conflict in the sphere of sex and marriage need not be suppressed and hushed up, but can be publicly dealt with in the formal setting of litigation. This leads to either reconciliation or divorce. The case will initially be heard before the neighbourhood court. The proceedings are the same as described for respect cases.

Theoretically, divorce[6] involves return of the bridewealth. In practice however, no such restitution occurs in many, perhaps the majority of divorce cases. In some cases the bride-givers will themselves offer to return the bridewealth and to dissolve the marriage: if they feel that the woman and her children are suffering under the neglect and the bad ways of her husband (drinking, violence, leaving the family without adequate housing, food and clothing, spreading venereal disease, and endangering her and her unborn children by breaking taboos on illicit sex). The same applies to marital conflicts arising out of wrong behaviour of the woman (adultery, inadequate housekeeping, failure to show sufficient respect vis-à-vis her senior in-laws) in which case it will be the bride-takers asking their money back.

The outcome of such cases depends largely on the inter-group relations between bride-givers and bride-takers. If the senior representatives of both groups have good mutual relations, and in general a high prestige, which they cannot allow to be threatened by the bad marital behaviour of a member of their group, an effort will be made to make him better his ways. The case usually ends in reconciliation and apology; a typical example is the following case. The proceedings are presented in some detail, as they nicely render the general flavour of Nkoya conflict resolution, and show the typical strategies employed.

E. The iron bedframe. Kabambi, a middle-aged man from Mukowe's village, has two wives. The senior one, Ennesi, he has had for many years; the other is Loshia, a young girl he married only recently. Shortly after this marriage Kabambi was asked by his new brother-in-law to lend him K4.[7] Kabambi refused and the brother-in-law offered to sell him an iron bed-frame for K6, which Kabambi agreed to. The bed had belonged to Loshia's deceased elder brother, who had left it to her when he died. Kabambi was keen to acquire ownership over this bed that his new wife was using; he feared she would remind him 'This is not your bed'. (The conjugal bed plays an important part in Nkoya sexual symbolism.) Ever since this time Ennesi had retired to her consanguineal kinsmen's village, only to come to Mukowe's for a few days of gardening. She refused to stay: but she did not refuse sexual intercourse – provided that Kabambi would come and sleep at her own village, which he refused. Obviously the senior wife feels threatened in her position by the younger co-wife, but for fear of being accused of sorcery (a standard allegation in the case of polygyny among the Nkoya) she cannot afford to express animosity with regard to this rival. However, no one would deny that she has a right to fair treatment from their mutual husband, and she often scolds him when she feels she is getting the worse share of the game and fish he brings home. This, however, is not sufficient reason to explain her absenteeism. Puzzled by Ennesi's behaviour, and annoyed, finally, by her refusal to return home, Kabambi decided to put the case before the neighbourhood court. The court is held away from the village, at an open space where Mukowe made chairs. Most headmen of the neighbourhood attend, as well as many elders and lesser men. The gist of the proceedings follows here (apart from the spouses, all taking part in the discussion are village headmen).

Shelonga: Look, Kabambi, you called us here, what is the matter?

Kabambi: My wife stays away and refuses to do anything.

Shelonga (turning to the woman): Well what is the matter?

Ennesi: I haven't got a good home, no clothes, no pot, no mosquito-net. I am eaten alive by the mosquitos. I don't have any good things in the house. My little sister (= co-wife) has got an iron bedframe but I am the senior wife and I don't have one.

Kapashi: Is this true?

Kabambi: No, if you think it necessary I can call children to bring and show what she has got inside her house.

(Children are sent on the errand and the result is truly impressive; Ennesi's possessions include two big iron pots on legs, three small pots, six plates, eight spoons. The only obviously missing items are blankets; but these she is likely to have taken away when she left Mukowe's.)

Kanjilo: Look, this house is full of possessions. Many people have only got one pot, and then not a pretty one like these. So what do you really want?

Ennesi: This is not what I mean. But I have no proper clothes.

Kanjilo: So what do you wear right now?

Ennesi: These are the clothes I bought myself, with my own money that I got from the sale of my maize.

(The exchange continues in the same vein. It finally becomes explicit that Ennesi wants a divorce, and that the only concrete thing she can mention as a ground is her co-wife's iron bedframe.)

Kanjilo: In the past, before the Whites came, did we have an iron bedframe to sleep upon? No. Did we have a mosquito-net? No. In that time, was there divorce just like that, for nothing? No. So why do you behave like a little girl now, why do you want to divorce over such a small matter?

Wankie: Look, all of you, I find this a very difficult case myself. The easiest solution would be just to divorce today.

(Nobody agrees with this solution).

Kapuka: Look, this is my sister. You cannot tell her to divorce, just like that. You are a big man, you are supposed to know how things are done in Court. This is no reason for divorce, at most we can caution. The only problem is really the bed. We don't know about her clothes or her blankets, but we see all the things that she has got in her house, so we don't believe her complaints about blankets and clothes either. The only problem is the bedframe. When this man bought it for his junior wife, he should also have given his senior wife a bedframe or K6. That is the only problem. This woman is my sister, I do not want her to divorce just like that.

Mukowe: I have no proper power over these people. Originally Kabambi lived far away from me, he only came to settle with me when we ourselves moved to this place. He never reported his troubles to me. Today is the first time that I hear all these things. Only Kabambi's wife came to tell me that she was leaving, never to return. 'Just ask your little brother (Cousin Kabambi) if you want to know why', she said. But when I asked him, Kabambi did not seem to know the reason. The best solution is really just to buy another bedframe.

Kapuka: We do have faith in Kabambi. For whenever somebody would fall ill, Kabambi would tie his blankets and bring them to sleep in that place until everything would be all right again. And when someone would die, it was the same. But since this woman started to vex him he has changed. He stopped doing all these things because of you, Ennesi.

Mukowe: Look, out of my own experience I can answer you back. I can reply to what you just said. When Kabambi's mother died, your sister slept there for only two days, no matter how many mourners came and how much work there was to do. On occasion of another funeral, she only came for one day. On yet another occasion, she did not even turn up at all. That is why this man is annoyed now!

(The court discussed the various aspects of the case, but found it hard to arrive at a verdict.)

Shakupota: The only problem is the bedframe, really. Kabambi should buy another bedframe as soon as possible. Then if in future a new problem arises, we can see whether someone really made a mistake, or whether it is all just a matter of jealousy (= the state of mind in which one resorts to sorcery).

Kapuka: My sister, now you should take away all your possessions from our village and go back to live with Kabambi again. He will buy a bedframe for you or give you K6. This is the end.

(Ennesi is obviously not entirely satisfied with this verdict; but since even her close relatives helped to arrive at the verdict, and agree with it, she has no choice.)

In this case we see how, for the sake of mutual interests of male consanguineal and affinal kinsmen, obvious indications of deeper personal and group conflicts are ignored and Ennesi is forced to yield to these interests. It would be interesting to assess, in a follow-up, whether the senior wife's dissatisfaction with the verdict has in fact precipitated a continuation of the conflict in the sphere of sorcery, divination, and ritual.

Divorce is not infrequently the result of a mutual agreement between the spouses, feeling that they should separate on the basis of incompatibility of habits and of character. Such divorce with mutual consent need not lead to a disruption of inter-group relations between bride-givers and bride-takers. In the public discussion of the case in the village court emphasis will be put on the personal conditions that worked against marital success – any more collective, structural conditions involving inter-group relations are purposely ignored. If the spouses are found to be irreconciliable, no pressures will be applied to let the marriage continue: the senior kinsmen fear to be blamed if in future the marital conflict might lead to disaster (violence, sorcery, death). An acceptable arrangement for the financial aspects of the marriage will be found, and whatever tension remains is expressed not through escalation and sorcery, but through mild joking between the former spouses and between the former husband and his successor. That inter-group relations have not suffered is ostentatiously brought out by the fact that the former in-laws continue to address each other by affinal kinship terms. The good 'post-marital' inter-group relations guarantee that the former husband will not try to make money out of a subsequent attachment of the woman, so no official divorce at the

Local Court is necessary. Such divorce arrangements are considered most honourable for all parties involved.

Relatively frictionless dissolution of marriage is, however, impossible if the marriage has been contracted over a wide geographical distance (which makes close day-to-day interaction between the affines unlikely); if the marriage has already survived for a long time; if previous reconciliation has not succeeded in improving the marriage; or if serious shortcomings, and escalated intra-family tension (e.g., recent deaths), conflict, and the associated sorcery, have reduced marital conflict to a grim battle for survival. Under such conditions various factors combine to take the formal dissolution out of the hands of the neighbourhood court and to entrust it to the Local Court.

The main factors working towards a considerable proportion of the marriage cases being tried before the Local Court are the following. The great majority of marriages is contracted in the village without any official registration; such marriages do constitute valid customary marriages before the Local Court. However, this Court does not acknowledge the validity of a divorce that is pronounced by a neighbourhood court. Therefore, it will admit the case of a former husband who, while divorced in the neighbourhood court, sees fit to sue a man who has taken his place. By consequence, divorced women are much more attractive partners for future marriages if they are in possession of a divorce certificiate issued by the Local Court. Fears of a former husband involving the Local Court are all the more realistic, since in sharp contrast with the neighbourhood court, this Court can impose fines as high as K200 (maximum) and can reinforce its rulings by appeal to the *district* police. Sometimes it is the subchiefs themselves who press for referral to the Local Court: they are aware that it would endanger their brittle informal position of authority if, contrary to the Local Court's explicit wish, they attempted to handle cases that are not mitigated by the desire for good post-affinal relations among the parties, and that therefore could lead to major conflicts, with affines (knowing what they could get at the Local Court) demanding sums of money far bigger than the neighbourhood court is supposed to handle. Moreover, there are certain cases which would furnish admissible grounds for divorce before the Local Court, but not before the neighbourhood court. E.g., according to the Local Court a wife is entitled to divorce and to considerable compensation if a man has left her (particularly to go and work in town) and has not contributed towards her expenses for at least one year. In the neighbourhood the absent husband's relatives would normally try to play down the wife's allegations of neglect, and the elders would seldom risk a personal conflict with the former. In such a situation a wife may consider it to her advantage to apply to the Local Court.[8]

With respect to sexual offences a pattern is followed similar to that of divorce cases. If good relations and a considerable overlap exist between the immediate kingroups of plaintiff and defendant, settlement will be in the neighbourhood court, and while a relatively small fine may be imposed, emphasis will be on redress of the offender and on the manipulation of honour: the group whose honour has suffered damage because they publicly failed to control a woman entrusted to their custody attempts to restore its dignity and to manoeuvre the defendant's group into a situation where they lose honour by having to admit that they failed to control one of their male members. If the structural requirements for internal settlement are absent the case is usually taken to the Local Court. Such a situation occured in example F.

F. Passion and politics. Alisi is a young, widowed daughter of headman Kabeshas' sister. When her husband's death put and end to Alisi's residence at the district centre (where she had joined Zambia's one party), she joined Kabesha's distant village. In this area the party had so far found very few sympathisers and Alisi proceeded to found a Women's branch of the party. Her work brought her in contact with Peter, chairman of the likewise budding local youth branch of the party. Peter lives in Mulempwe village at the other side of the valley; here he had only remote kinsmen and is rather isolated, as regards his kinship-political position. The acquaintance developed to a stage where an enraged Kabesha has to chase Peter out of Alisi's hut in the middle of the night. The sexual offence, in conjunction with Peter's insults of Kabesha when caught *flagrante delicto*, constituted an obvious case. The relative social isolation and low popularity of both the plaintiff (cf. A) and the defendant, the absence of valued relationships between their respective villages, and the knowledge that the offences constitute an admissible case before the Local Court where they would fetch higher damages than before the neighbourhood court, led to the decision to have the case tried at Kapondwe. Here Peter was found guilty and payment of damages was imposed on him.

6. CONCLUSION

In contemporary Nkoya rural society the Local Court is, as to its geographical location, its personnel, and its functioning, peripheral to the mainstream of the social process. As compared to other institutions of conflict regulation (intra-village *ku-ambola*, the ad-hoc neighbourhood court), the Local Court is infrequently used for very specific types of cases and under specific conditions, such as were outlined in the preceding pages. The Local Court, although the only formal judicial institution stipulated within the modern administration of the area, is not in the focus of the judicial process; and such conflicts as it deals with are hardly of decisive importance to the individuals and groups involved – as compared to those conflicts which are resolved without reference to the Local Court.[9]

The Local Court, since it is there and since it commands powerful sanctions (ultimately upheld by the nation-state), superimposes upon the internal Nkoya institutions an additional judicial framework. It endeavours to define and to promote such rights and obligations as it presumes to exist between individuals. Neither the definition of its legal premises, nor its authority, nor indeed its personnel, are to any significant degree determined by the social processes within Nkoya rural society. Precisely because the Local Court is external to these processes, it can efficiently deal with conflicts between parties who are not tied to each other by multiplex roles in everyday village situations (and whose conflict therefore would directly affect a host of other people in their environment) but who on the contrary have a specific, one-stranded relationship involving fairly specific rights, obligations, and grievances.

While present-day sexual and marital relationships frequently approach this ideal-type, the bulk of social relationships in Nkoya society is still of the inclusive, multiplex nature: they involve people who are tied by, at the same time, kinship; economic, political, and ritual interests; common residence within the same village or neighbourhood. In these latter situations, involving such a peripheral agency as the Local Court may mean a temporary advantage (in terms of financial gain and revenge) to one or two individuals involved. But it will also inevitably disrupt the existing pattern of relationships to such an extent as to threaten seriously individual security, perhaps even survival; and this also applies to those few who superficially appear to benefit from the Local Court's ruling. The latter's turning to the Local Court is generally resented by the other party (and often by public opinion as well); even if the Local Court manages to sort out the concrete issues of the case, new ill-will is bred, the underlying conflicts over authority, status, and autonomy tend to linger on, and the risk of crisis (sorcery, fission) often remains unabated. Therefore, given well-developed internal alternatives to the Local Court, which are still endowed with sufficient authority in the eyes of the participants as well as tolerated by the Local Court and higher-level authorities, there is little wonder that most conflicts seek their solution outside the Local Court. This is particularly so since, closely related to their immediate conflict-regulatory function, *ku-ambola* and the neighbourhood court provide an arena where, as a direct reflection and continuation of the extra-judicial social process, basic ideals of Nkoya society are expressed, and where the status, authority and power of significant social groups, social categories, and their senior representatives are continually examined, competed for, and redistributed.

What are the implications of my argument?

Not, I should emphasize, a posthumous attack on Gluckman's extremely valuable and seminal work. There is not the slightest suggestion that his masterly description and analysis of the judicial system of the Lozi proper should contain any major distortions, even if there is a marked difference with the judicial situation in a Lozi subject tribe, thirty years later. On the other hand, inadequacies of my own research (Van Binsbergen, forthcoming) may explain part of the discrepancy.

In addition, there are several systematic explanations of the discrepancy: the specific historical differences between the central Lozi and the Nkoya variant, within the former Barotse state; and, beyond this, a different research approach.

Comprehensive social change over several decades, including the attainment of national independence and the incorporation of the Barotse administration into the national administration of Zambia, may appear a ready explanation (Caplan 1970; Gluckman 1967a: 368f; Van Binsbergen 1975, 1976a, b, c). Yet what data I have on the Nkoya judicial situation in the 1930's–1950's suggests that also in the time of Gluckman's fieldwork a similar discrepancy existed.

There are two crucial points which, although never denied by Gluckman, have so far failed to attract sufficient attention among his commentators. First, Gluckman's research was confined to the Mongu-Lealui area: the small core of the Barotse state, where Lozi speakers then outnumbered any other groups and where the Lozi king's power and authority were most effective. Secondly, the Barotse state as described by Gluckman was only of recent origin and in full expansion – and expansion of the Lozi legal system, also during the colonial period, was an aspect of this. As late as 1937 the colonial administration helped to establish a Lozi appeal court (Naliele *kuta*) headed by the son of a Lozi Paramount Chief, in the centre of Nkoya country. A major reason for the colonial administration supporting this move was that the imperfect incorporation of the area into the Barotse indigenous organisation made it until then impossible for disputes to go beyond the highly competing local chiefs and *indunas* and to use such appeal opportunities as the central Barotse judicial system provided (G.C.R. Clay, personal communication).

On one level of analysis the Nkoya (and perhaps other subject tribes on the woodland plateau of the former Barotseland, now Zambia's Western Province) occupy, as far as their legal system is concerned, quite a different position from the central Lozi, whose institutions used to focus on the kingship and the land, against the background of the unique Zambezi flood plain-ecology. The difference in effective incorporation into a larger state system does explain in part the discrepancy between the judicial situation among the central Lozi and the Nkoya. On top of this came then, after independence, the general dismantling of the Lozi legal administration and of the judicial role of the Nkoya chiefs (section 2); these recent changes further added to the peripheral nature of the Local Court among the Nkoya.

However, these structural differences between the Central Lozi in Gluckman's time, and the contemporary Nkoya, mainly concern what one might call the intermediate social-structural level: the supra-local organisation which is superimposed on the lowest, village level – but which is in itself determined, to a high degree, by national and international conditions: the governmental and industrial power distribution, world markets of labour and goods, urbanization, etc. However large the historical differences on the intermediate level, on the grass-root level of the village there exists a striking similarity between present-day Nkoya and the Lozi village society of the 1940's, and indeed between these two, and a great many other village societies throughout Central Africa. The small villages, the high geographical mobility, the competition for political and residential following along kinship lines, the competition for titles carrying high prestige, the continuous re-alignment, and fission reflecting the conflicts engendered in this way, the part played by sorcery and sorcery accusations in these processes, the shifting agriculture with a fringe of animal husbandry as providing an additional, ecological basis for village dynamics – these are all recurrent themes in the anthropology of Central African villages (Barnes 1954; Colson 1958, 1962; Cunnison 1959; Marwick 1965; Mitchell 1956; Richards 1939; Turner 1957; Van Velsen 1964; Watson 1958).

Alternatively, on the highest level of national and international politics and political economy, most members of contemporary Nkoya society along with the overwhelming majority of rural Central Africans since the early decades of colonial rule (including most of Gluckman's Lozi), fall within the class of peripheral peasantry. In this respect their situation is also far from unique. Determined by central conditions way beyond the control of the villagers, this situation is characterized by a paucity of local cash opportunities, dependence on urban-rural relations, and an increasingly direct influence of central agencies in the rural aras. The impact of this macro set-up upon the contemporary rural social and judicial processes can hardly be overestimated.

If both on the lowest and on the highest structural level the Nkoya and the Central Lozi are not too exceptional among Central African rural societies of the twentieth century, then the salient points brought out in my analysis can certainly not be explained exhaustively by mere reference to intermediate-level differences between Nkoya and Lozi. I would moreover, suggest that some of the Nkoya patterns outlined in the present paper may also be found to exist in modified form in other Central African societies today.

This finally brings us to an important methodological point. Whatever the historical and ethnographic peculiarities of the Nkoya, I suspect that my findings also, and to a considerable extent, depend on a difference of perspective adopted in my research, as compared with that of other legal-anthropological studies made in Central Africa. If one concentrates on formal court cases as the unit of study, then the numerous instances of conflict and conflict regulation which occur on the village scene but which never enter this formal setting simply fall outside the scope of the research. If, as I have tried to do, one concentrates on the ongoing social process in the village, taking as one's unit of study such social conflicts as arise, and tracing the social processes through which these conflicts are brought to an end, then litigation before a formal Local Court necessarily appears as only one of the options open to the participants; and it may well turn out that they pursue this option rarely, due to structural conditions which one may then set out to identify. Strictly speaking, the two approaches, while both legitimate and complementary to each other, yield incomparable results.

While one may wonder how limited an insight into a formal judicial system can be gained if the latter is studied as just one of many options within the overall system of conflict regulation (my weakness), one may as well ask if a judicial system can be properly understood if we continue to study it on the exclusive basis of one pre-conceived model, the formal court situation.[10]

NOTES

1. Fieldwork was carried out in the period February 1972–April 1974. I am indebted to the following persons and institutions: my informants and the Zambian authorities for their warm co-operation; the University of Zambia for allowing me to devote ample time to research while I was a lecturer in the Department of Sociology, and later for research facilities provided by the Institute for African Studies; to my wife, Henny E. van Rijn; to D.K. Shiyowe for excellent research assistance; to M. Gluckman, A.J.F. Köbben, H.J. Simons, and especially J. van Velsen for encouragement and advice; to the Netherlands Foundation for the Advancement of Tropical Research (WOTRO) for supporting the writing-up of the field-data; and finally to R.L. Abel, W. Bleek, R. Canter, G. Clay, A.J.F. Köbben, H. Mwene, S.A. Roberts, H.J. Simons, and J. van Velsen for valuable criticism of earlier drafts.
2. All names of people have been altered, as have the names of Nkoya localities.
3. I.e., Kololo, which (contrary to the original Lozi, or Luyana, still the official Lozi court language) is not intelligible to Nkoya speakers, unless they have expressly learned this language.
4. At least, as long as the relation with the dead has not yet developed to a crisis: supernatural illness, possession, post-mortem sorcery; in the latter cases, religious specialists are resorted to as the main link between the living and the dead: Van Binsbergen 1972, in 1976 c, and forthcoming.
5. It is common that a divorced woman brings her infant children into the household of a later husband; problems will begin to arise by the time these children have reached school-going age, involving expenses for school uniform, etc.
6. Divorce is relatively frequent in Nkoya rural society. A preliminary estimate indicates that over 60% of all marriages end in divorce (instead of death). For detailed quantitative analysis, see Van Binsbergen, forthcoming.
7. K (Kwacha), the Zambian currency. At the time of research K1 was about Hfl. 4,—.
8. This is one of the rare instances of recognized discrepancy between the jurisprudence of the Local Court and the neighbourhood court. Disputes over land (particularly over highly-valued riverside gardens, pressure on which is beginning to build up now) provide another example: while land disputes are hardly admissible before the neighbourhood courts (due to Nkoya ideal conceptions of land-holding), they are occasionally tried before the Local Court.
9. I am aware that my rather intuitive assessment of relative importance of conflicts should be refined by explicit operationalization and measurement.
10. In later reassessments of his Barotse legal research, Gluckman did admit to having studied the Barotse court cases too much in isolation, and to have ignored their relation with the ongoing social process in general (1967a: 371f; 1967b: XVI).

Family dispute settlement and the Zambian judiciary: local-level legal adaptation* 4

RICHARD S. CANTER
Boston University

My concern in this paper is the adaptations which have occurred in Zambia between the National government's local court and local-level forms of dispute settlement. I will examine the conditions under which rural Zambian families turn to the National judiciary to settle their internal disputes, and the role which the local court plays when faced with family dispute settlement.

The Zambian government's local court, the lowest level court in the Zambian judicial hierarchy, is in most cases the forum of last resort in family disputes. Family forums for dispute settlement (*Nkuta)*, though not officially sanctioned, operate successfully through mediation to resolve the bulk of disputes which come before them. When family mediation is unsuccessful, cases are generally appealed to the village moot where mediation is attempted by village authorities. Should village mediation fail, the case will be appealed to the local court for adjudication.

From an analysis of dispute settlement behaviour at the local level, through the use of 'extended case' material, two developments may be observed which reveal significant adaptation of traditional forms of dispute settlement and the local court procedures. The first is the socio/legal expectation on the part of the community and the local court that a mediated settlement should be attempted before bringing a case for

* Field work in Zambia on which this research is based was supported by the Institute of Health (National Institute of General Medical Science) training grant number GM-1224.

For their critical comments and readings of earlier drafts of this paper I wish to thank Elizabeth Colson, Richard Abel, S.A. Roberts and Jaap van Velsen.

adjudication. The local court assumes that a case has first been heard within the appropriate kinship and social networks which would have 'corporate concern' over the litigants and their conflict. This expectation maintains the jural authority of family and village leaders while allowing free access, through 'appeal', to the local court.

The second development concerns the decision-making role of the local court. In family disputes the court calls a 'family authority' as 'expert witness'. The family authority will be a kinsman who stands in a superior kinship relationship to the litigants, and most often of the ascending generation. Fact-finding is assessed mainly from the testimony of the family authority, and the decision-making role of the court reflects his opinion as to fault in the family dispute. Although the family authority was unable to foster a mediated settlement, by adhering to his testimony the court backs his decision with the authority of the National government. Where a family authority is non-committal in his testimony, the court tends to render a non-definitive decision, awaiting a more definitive family opinion. The court seems unwilling to undermine the authority of the family by becoming an alternative forum for family dispute settlement, but attempts to seek responsibility for decision making from within the family, whereas it exercises an independent decision-making role in non-family disputes.

THE SETTING

The area under study is the Lenje speaking chieftancy of Mungule situated in the Central Province of Zambia. Mungule is one of six Lenje chieftancies which are administratively recognized by the Central Government. In the past quarter century the area has become increasingly multi ethnic as migrants from all over Zambia and immigrants from Rhodesia, Tanzania, Angola, and Malawi have taken up residence to exploit the good potential for cash-cropping. Mungule lies approximately ten miles north-west of the Zambia capital of Lusaka and is crossed on its Eastern border by the railway which connects Livingstone with the copperbelt. A rich market exists both in the capital and on the Copperbelt for the cash-crops grown in the chieftaincy. Today, the population is approximately 28,000 people, 65% Lenje, 35% multi-ethnic.

Like most rural areas in the independent nation-states, life in Mungule is profoundly affected by the policy decisions of the Zambian government. A decision to curtail trade with Southern Africa will within a short time determine the price and availability of staple goods – sugar, salt, soap, etc. – in the rural area. National policy changes which offer free medical care and education are having a dramatic effect on rural health care and schooling. Yet, in the day to day workings of the chieftaincy, the daily events which touch people's lives – good fortune, disputes, the desire to expand one's economic potential, the competition for status and power, – are played out against family, village, and chieftaincy networks and alliances. To a great degree, the events which most clearly affect people's lives are generated within the boundaries of their local-level world. Accordingly, it is the local-level political and legal systems which order the events of this world.

CONTEMPORARY-TRADITIONAL LEADERSHIP

With few exceptions, local-level politics and law are controlled through the traditional offices associated with the ruling Lenje elite: chief, deputy chief, local court members, headmen, and elders who represent large matrilineally-oriented kin groups. Even national office holders, at the local level, are drawn from the ruling elite.

I have chosen the seemingly contradictory term 'contemporary-traditional' to describe the Lenje elite, as I believe that it best categorizes their political and jural power base.

If this were a paper on the social, political, and economic changes which have affected this area, one would be able to describe the adaptability, progressiveness, and forward-looking attitudes of these people. They have moved with the major forces which have transformed community life; yet, their power derives from their legitimate control of traditional offices. They have not resisted change, nor have they been overwhelmed by it. Hence, the categorization 'contemporary-traditional.' This dichotomy can also be used to describe the ideology toward legal change which seems implicit in the decision-making role of the local court as it hears family disputes.

THE LOCAL COURT

Originally, the local court was the 'chief's court', where cases of major consequence were heard which could not be settled at the village level. In the early 1940's, the British Colonial Government, using their policy of indirect rule, institutionalized the 'chief's court' into the 'native court' and began paying the chief and his assessors government salaries. All civil cases between Africans within the chief's area could be brought before the 'native court'. Through statute and legislation, certain rules and procedures were enforced, but primarily local customary law and procedure characterized the working of individual 'native courts' in rural areas. This situation remained more or less constant until 1968, when all Zambian chiefs were removed from the now-called 'Local Courts'. Court members, the court president, and court assessor, are now nominated by the chief, and their tenure must be ratified every three years by the people.

The Mungule Local Court has five staff members, the President, Assessor, Court Secretary, and two court messengers. The latter three are civil servants chosen by the government. The Court President and Assessor have been sitting on the court for almost twenty-five years. The Court President is in his late fifties and the Court Assessor is in his early seventies. Both are village headmen, and both are members of families considered to be the original Lenje migrants to the Mungule chieftaincy. Both are multi-lingual, which allows migrants to give testimony in their mother tongues. The Court President speaks fluent English, though this language is hardly ever used in the court.

THE DATA

The cases used in this paper were observed and recorded by me at the Mungule Local Court during a 3-month period in 1971. All cases which came before the court during this period were recorded, giving a sample of about 150 cases. Of these, fifty were chosen for 'extended case analysis'. Court members, litigants, witnesses, family members, and other remedy agents who had heard the dispute were interviewed. Where possible, the pre-history of the dispute was elicited. In the summer of 1973 I began an enquiry of the consequences of the settlement. The eight cases presented here are from the extended case sample. The first two are included verbatim. In the following six I have exerpted the testimony of the 'expert witness' and the judgment of the court. I have checked my findings against all other family cases in the sample and with two exceptions the findings were borne out. The first exception was an assault case between a mother and a son, which was the only case in the total sample which came directly to the Local Court. The second exception was a family case between new migrants to the area who had no locally based kinship network. In this type of case, the decision-making role of the Local Court reveals independent decision making without the use of the 'family authority' as 'expert witness'.

THE CASE MATERIAL

Abbreviations:
C.S. = Court Secretary
C.P. = Court President
C.A. = Court Assessor
D. = Defendant
P. = Plaintiff
W. = Witness
1 kwacha = $ 1.40. in 1971

Case 1. Slander. Sister/Sister.
Plaintiff – late 40's; Defendant – mid-30-s. Ethnic group: Lenje/Lenje.

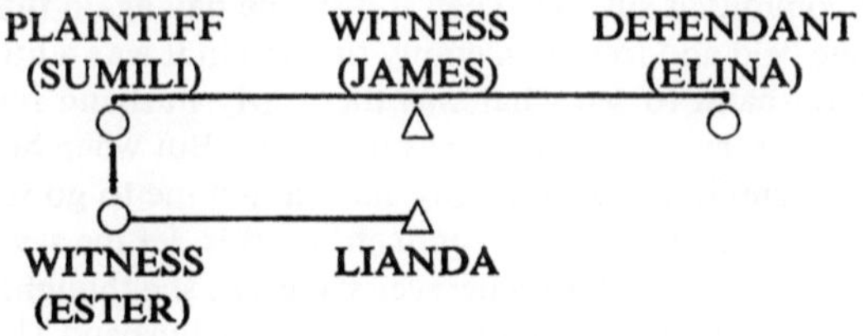

C.S. Elina, Sumili is accusing you of having accused her of being a witch *(muloshi)*. Do you plead guilty or not guilty?

D. Not guilty.

C.A. Sumili, do you have any witnesses?

P. Yes, James is my witness.

C.M. James, out of the Court please.

C.A. Elina, do you have a witness?

D. Yes, Ester is my witness.

C.M. Ester, out of the Court.

C.A. Can we have a statement from you, Sumili?

P. It was one day that I saw three young ladies come to my place. When they came there they informed me to come to James' house to go and have a *Nkuta*. I went, and when I arrived there I sat down, and James asked if my grandchild would take some tea, and the child did. Then the three young ladies came in and my younger sister (the D.) started beating me and telling me that I was a witch who had bewitched her deceased husband Thomas. After beating me, James came to separate us. Then Elina went around in the compound saying, 'All of you should know that Sumili is the witch who bewitched my husband Thomas.' She went here and there preaching the same words. James tried to explain that this was very wrong. And I said to him, 'How can I be accused of witchcraft? I'm a grown up person. All of my brothers and sisters who passed away, I was never accused before of witchcraft. How come now I would bewitch someone who is not even my relative except by marriage?' All this disturbed me so that I felt that I would come here to court to see if you could settle all these disputes.

C.A. Elina, have you heard what your sister has just stated? Is it true or not true?

D. It is untrue. What I only know is this. This sister of mine first of all was staying at Lalungwa mabwe, from there she went to Mamba village, from there she was chased and went with her husband to Mumbwa, from there she went to join our daughter in Lusaka. Then her daughter bought a certain place at Kabanana where my husband and I lived. Then my sister came in and I got one pot and one plate from her. This became the main topic wherever she went. She said 'Elina has taken my pot and my plate. You can't bring in anything.' She went up and down preaching against me because I took a plate and a pot. One day I felt I was getting very disappointed because my own sister should do such a thing, so I felt that I should go and commit suicide. Then I ran away, and my husband Thomas and my sister and other people went to see the witchdoctor. The witchdoctor said, 'I think that Elina hasn't committed suicide yet. She is still living. She is at Nkomesha. You go and you will get her there.' They came in and got me; I had not committed suicide. Then it was one day again that this sister of mine went to the field and found an empty tin, and in it was a little bit of snuff. She called my husband to see what was there. My husband refused, but she pleaded that he go there to see what was in the tin. But when he went there he found that it was snuff. The second day she wanted me to go see what was in that small tin, which I did. And to comment on this, let me say that my sister whatever she saw on the road, or wherever she went, she thought she saw some medicine. She always thought that it was my deceased husband Thomas who was trying to bewitch her. She called me and my husband witches. That second day when my sister called me to see the medicine in the snuff box, I refused to go. But she persisted. At last I went there and checked and found that it was still the same thing. The next morning when I was out in the village I found out from some people, 'Your sister was drunk and she was saying that, "You know what I'm doing at that field. I pluck all the maize off so that I can have good spacing between the stalks, so it will be very healthy. But when I go the next day, I find that someone has made them grow close again there, just as alive as the day before when I plucked them off. And I know who is doing it; it should be Elina and her husband, and nobody else."' She went from place to place complaining, 'I don't know what I'm going to eat with my children this year. My sister is bewitching my maize. I thin the maize and when I go back the next morning I get the same maize growing that I plucked'. I think that this information annoyed me, and I even went to her place and shouted at her and warned her, 'That's why you don't stay at the same place for a very long time. Always people chase you from their places because you are a bad woman.' Not even three weeks past, my husband became sick. He couldn't pass water. At last he was passing puss. One of his sons took him to the hospital, as far as Kabwe. All that failed, and at last he passed away at his village in Nkomesha. During all that time that my husband was sick, my own sister used to accuse him of being a witch. That he was the one bewitching her garden, that he was using some charms which put insects in her crops. And she said, 'I'm sure Thomas will die because of the witchcraft he has been committing on my fields every year.' And also accusing me of being a witch. After all, I'm a bit too late. It should have been me who first summoned my sister. When I came back from the name inheritance where I was inherited by the new husband of mine, I heard that one of the sons of Sumili was killed, and they were accusing his sister Ester. But me I told them, 'I don't believe in this story, and I don't think Ester can do it that is her own brother.' So all that thing ended like that, until at last my older sister Sumili one day met Ester at the beer hall, and there she raised up that topic, and then later there was a fight. (Sumili and Ester are mother and daughter.) There Ester said to me, 'Even your own husband Thomas was bewitched by my own mother Sumili.' What Sumili told me was 'that Thomas was a witch who went dancing at night at their houses. But when he came to my house he found that my charm was very strong, and when he came in I saw him, and I pierced him with that small horn of mine, and the bloodstains were seen from my house to his house. That's how Thomas died. It was me, Sumili, who killed him when he came to bewitch me at my house during the night'. You know before Thomas died this sister of mine used to come to our house trying to get some medicine so that she could bewitch the husband of Ester, and the husband of the other daughter. I used to tell her that my husband is not a witch, he has no medicine for bewitching people. Another day she came in and wanted some medicine which you put on the fire, and the smoke from that fire would break love between her own son and his wife. But I told her that I didn't have that. Later on she managed to go to Matero and there she got some medicine. So I told Ester, 'Listen, not only did she bewitch my husband, but she wants to bewitch the love between you and your husband. She wants to put medicine on your fire'. Now we decided to summon her to James' place for *Nkuta*. James told us to come on Sunday. When we came – me, Ester, her husband – we found Sumili not there, so we went to call her. When we got there with her, we saw James shouting at some of his nieces, and was chasing them. 'You go to Mumbwa to go and see your fellow Kaondes. That's where your father's from. You're not supposed to be at this place.' When we saw that, we knew that the case wouldn't take place; there won't be any *Nkuta*. James is up to something. In my own thinking, I thought it's some sort of plan. There is some sort of arrangement to confuse the *Nkuta*. So before anything was said, what I did was to hit this old woman, but she was holding a baby, so I thought if I hit her hard the baby is going to die, so what I did was to just throw myself on her body, and sure I kicked her. I did it because of her misbehaviour. She is very good at gossiping, wherever she goes she talks about my witchcraft. That's why I felt that before I even saw a summons we should have come here to Court with her, to come and get a letter, and we would have taken the letter to Kamchobi (famous Soli witchdoctor) to go and tell us who is the witch, she or I. I think that's the end of my statement.

C.A. Elina, you say that you beat this old woman here. Did you really beat her?

D. Yes, I beat her.

C.A. Now what annoyed you to beat her? Did she say any words to you when you arrived there?

D. It was from her previous talks. That's what annoyed me.

C.A. Elina, do you agree that you accused her of being a witch?

D. No, I don't agree. What I only know is that I talked to her that we should get a letter from you here at the court or get a letter from Chief Mungule, so we could take it to Kamchobi the witchdoctor, to go and clear off all what we've got on our bodies, because being a witch is not a good thing.

C.A. Do you tell me that you didn't utter the word that she was a witch?

D. No, I didn't say that. My only words were that she and I should go either to Chief Nkomesha or Chief Mungule or the Court to go and get a letter and take it to witchdoctor Kamchobi, and go and clear all the medicine we've got on our bodies, whether it be me who will be found to be a witch, then my charms should be cleared from me, if it should be my sister, then all the charms should be cleared from her body.

C.A. Can you call the witness of Sumili? James, you are here this is the court now. What are you to both of these people?

W. Sumili is my elder sister and Elina is my younger sister.

C.A. Do you know anything about their coming to court? Do you know the case that they have come here for?

W. Yes, I know the case. There was one Saturday when I saw Elina and my niece Ester and they wanted me to have a family Nkuta. They said they wanted to settle some witchcraft case. I said, 'Who is a witch?' They said, 'Sumili.' I told them to come on Sunday. They all came in and I sent someone to call Sumili. Before they came back I got annoyed with my niece. I said, 'What are you doing, you people? I think you want to go and pull Sumili from her place. This is misbehaving.' As I was getting annoyed, Sumili came in and was seated. Not even a word was said, and I saw Elina jump on Sumili and started beating her. I went and pulled her off, and she ran away and was shouting in the village, 'Here is the witch who bewitched my husband Thomas.' I was very ashamed and I didn't settle any case. That's all that I know. But I said to Elina, 'Sumili is our oldest sister. She has kept us up to now. How come suddenly she should bewitch someone who is not even of our family except by marriage?

C.A. Elina, what is the relationship between you and James?

D. He is my brother.

C.A. What he said, is it true?

D. The only real truth in his statement is that I jumped on the body of my sister and beat her.

C.A. Is it true that you said that she was a witch?

C. No, I didn't say that. After all, it was Sumili who told Ester that she was responsible for the death of my husband. That's the only thing that I know, and what annoyed me more is that when I went to James' place we did not go there to settle the case of someone being a witch, but we went there to talk about some kind of bewitching which would cause the husband and wife to separate. (The specific medicine used to cause the separation of a husband and wife is called *Kafundula*).

C.A. All right, can we have your witness. Ester what is your relationship between these people?

W. This is my mother, and also this is my mother. (Sumili is her biological mother.)

C.A. Can we have a statement from you?

W. What I only know is that one day my mother Sumili came to my place and brought in one of her grandchildren, and she ordered me to plait her hair because she was going for a beer drink. I did it and she left. Then later in the evening she came in and wanted to get the grandchild to go with her to her home. But the child was crying and was not interested in going with the grandmother. I told my mother 'I think the child wants some bread.' But as I went into the house I found that my mother was beating our grandchild and pulling her to her home. Then the next morning Elina came in at our place, and I told her everything. Sumili was kicking the child. After I told her then Elina started telling us the story. 'Listen, this is very bad what Sumili is doing because even before my husband died Sumili was coming at our place trying to get some medicine *(Kafundula)* so that Lianda and his wife would divorce. I told her that this medicine was not known by me or my husband.' When my younger brother Lianda heard that, he wanted an explanation why she wanted to break up his marriage. So he went to James' place and asked him to hold a family *Nkuta.* So we arranged it. We came in – me, my husband, Lianda, Elina – when we got there we got into a place of insults. James continued despising us, until at last my mother was annoyed and said, 'Listen, Sumili, you have always been confusing all these *Nkutas* here. Then Elina jumped on Sumili. That's all I know except that when we went there we were not going to discuss any witchcraft case, but to talk about the medicine *Kafundula.*

C.A. Can you explain what Elina said after the fight?

W. No, I can't say, because it was my uncle who was separating them. I can only tell you what was said during the fight.

C.A. All right. But what words that Sumili said do you think annoyed Elina?

W. What Sumili said which may have annoyed Elina was, 'You, Sumili, it is you who have been encouraging these young girls from Matero to do all this nonsense here at Kabanana; without you all this should have not happened.

C.A. Is that all?

W. Yes, that is all I know.

C.A. Why was it Elina who beat Sumili? Shouldn't the daughter-in-law (wife of Lianda) have been the one who was annoyed with her?

W. Yes, it should have been the daughter-in-law who was more annoyed with her.

C.A. Does anyone have anything else to say?

D. Yes. It should have been me who got the summons for Sumili before she got it for me. Or we should have got a letter from here to go see Dr. Kamchobi, so he could clear us of all the charms we have.

Judgement:

C.A. The Court has heard all the complaints ... (reiterates). Now I come to the point of advising you, Elina. Elina you are mistaken, and your main mistake is that if you yourself heard that Sumili had bewitched your husband you had no right to beat Sumili because Sumili is your own sister. If Sumili is accused of bewitching your husband, it is not you who should say it. That should be the family of your deceased husband who can do it. Because when that thing comes in, it will come in for both of you. And James and Ester, because your people are of the same family. Now I am surprised to learn that it was you who ran around the village saying that it was Sumili who bewitched your husband. It is high time that some of you started thinking. If you heard that Sumili had bewitched your husband, you're not supposed to shout about it. Because if the relatives of the husband hear about it they may either summon you or put you in trouble. They may even kill your own sister. If you hear about such a thing you have to keep it in confidence because you are bringing this case on your own body. Because if Sumili gets it, you've got to get it too. And again, you shouldn't have fought your own sister. It is your daughter-in-law who should have brought this matter because she is the one who Sumili was intending to bewitch. And here we would have been very ready to find out why Sumili was trying to bewitch her. All those medicines you have been talking about, they didn't involve you. They involved your daughter-in-law and Sumili. So how come you can go and beat your own sister? There's another thing that I have to tell you, woman. You are too good at gossiping. You just hear a little thing and you go shouting, 'My sister is a witch.' That's nonsense. You're not supposed to do it. She does not have a mark that she is a witch whereby you could go up and down singing that Sumili is a witch. I repeat, it is high time that you started thinking, and reasoning, and knowing what you are doing. And we come to James. He has been very frank. He has told us the truth in this court. He said that he tried to stop you from fighting your own sister. And you shamed him by shouting in the village that your sister is a witch. And what you should know is that you have made your older sister not live properly. You have beat her; you have spoiled her name in the village. What about if she dies? Then all those *Kapewo* (bad spirits of a deceased person) will come on you. And this is the thing that you have seen all these *Benemukuni* (Lenje) trying to wash all these medicines at the cross-roads because they don't want that *Kapewo* or *chibanda* (ghosts or bad spirits). You get all those things if someone dies with a bad feeling for you. Then all those bad spirits from him will fall on you. And I have to tell you that you really made a mistake, Elina, and to clear up the spirit, and the heart, and the name of your own elder sister Sumili, you are going to pay her 20K. And you, Sumili, if she doesn't pay you 20 K, you come and report to court and we shall force her to pay you. If you are not satisfied you may appeal. Out of the boxes.

Comment:

This case involves two Lenje sisters with a 20 year history of conflict. The case as it was heard before the Local Court reveals a great deal about the past relationship of the sisters. The history of this conflict suggests that the accusation of slander was but a minor aspect of the ongoing conflict. Though the court assumes the history of the conflict, its decision relates ostensibly to the particular conflict of the moment.

This case – slander for the accusation of witchcraft – is an example of the expected dispute settlement behaviour, and exemplifies the decision-making role the court uses to maintain the authority of the family. Initially, oldest brother attempted to resolve the conflict by holding a family *Nkuta*. Before he could hear the case, the situation deteriorated into a free-for-all. This may be because he had already expressed his inclination to side with the defendant.

What is not obvious from the testimony is that he later asked the village headman to attempt to resolve the dispute. Knowing well the long history of the conflict, the village headman declined, advising that the case be taken to the Local Court. In an interview with the village headman, I asked why he had not attempted to hear the case. Somewhat incredulously he replied, 'They're sisters. They have been fighting for twenty years. What could I do?' His perception was that given the relationship and the history of conflict, a mediated decision stood little chance of resolving or cooling the conflict. The context of the case called for an adjudicative decision. This information was transmitted to the court members by the headman before the case, when he accompanied the litigants to court.

During the case the sisters were allowed a free forum for their testimony of past and present conflict. It appears that this is the means by which the court will assess the facts in the case. Actually, fact-finding seems to be assessed from the older brother's testimony. He is called as a witness and the dialogue between him and the court assessor is crucial to understanding the court's decision-making role.

C.A. Can you call the witness of Sumili? James, you are here, this is the court now. What are you to both these people?

James Sumili is my older sister, and Elina is my younger sister.

C.A. Do you know anything about their coming to court? Do you know the case that they have come here for?

James Yes, I know the case. There was one Saturday when I saw Elina (the defendant) and my niece Ester (the daughter of the plaintiff, and niece of the defendant – she addresses both women as 'mother') and they wanted me to have a family *Nkuta*. They said they wanted to settle some witchcraft case. I said, 'Who is a witch?' They said, 'Sumili'. (This part of the testimony should not be taken too literally. He knew about all the past events, but here is stating how he became involved in an attempt at family dispute settlement.) I told them to come on Sunday. They all came in, and I sent someone to call Sumili. Before they came back I got annoyed with my niece (Ester). I said, '*What are you people doing? I think you want to go and pull Sumili from her place (banish her from the village). This is misbehaving.*' As I was getting annoyed, Sumili came in and was seated. Not even a word was said when Elina (Defendant) jumped on Sumili and started to beat her. I went and pulled her off and she ran away shouting in the village, 'Here is the witch who bewitched my husband Thomas (deceased).' I was very ashamed and I didn't settle any case. That's all I know, *but I said to Elina, 'Sumili is our oldest sister. She has kept us up to now. How come suddenly she would bewitch someone who is not even in our family except by marriage?* (He does not believe that Sumili is responsible for the wrongs which Elina believes she has committed.)

The case goes on at some length, but finally the court gives its judgement. It finds in favour of Sumili and against Elina. After reminding Elina of the dire consequences of witchcraft accusations within the family (the moral role the court plays in family disputes), the decision is rendered very much in line with the the testimony of James.

C.P. ... And we come to James. He has been very frank. He has told us the truth in this court. He said that he tried to stop you (Elina) from fighting with your own sister. And you shamed him by shouting in the village that your sister was a witch (this is what the case before the court is about, the accusation of witchcraft). And what you should know is that you made your older sister not live properly. You have beat her; you have spoiled her name in the village (slander) ... And I have to tell you that you really made a mistake, Elina, and to clear up the spirit, and the heart, and the name of your elder sister Sumili, you are going to pay her 20 Kwacha.

As will be further illustrated below, when a family authority in his or her testimony gives a strong opinion about fault among members of the family unit, the court's judgement reflects the family authority's findings. Put another way, in family cases fact-finding is less an independent assessment by the court and more a reliance on the testimony of the 'expert witness'.

Case 2. Slander. Nephew/Aunt.
Plaintiff – early 30's; Defendant – early 30's. Ethnic group: Lenje/Soli. (The plaintiff's mother is Lenje; his father Soli. In this area it is the ethnic affiliation of the mother which determines the classification of the child.)

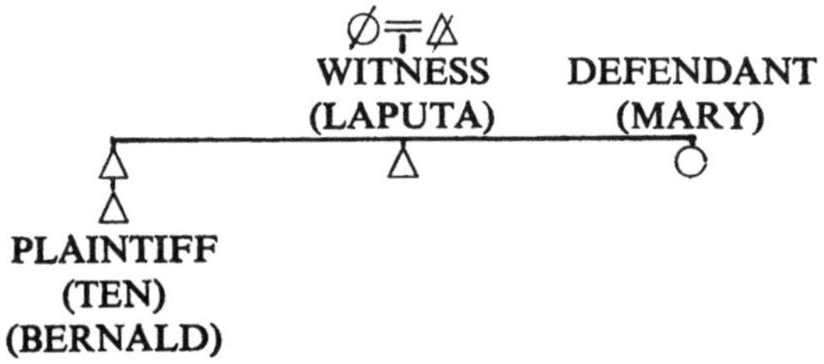

C.S. Mary, you have been brought before the Court and are being accused of defaming Bernald's name by calling him a thief because he stole your 3K. Do you plead guilty or not guilty?

D. I plead guilty.

C.P. Ten, can we have your statement?

P. I remember it was one day that I went to Lusaka and slept at Kanyama, bought a bag of mealie meal, and when I came to Kanjombe I got my father. We had very good transport. We came to Kalimba and drank and drank. From Kalimba we went to Laputa's place and there I left my mealie meal. Then I came back to my house and spent the night peacefully. The next morning me and my wife left for the field. As we were working my wife said to me, 'Your mother says that we have to go and collect the mealie meal.' I told her, 'No, listen, we won't go and get all that mealie meal from there. I have heard that all the family has gone to the funeral in Chumbela village, so we can't go there in their absence or all the mealie meal will be mixed up'. We went home and slept. At night I heard someone, and that was my mother asking us, 'Is there anyone today who had gone to Luputa's houses?' I told her nobody's gone across this road. Then early the next morning I heard Mary come to our place. She said someone broke into my house yesterday when I was away for the funeral. This has been the second time. Me and the Headman Chibilika went with her. When we arrived there she said, 'You can see the footsteps here. These footsteps should be Ten's (The P.). Ten is the only lame man here. (Ten walks on the toes of one foot). Then I heard from Laputa (the W.), 'Yes, even last year he is the one who broke into my house.' Then I answered them, 'Listen, you gentlemen, you are lucky because you have not born any child who is lame. If you had one you should not have said such nonsense.' And then I had to give them an example: 'Let's say you are trying to go in for women at night, and you don't want people to hear your footsteps. What do you do? Don't you use your toes? You walk on your toes. It is not good of you to say this to me. I'm speaking in the eyes of God that I'm not the one who did it. If this Court had any Bible I would make an oath on it. Also wherever I have been going, this lady keeps saying, "There is a thief. There is a thief". That's why I have summoned her. Now she can clear my name before the Court.

C.P. Mary, you have heard the statement from Ten?

D. Yes, but I didn't even say those words.

C.P. Okay, let's have your statement.

D. What I know is that on Sunday we went for the funeral. When I came back my sister-in-law informed me that someone broke into my house. We spent that night, then the next morning. I started shouting again: 'Me, I'm a poor woman. I'm not married. The 3K was for my transport money to Lusaka.' As I was saying all this then my brother came in and told me, 'No, sister, don't worry. There is no one here who can steal money except the very one who steals from this village. That is Ten. And after all, whose footprints did you see by the window? They are those of Ten.' Then I told Ten that he had stole my money.

C.P. You have said that you plead guilty. Can you satisfy us that you really saw Ten steal your money?

D. Yes, we saw his footprints. If it was just someone trying to walk on his toes, we can see the difference. Therefore I am satisfied that it was Ten who stole the money.

C.A. Ten, you are accused that you stole the money.

P. If only there was a Bible, I should have sworn before God.

D.P. Listen, if God was answering on earth I think there should have been no cases. Listen, Ten, do you tell us that you have not even stolen once?

P. Where? Where did I steal?

C.P. But we've heard that this is your second time to steal.

P. She is telling lies. Otherwise I should have sworn as I told you.

C.P. (to the D.) Do you have someone who can witness that he stole the money and that this is the second time?

D. Yes, the one whose house was broken into.

C.S. What's your name?

W. My name is Laputa. (The uncle of the P. and brother of the D.)

C.P. Has Ten ever stolen from your place?

W. Yes, he has done that. It was about a year ago that I found that my house was broken into and that 30K was missing. I said someone who is stealing from me is coming from a very near place. I think I won't say anything, but one of these days I'll get hold of him. It didn't take very long. Someone came to my place and told me that someone had broken into my house. When I went there I found that the footprints were of Ten's. He had stolen 7K50n. I saw the track of his bicycle and I followed it. The track went straight up to the place where he was drinking beers. Before I said anything I went to talk to his father. I told him, 'You come and see the track of his bicycle.' Then when I asked him, Ten agreed: 'What can I say if my parents have accused me of stealing the money? Don't worry, uncle. I'll pay this amount at the end of the season.' That was last year, and he didn't pay it. Later on I told him, 'Don't pay it. After all, you have eaten your father's property.' I didn't worry until I heard this case and saw the footprints. You know you Court members that there is a certain period when the cattle graze on maize. That is just like a thief with money. So let's not worry about him. I'm very disappointed that I should stand in Court witnessing against my own nephew and my sister. I even told the father of Ten, my older brother, 'All these things are happening because you are taking the commands of your wives. Whatever your wife decides you follow it. That's why you are here trying to defend your son. You are doing it through the influence of your wives. Later this will bring a separation between the three of us (two brothers and the sister). One will live on his own and one will live on his own. This will cause a lot of inconveniences among ourselves. What we can only do, this is our son, if he makes a mistake we should say okay, your father's side fails to go along with you, you go and try your mother's side. Then we send him to his mother's side. And those *benenongo* (Pot clan) will know about his character, and if they fail to keep him I know that he will come back again.'

Judgement:

C.P. (Reiterates charges) ... What you should know is that all parents know the behaviour of their children. They always give a very simple test to find out which of their children is a thief. Some get money, some get a piece of meat. If there are three children they put the money or the meat in the house and watch as each one goes in. Then after each goes in they check the house. That one who has got that habit (stealing) they will know. Now you being the own nephew of Mary, she has the right to accuse you. You are her child. This sort of thing even happens when someone is working. You make a mistake and the boss puts it down. You make another mistake and he puts it down again. Later on he will tell you, 'I'm sorry, my friend, you are not doing anything good for me.' That's as good as a parent. A parent will always try to find out the child's mistake and will know. You Ten have been born from that village and there are many others who are born there too. But they were not accused of stealing, and you were. You have been accused twice by Laputa. You didn't come here and summon Laputa that he has defamed your name. Did you come and summon your uncle when he accused you? You even agreed that you would refund the money, which you have not done. The Court feels that all the accusations you have brought here against Mary are not answerable. Mary, you are acquitted. We can't see any case against you. If you are not satisfied you may appeal. Out of the boxes.

Comment:

The original conflict in this case, theft between family members, was handled at the family level. The case heard at a family *Nkuta* produced the decision that the plaintiff (Ten) should repay his uncle (the witness). When time passed, it was decided that nothing should be done because, 'After all, you have eaten your father's property.' (The theft occurred between people who might inherit from each other). The same type of settlement was considered when the plaintiff was alleged to have stolen from his aunt. (The conflict was kept within the family, and the plaintiff was warned that if he continued stealing from his father's relatives he would be forced to leave the village and reside with his mother's relatives.)

The plaintiff decided to summon his aunt to court charging her with slander. The defendant agrees that she has accused the plaintiff of theft and pleads guilty. The court calls the uncle of the plaintiff, brother of the defendant, as the 'expert witness'. The witness clearly states that the plaintiff has a history of stealing from the family. He then indicated to the court his embarrassment for having the case go outside the family's control. The witness states: 'You know, you court members, that there is a time when cattle graze on maize. That is just like a thief with money. *So let's not worry about him.*' (The uncle is saying that the plaintiff cannot help himself when it comes to stealing from the family, but that the family is willing to handle the situation among themselves.)

He continues indicating to the court that the family would rather handle the case itself. 'I'm very disappointed that I should stand here witnessing against my own nephew and my sister.' He then goes on to state how the family will handle the dispute (the threat of banishment). The court's decision elaborates to the plaintiff his uncle's analogy between cattle eating maize and a thief stealing from his family (see judgement). Finally, the court acquits the defendant, although she had pleaded guilty.

Again, decision making is congruent with the testimony of the family authority. The court appears to make its decision by reaffirming the decision implicit in the family authority's testimony.

In the following family cases, for the sake of brevity, I have exerpted the testimony of the family authority and the decision of the court. The first three cases are examples of family disputes where the family authority gives a strong opinion about the case and the court follows his testimony. The last three cases illustrate weak family opinion and show the reluctance of the court to impose an independent decision in family disputes.

Case 3. Inheritance. Father's son and Father's sister's daughter's son. Plaintiff – mid-30's; Defendant – mid-30's. Ethnic group: Lenje/Lenje.

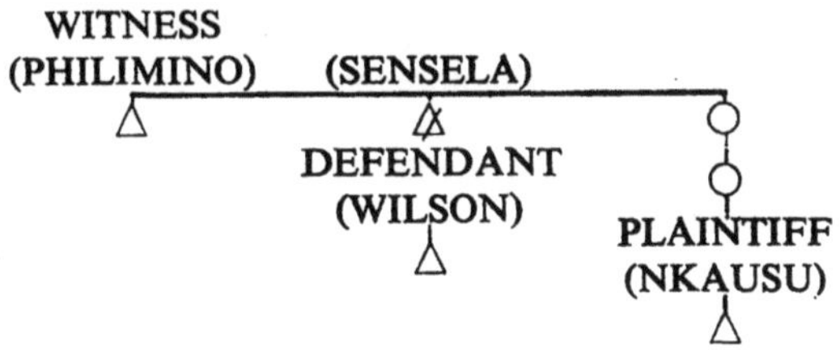

Inheritance cases, as a rule, only reach the local court when some specific problem arises over the transfer of an estate. The division and inheritance of an estate is hammered out over a 6- to 12-month period among members of the deceased's mother's and father's matrilineal relatives. Who would inherit what, was made clear by the family in 1967 after the death of the defendant's father, who was the plaintiff's matrilineal uncle. In January of 1971, the case came before the court on a technicality: who actually owned a grinding mill inherited by the plaintiff from his uncle's estate. The defendant, the son of the deceased, claims that the grinding mill inherited by his cousin (the plaintiff) was jointly owned by himself and the deceased, and therefore the family gave away property which was not part of the estate. He has locked up the grinding mill until he is compensated for his share of ownership. The plaintiff has brought the case to get the defendant to unlock the grinding mill so that he can use what he believes is rightly his property.

The case is somewhat complicated by the fact that the plaintiff not only inherited the property of his deceased uncle but also inherited his name. To the Lenje, this means that he receives the 'lion's share' of the deceased's estate, his name and kinship and social obligations. This now makes the plaintiff the 'father' of the defendant. Both are in their mid-30's.

The question before the court is who paid for the grinding mill when it was originally purchased in 1962. If it was paid for by the deceased, then the plaintiff has full rights to his inheritance. If it was paid for jointly by the deceased and his son, then the family had no right to transfer the property.

Over a four-year period this case has been heard at both family and village courts. The defendant always claiming that he had rights in the grinding mill. First he claimed that he wanted part of the profits. Then he claimed that he had bought a new engine for his father. Now he claims that the mill was jointly purchased by his father and himself. There had been two grinding mills in the deceased's estate, one which went to the defendant and the other to the plaintiff. This case is over the original ownership of grinding mill no. 2.

As expert witness, the court calls the younger brother of the deceased. The dialogue between the court and the witness was as follows:

C.A. Is there a relative of your father here, who was there when you bought the grinding mill with your father?

D. Yes, the younger brother of my father. He knows everything.

C.P. Philimino, can we have your statement? Philimino Lusaka, you know you are an old man and these are your relatives. And what we want from you is to tell us the truth.

W. What I only know myself is before Sensela died he informed me that he was going to purchase a grinding mill (no. 1) with his own son. From what I know they paid 50/50. No one paid more than the other. Before he died I had to ask my brother. 'Brother, you are growing old. Dying is almost like sleeping. Please can we have all these things clarified. Who is the owner of this new grinding mill (no. 2)?' What he told me is that this grinding mill (no. 2) has been bought out of the profits gained from the old grinding mill (no. 1) ... I'm satisfied that the grinding mill (no. 2) was bought out of the profits from the old grinding mill and not out of Wilson's (the defendant's) pocket. And after all, before his father's death, Wilson never told me: 'This other grinding mill (no. 2),

I bought it out of my own money.' He has been very quiet. When we asked at our home (held a family *Nkuta*) and when we heard that there was some conflict and sat down with some of the Indunas (village *Nkuta*), then Wilson claimed that he bought a new engine when they were sharing the grinding mill (no. 2). He wanted this man (the plaintiff) who has taken over the grinding mill to pay him about 400 kwacha for the new engine. All that we solved (at the village *Nkuta*). Nkausu was going to pay him for a new engine. It is the first time that I have heard that he bought the grinding mill (no. 2), which is at my village, with his own money. *That is a lie*. What made him lock the door is that the other one has not been paying him back for the new engine.

C.A. But who do you think is wrong between the two people here? (Over the actual original ownership of grinding mill no. 2).

W. Wilson (the defendant) *is wrong*.

Judgement:

C.P. Wilson, today, just when you leave here, go and open the grinding mill (no. 2). That grinding mill is completely in the hand of Nkausu ... You go right now and unlock the grinding mill so that it should be working.

Case 4. Divorce. Wife/Husband.
Plaintiff – early 20's; Defendant – early 20's. Ethnic group: Soli/Nyanja.

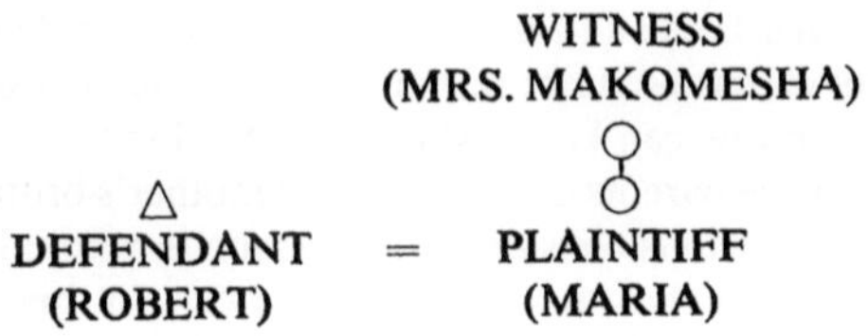

In this case, the wife has brought the husband to court charging him with neglect and seeking a divorce. She claims that he hasn't supported her or their children for six months. The husband pleads innocence because he has been away as a migrant labourer. The court asks him what he thinks of the wife's demand for a divorce. He states:

D. No, I don't want a divorce. I still love my wife.

C.P. But how can you love her when you have neglected her? Even your own children? Give us some reason why you should refuse (to be divorced).

D. (Silence)

C.P. Marie, are your parents here?

P. Yes, my mother is here.

C.P. Let's have your mother. Mrs. Makomesha, what is your opinion?

W. My daughter has been neglected for a very long time. It is me who has been acting as her husband, clothing her, feeding her, clothing her children. Some time ago we called an *Nkuta*, but my son-in-law still pleaded that he wanted Maria as his wife, and we urged her to go back to her husband. (Indicates proper processing of the dispute.) This trouble hasn't ended. *I feel they should divorce*.

Judgement:

C.P. Maria brought this case against Robert, in which Robert has been accused of neglecting her. Robert didn't support his wife in any way, didn't want to stay with his wife at home. Also the mother of the girl stated the same – he neglected his wife. Robert gives no evidence that he did not neglect her, but still he says he loves his wife. I say that we are not here to force a horse to drink water, and I therefore say that this should be the end of the marriage ...

Case 5. Divorce. Wife/Husband.
Plaintiff – early 40's; Defendant – late 40's. Ethnic group: Lenje/Lenje.

This couple has been separated for over a year, the wife living on her own in a nearby village. The conflict between the couple has a long history, and their marital disputes have been heard before family and village courts over the years. Since they have been separated, the wife claims that when the husband gets drunk he comes to her home and tries to beat her. The husband does not deny the allegations, but claims he is not responsible because he is drunk. 'If a fellow is drunk, do you think he can know what is happening?'

The court asks for the parents of the wife. Her mother's brother is the witness. (The guardian of a woman is considered the person in whose house the woman was living when her husband came to take her away. In this case the wife was living avuncularly, and therefore her uncle is considered her guardian.)

C.P. Can we have the parents of Lukaki, please? Let's hear from you. What is your opinion? What do you know about these two people?

W. Daniel (the defendant) is a troublemaker. Whenever he comes from beer drinking he comes home and insults his wife. The wife has got to run up and down, and always she comes to my place. I should say that the wife left Daniel's place a year ago, and she has been staying at her own house ... *My opinion is that they should divorce* because later this drunkard would kill my daughter, because he always threatens to kill her.

Judgement:

C.P. (After giving Daniel a long lecture on the evils of drinking) ... I have never seen a more confused person than you, Daniel. You are a big man, and I inform you, from today you are no longer married. You are not married to Lukaki, you have been divorced by the court. You have divorced yourself, Daniel. You are lucky that you had plenty of children with this woman. You were her first husband. But because of your madness, drinking too much beer, the court has decided that you should divorce.

It might be assumed from the above cases that the evidence irrespective of the 'expert witness' was so overwhelming that the court's decision would have been the same without the opinion of the superior kinsman. The following cases in which the 'expert witness' was not forthcoming with a definitive opinion illustrate the reluctance of the court to make independent decisions without the concurrence of a family authority.

Case 6. Divorce. Wife/Husband.
Plaintiff – late 30's; Defendant – mid 40's. Ethnic group: Lenje/Lenje.

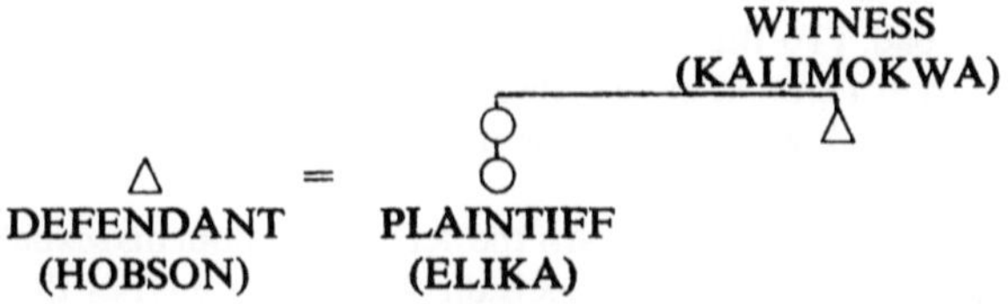

In this case the wife is seeking a divorce claiming that the husband commits sexual perversions. They have been married for 22 years. Within the testimony of the wife she tells the court that there had been a family *Nkuta* where her husband was fined for the sexual acts she now claims justify a divorce. The husband does not deny her allegations, but he claims that she left him, went to town, contracted venereal disease, came back, infected him, and he in turn infected his second wife. His second wife's family held an *Nkuta* and charged him one ox for infecting their daughter. Now he wants to know the man who infected his first wife so that he can claim compensation from him.

The day the case was heard, the guardian of the wife was not present, and the court refused to pass judgement, although it had heard all the testimony of the litigants. Two days later the case was continued, only the testimony of the guardian was given, and then the court passed judgement.

C.A. Are the parents in?
W. Yes.
C.A. What's your name?
W. Kalimokwa (The wife's mother's brother by name inheritance).
C.A. What's your relationship to the plaintiff?
W. She's my niece.
C.A. What do you know about these two people?
W. What I've heard myself is that the husband sucks the wife's breasts.
C.A. No, no, no. We are not after that business. Your child has brought a summons. She wants to divorce her husband. What do you know about that?
W. What I know is that my niece has been running away from her husband and coming to my place, and I would persuade her to go back to her husband.
C.A. We don't want all that. What is happening is that your daughter has summoned her husband for a divorce. What about that?
W. I don't know what happened in their house. What I know I have already

told you. The husband even agreed (at a family *Nkuta*) that he sucks the breasts of the wife, and he paid 4 kwacha for doing it.

C.A. No, we are not after that here. What about the summons?

W. All right, if they want a divorce, then they can have a divorce. I've got nothing to say.

Judgement:

C.A. We adjourned this case so we could hear from the wife's parent. But he says it is up to them. This is wrong. He should be concerned about the outcome of his child's marriage. He should explain to the court how his son-in-law treated him – good or bad. (To the witness) Out of you we have heard nothing. If it was me as a parent I should have stated everything. I love my son-in-law, or I don't love my son-in-law. These are the mistakes of my son-in-law, etc. ***But you haven't given us anything definite.***

(The court assessor goes on to warn the defendant about his sexual behaviour, but about this case he renders no decision. Instead he advises that the family hear the defendant's case against his wife for compensation for infecting him, and after that the court will consider hearing the case again.)
No divorce granted.

The last two cases of non-commital family witnesses further illustrate the point that the court is loath to make independent decisions in family disputes without the concurrence of a family authority.

Case 7. Divorce. Wife/Husband.
Plaintiff – late teens; Defendant – late 20's. Ethnic group: Senga/Kaonde.

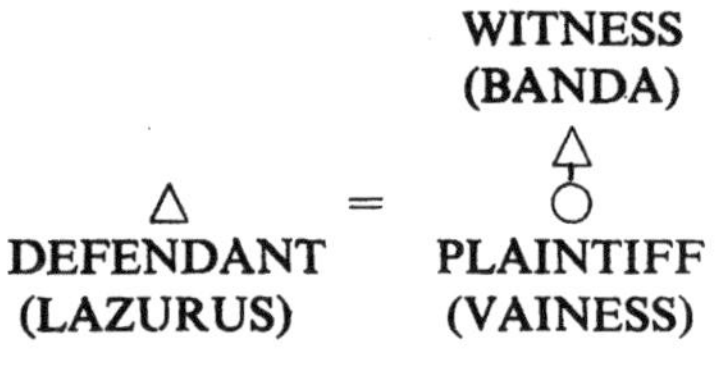

In this case the wife accuses the husband of having chased her from his house because he believed that she was involved with his brother. The husband does not deny the charge but counters that his wife accuses him of being impotent. He claims that he does not want a divorce, but she insists that she does. The court asks to hear from the guardian of the woman.

C.A. Call the parent of the girl.

C.S. What's your name?

W. Kaiser Banda. (The father of the plaintiff).

C.A. What can you tell us about these two people. Your daughter wants a divorce.

W. I can't say anything. I don't know what's cooking in their house. That is the house of my children, so I can't say anything. What I want to tell you is that my son-in-law chased my daughter from his house. But when she came in I advised her to go back to her husband. My daughter said, 'I can't go there because the only treatment I get is being beaten.' I think what I'll do is summon him to court so that the court members can advise him.

C.A. Listen, Kaiser Banda, you are the parent of this girl. You should know better than the court what to do with your daughter.

W. Listen, Sir, I can't say much because that house is for my children. Whatever happens there I just can't tell.

C.P. It's all right, Kaiser Banda. You can go and sit down. (Said with disdain.)

Judgement:

C.P. We have heard the complaint. We asked the parent, but he said that he doesn't know anything. He can't tell us because it doesn't involve him unless it happens in his house. Lazurus (the defendant) if we shall hear that you are jealous of your own brother, and that you suspect that your brother goes in for your wife, if we shall hear it next time, '*Ngola mulakuyi chatila ku muyeye kutambeyi kumiti*' (Something you hold in your hands will slip out). I warn you that if this report comes up here, the only thing will be divorce.

Case 8. Divorce. Wife/Husband.
Plaintiff – early 50's; Defendant – early 60's. Ethnic group: Lenje/Lenje.

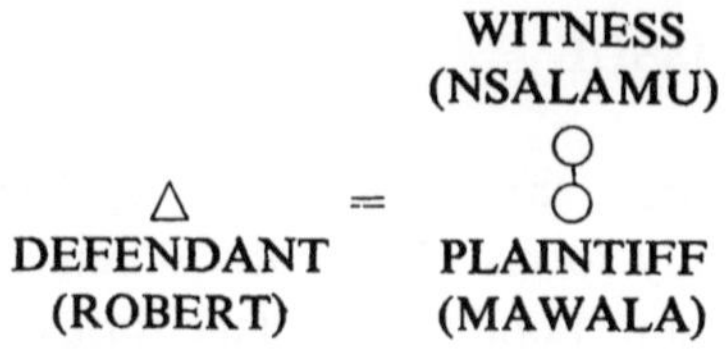

In this case the wife is seeking a divorce, claiming that her husband taunts her about being barren. They have been married over twenty years and have no children. This is the second time that the wife has come before the court asking for a divorce. The husband claims that she spends a great deal of time away from his home, but that he still wants to remain married. The court calls as witness the mother of the plaintiff.

C.P. May we have the parent before the court?

C.S. What's your name?

W. My name is Nsalamu.

C.A. What do you know about these two people here?

W. Actually, I can't tell because I don't know what happens at their house. But what I know is my son-in-law is a troublemaker, and he is always threatening to commit suicide. That's why we are fearing that he is going to commit suicide at our place.

C.P Listen, Nsalamu, what we want is your opinion. Do you still love your son-in-law?

W. No, no, no. I don't love him anymore. Otherwise I'll land in trouble because he is always threatening to commit suicide.

C.P. Nsalamu, would you mind explaining to us what are the main causes that make him say that he is going to commit suicide? Don't you know?

W. No, I don't know anything. But yet I only know what I hear. Whenever he comes to our place he only has jealousy. He thinks his wife has some other man at our home. I think that that may be the reason why he says that.

C.P. Can that be the main reason why he tries to commit suicide, because of jealousy?

W. I may not know, but it may be that that's the very thing. (The witness refuses to speak on the issue – should her daughter be granted a divorce.)

Judgement:

After lecturing the defendant on proper family behavior, the court president says:

C.P. (to the defendant) I warn you if you are the one who is not respecting the family of your wife, if you continue saying, 'I don't love you because you don't bear children, and I want to marry someone else' – if that is repeated 'something you hold in your hands will slip out.' And you, mother, (to the plaintiff), you are going back to your husband, and if the same mistake happens again, come to court and we shall help you.

THE ACADEMIC ISSUE

The above cases illustrate the adaptation of legal processes which have evolved between family forms of dispute settlement and the National judiciary. The survival of family and village forms of dispute settlement depends upon the expectation of the community and the Local Court that individuals first attempt to process their disputes through mediation. When this form of dispute settlement proves unsuccessful, the Local Court is then willing to hear family cases. In its decision-making role it attempts to bolster rather than usurp family authority.

Though the court is willing to be a conduit for family decision making, backing the findings of a senior kinsman with the adjudicative powers of the National government, it seems unwilling to make independent legal decisions without family concurrence. This too can be seen as an attempt to maintain the authority of basic kinship units, through the socialization function of the court. Ultimately, the court has defined its decision-making role as one of affirmation of family opinion, rather than being an independent decision-making body as it is when faced with non-family disputes.

Apart from the question of legal adaptation, I believe that the above findings speak to a more significant and larger issue. In conclusion, I would like to discuss the question of local-level legal adaptation in light of the crucial concerns of National policy-making.

POLICY-MAKING AND DIRECTED LEGAL CHANGE

The particular interrelationship between the National judiciary and the local-level legal system is the outcome of thirty years of dual legal control between local-level political authority and National political authority. The Local Court has maintained a delicate balance between the political power of the Nation/State and the realities of local-level political control which are built on strong family and village alliances.

Under the present adaptation the jural authority of family and village leaders is actually and symbolically reaffirmed through the processing of disputes. Their occasional lack of success is secondary to the reaffirmation of their expected dispute settlement role.

From the point of view of directed legal change, this kind of information would be crucial for policy-making decisions. To date, policy changes have mainly focused on so-called 'customary' laws and principles. By adopting the use of the 'extended case method', an inquiry into the present state of African family law would refocus our attention beyond mere principles and laws to the areas of local-level dispute settlement which are socio/cultural adaptations to the contemporary forces affecting rural African societies.

In countries like Zambia, an understanding of local-level law, though important, masks other legal adaptations which express the role of dispute settlement systems as they are shaped by the needs of a rapidly changing society. To give balance to our understanding of local-level African family law, the 'interstices' of legal process should be as important as the rules which inform the legal system.

The adaptations, adjustments, and accommodations which local-level legal systems have made with former colonial and present independent governments reveal legal necessities which must concern those committed to realistic legal change. It forces us to consider the larger question of African family law-systems, with African family law significant but not our total concern.

To claim or not to claim: changing views about the restitution of marriage prestations among the Anufòm in Northern Togo* 5

EMILE AND ELS VAN ROUVEROY VAN NIEUWAAL
Afrika-Studiecentrum, Leiden

INTRODUCTION

In this paper we intend to describe the system by which women are reciprocally given and received in marriage, and the accompanying marriage prestations, as it exists among the Anufòm, an ethnic group in Northern Togo.[1] That this system is not just a construction in our minds, but one with which the participants are daily concerned, should become clear from the description.

The system of marriage and marriage prestations is the subject of a great number of disputes brought before the two most important judicial institutions in the area: the *Tribunal Coutumier de Ire Instance* (the lowest government customary law court) and the Court of the Paramount Chief of the Anufòm. There is significant disparity not only between the traditional ideas on these subjects as expressed by the Anufòm and as formulated by these two courts in their judgments, but also between the views of the *Tribunal Coutumier de Ire Instance* and those of the Court of the

* This article, which was first published in *African Law Studies*, No. 12/1975, results from a study of customary family law in the Anufò area in the *circonscription* Mango, in Northern Togo. The study was carried out between July 1969 and July 1970, and between February 1971 and October 1971. Data were collected in the town of Sansanné-Mango (capital of the *circonscription* Mango) and in the surrounding rural area, mostly in the village Ayikpèrè (see also note 9). This research was supported by The Netherlands Foundation for the Advancement of Tropical Research (WOTRO), The Hague, and under the supervision of Professor J.F. Holleman, University of Leiden. The authors gratefully acknowledge John Griffiths of New York University. We are indebted for his insights and criticism during the preliminary work for the publication of this article.

Paramount Chief, as we will illustrate through a detailed examination of two cases.

THE ANUFÒ MARRIAGE SYSTEM

The Anufòm are a small ethnic group numbering about 20,000. They live in northern Togo, in and around Sansanné-Mango, a town of approximately 10,000.[2] Their name, Anufòm, refers to their origin from the region of Anò in the Ivory Coast, between the rivers Comoé and Nzi. During the second half of the eighteenth century a group of Anufòm set out from Anò. They engaged in several military exploits (some in the service of the king of Gonja and in the service of the Mamprussi), one of which finally led them to their present habitat.

Anufò society consists of three social groups of different status (and partly different ethnic origin), membership of which is hereditary in the male line. The leaders of the Anufòm, formerly the army commanders (sg. *donzo*, pl. *donzom*[3]), form the ruling estate. Subordinated to the ruling estate is the estate of the commoners, the former soldiers (sg. *ngye*, pl. *ngyem*). Next to them there is the estate of the learned muslims (sg. *karamò*, pl. *karamòm*), who act as councillors and magicians to the rulers at their request. The *karamòm* are not subordinated to the *donzom*, nor do they have any ambition to leadership of the society; their relationship was defined by a pact, concluded before leaving Anò, by which the two groups promised each other mutual aid and respect. When the Anufòm arrived in North Togo, two centuries ago, only the *karamòm* and a few *donzo* lineages were muslims and it was not until the first decades of this century that the whole ruling estate and part of the commoner estate gradually adopted Islam. Today in the town of Sansanné-Mango most Anufòm are muslims, but in the rural areas most have still not been converted. All three estates speak the language of the original people of Ano, a form of Agni-Baule. The *karamò* of Dyula origin and those *donzom* who are Mande by origin still speak Mande on ritual occasions.

Although they constitute only one third of the total population in the *circonscription* (province) Mago, the Anufòm have for centuries dominated the other ethnic groups in this region of Togo, and the Paramount Chief of the Anufòm is accepted by the Anufòm and by others within the *circonscription* Mango as the highest traditional authority. Before the pacification of Northern Togo by the Germans at the end of the nineteenth century, the Anufò economy was based on raiding the surrounding country and levying a tax on the subjugated population. Today all three estates derive their principal income from hoe cultivation.

The exchange of women

The most important social unit of Anufò society is the patrilineal descent group, the *awuru*. In its maximal form it has a depth of seven generations, descent being reckoned from the original ancestor who came from Anò. Every such maximal lineage is subdivided into lineage segments ranging in depth from three to five generations. These smaller descent groups, also referred to as *awuru*, are the units which usually act more or less autonomously in everyday matters such as the giving and receiving of women in marriage. Each maximal lineage and lineage segment had a head, who has to be the eldest man of the oldest living generation. It is seldom that a maximal lineage as a whole will be actively involved in such transactions, though the lineage head should be informed of all marriage transactions.

The patrilineal descent groups of the Anufòm are not exogamous. Among the *ngyem* the exogamous unit is the lineage segment with a depth of three generations. Among the *donzom* the nearest kinswoman a man is allowed to marry is his FFBSD. Among the *karamòm* even marriage between parallel cousins (with FBD) is possible, although it is considered preferable to marry a daughter of one's father's half brother, *i.e.*, a brother with the same father but another mother.

The Anufòm hold explicit ideas about the advantages and disadvantages of a 'marriage within the lineage' as against 'a marriage far away', *i.e.*, a marriage with a member of another lineage.[4] For example, marriages within the lineage are supposed to enjoy greater stability, carry an expectation of fewer prestations from the groom and his parents to the parents of the bride and afford the satisfaction of further strengthening bonds with one's nearest and dearest kinsmen. On the other hand, marriage outside the lineage can serve to confirm an existing and valuable friendship and to create or cement a useful alliance with another lineage. Since the Anufòm are under no obligation to marry the women of their lineage to men of other lineages, when they do so they part with something they can 'use' themselves equally well. This fact is thought to increase the value of the gift of a woman in the case of 'a marriage far away'.

Reciprocal giving and receiving of women in marriage between lineages is restricted to lineages belonging to the same estate. Mutual exchange between lineages from different estates is made impractical by the impossibility of, or very strong objections against, some types of inter-estate marriage: a *karamò girl* cannot be given in marriage to a *donzo* or *ngye* man, and a *donzo* girl cannot be given in marriage to a *ngye* man. Thus, if a *ngye* lineage gives a daughter to a *donzo* or a *karamò* lineage, they will not receive a woman in return. Permitted and prohibited marriages between the three estates are shown in the following diagram (the arrows represent permitted and the crossed arrows prohibited marriages).

Diagram 1. *Permitted and prohibited marriages*

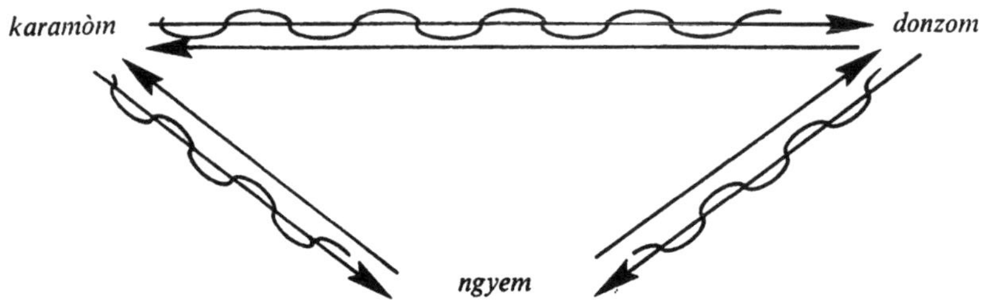

From the genealogical material we collected, it appears that, on the whole, the principle of an equal exchange of women between lineages is carried out in all three estates. In the following description of the system of exchange of women we will limit ourselves to the estate of the commoners, because the principle of exchange is formulated most clearly by them. While exchange relations between lineages of *karamòm* or *donzom* are established and perpetuated in much the same way as with the *ngyem*, *ngyem* speak of 'paying back a woman's debt' where *karamòm* and *donzom* prefer to speak of 'giving a woman' even if the woman given is a return gift.[5] Only among *ngyem* is the obligation to reciprocate a woman considered something that can be enforced before a court.

The basic rules of the exchange system can be formulated thus:

1. If lineage A has received a woman in marriage from lineage B, lineage A must compensate lineage B for the loss of this woman's procreative capacity by returning one of its own women to lineage B.
2. This obligation of lineage A to return a woman to lineage B is considered to be a debt[6] which cannot be settled in any other way. The idea that money, cattle or other goods might serve as substitute compensation for the loss of the procreative capacity of a woman is rejected, and when in former days the Anufòm sometimes paid for women with

cattle or money, such transactions were considered merely as a 'purchase' of a female slave or prisoner of war and there was no question of an alliance with the lineage of the purchased woman. Nor can one lineage's obligation to furnish a wife be satisfied by another lineage. We shall hereafter refer to the obligation to return a woman as a 'bride-debt'.

A lineage which receives a woman is not obliged to repay the bride-givers immediately. Often a woman is given in return only after the first woman has born children and in many cases the repayment of the debt is postponed until the next generation.

That it is the right to the procreative capacity of a woman which is exchanged between lineages may be shown by the following additional rules:

3. The right of lineage A to the children of a woman received in marriage from a lineage B is only fully established when a woman has been returned by lineage A to lineage B.
4. A lineage which has received a woman who remains childless is not under an obligation to give a woman in return; on the contrary, they are often offered a second woman to replace the barren one.

Even if a wife deserts her husband, his lineage will honour their bride-debt, provided that children have been born from the union. Should the same woman bear children to her lover, he as well will do his best to give a woman in return to her lineage. Similarly if a widow does not remarry with a man from the lineage of her deceased husband (as the prevailing levirate custom requires) that lineage will still return a woman for her, provided she has born her first husband children. Finally, a marriageable woman is often referred to as an *awuru*, a patrilineage, in the sense of a future patrilineage.

It follows from the foregoing that Anufò lineages, especially among the *ngyem*, have to follow an external policy in marrying off their daughters to other lineages. The marriage policy of a lineage gives rise to much internal discussion among its adult male members, a discussion in which the opinion of the father of the girl concerned is of the highest consequence. The head of the lineage segment concerned makes the ultimate decision and bears responsibility for it towards other lineages. A father cannot be forced to marry his daughter to the candidate preferred by the lineage head and elders. He will, however, hesitate to oppose a reasonable proposition from them, since he depends on their goodwill for the payment of the bride-debt incurred by his own or his sons' marriages.

There are considerations which serve to guarantee the discharge of the obligation to return a woman, for example:

- A high value is placed on good relationships between two lineages; this should not be jeopardized by a failure to reciprocate.
- A special relationship exists between a person and his (or her) mother's patrilineage, his *na-awuru*[7]. A woman will often take her children to her father's lineage to cure or prevent illness by seeking the aid of her ancestors, the protection of the mother's patrilineal ancestors being considered more effective in case of illness, barrenness, etc., than the aid of a person's own patrilineal ancestors.

Moreover a man has some very special rights in his mother's patrilineage, the most important of which is his claim to a woman from his mother's patrilineage, the *na-awuru-bara*[8] (marriage between a man and his MBD being preferred). A man is only entitled to demand his *na-awuru-bara*, however, if the bride-debt incurred by the marriage of his mother has been paid by his patrilineage.

Diagram 2 gives an example of a bride exchange relationship between two patrilineages for over six generations. Both lineages, which belong to the non-islamized *ngyem*, live in the small Anufò village Ayikpèrè.[9]

Diagram 2. *Exchange of women over six generations between the patrilineages of KOSSI and MBAMBIM*

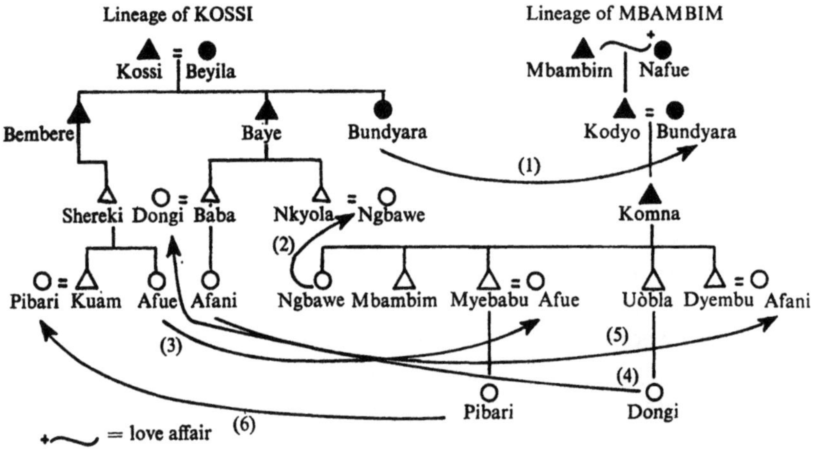

When a bilateral exchange of women has taken place, the following situation obtains: lineage A has given a girl to lineage B and lineage B has given one of its daughters in return to lineage A. The children from the woman of lineage A (who belong to their father's lineage, B) have lineage A as their *na-awuru* and the children from the woman of lineage B (who belong to their father's lineage, A) have lineage B as their *na-awuru*. The sons of both women may expect a girl in marriage from their *na-awuru*, and when these marriages have been concluded the next step towards a solid alliance between lineage A and B has been made. Once such an alliance is finally established it will last as long as daughters in both lineages are available.

A commonly accepted pattern of exchange, involving one wife-receiving and two wife-providing lineages, is for two brothers to use each other's daughters to redeem their own bride-debt, thus:

Diagram 3. *Reciprocal payment by brothers of each other's bride-debt*

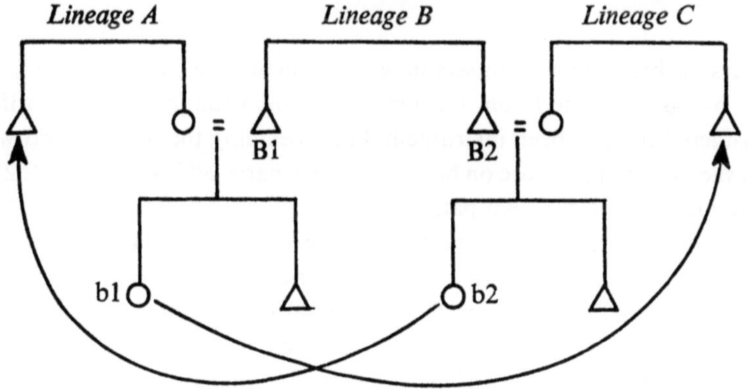

B1 and B2 are brothers (lineage B); B1 has received his wife from lineage A and B2 his wife from lineage C. To pay the debt of his brother B2, B1 gives his own daughter (b1) to lineage C. This obligates B2 to his brother B1 (as far as a 'debt' can be spoken of between brothers) and B2 in his turn will be obliged to marry off his own daughter (b2) to lineage A in settlement of the debt incurred by his brother's marriage. This arrangement is very frequent among the Anufòm, and is considered the ideal form of exchange. In this way paying a bride-debt with the daughter of the bride (which is considered undesirable because the original bride-giving group cannot marry this girl, to them a sister's daughter or father's sister's daughter) can be avoided. The bond between the two brothers is emphasized, and in addition both men will have an interest in keeping all four marriages intact.

Another pattern, often seen in the case of a polygamist who has no brother willing or able to provide a daughter, is to offer a daughter of one wife to redeem the bride-debt incurred for another wife.

Diagram 4. *Cross-repayment by polygamist with daughters of two wives*

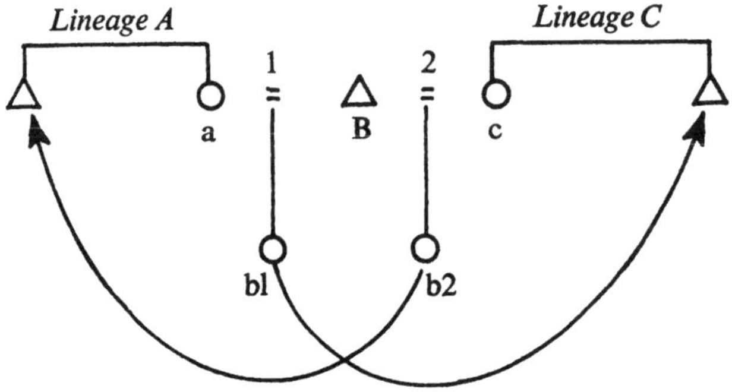

B pays the bride-debt of his second wife (from lineage C) with his daughter (b1) by his first wife (from lineage A). In this situation this first wife is considered to have been instrumental in redeeming the debt of a co-wife, and she can exert pressure on her husband to marry off his daughter (b2) by his second wife to her own patrilineage A.

Among all Anufòm, but particularly in the social estate of the commoners, most marriages are concluded in accordance with the system of bride-exchange. Genealogies from over 400 inhabitants of the Anufò village Ayikpèrè[10] show that the system of bride-exchange has been practised consistently over at least the last five generations. Nevertheless, as a lineage is not always able to return a woman in this or the next generation, the system not infrequently gives rise to problems. The alliance between two lineages is also at risk every time a girl refuses to marry the fiancé to whom she has been promised or a woman leaves the husband to whom she has been given. The system is especially rigid because it is impossible for a lineage which has no daughters available to transfer its debt to a third lineage. Lineage C would never agree to give a daughter in marriage to lineage B on behalf of lineage A, in order to continue an already existing marriage alliance between lineages A and B.

Divorce is a subject with which we are not here directly concerned, but it is essential to say a few words about it. A true divorce, resulting in a severance of both marital and interlineage ties, involves a difficult adjustment and can only be effected by agreement of the two lineages concerned. The *de facto* separation of a husband and wife does not necessarily mean a disruption of the relations between their lineages. The husband will continue his relations with his parents-in-law in the hope that his wife's patrilineage will offer him another girl and because he does not want to jeopardize the rights of his children in their mother's patrilineage. The Anufòm say that a woman can be given in marriage only once in her life; even if she has left her husband for another man she must perform the widow ceremonies (seclusion for some time) when her husband has died, and likewise her ex-husband must perform the duties of a widower after her death.[11]

Marriage prestations

Wooing may commence by a young man rendering services to the father and mother of a girl, visiting them regularly and bringing small presents, like a bowl of millet beer or some cola nuts. His object is to establish a friendship relation that will result finally in the girls' parents promising him their daughter in marriage.

From the moment a man has been promised a girl until he actually marries her, he must render personal services (such as assistance in farm labour) and offer gifts to his future parents-in-law. These services and gifts are called *ashibyèya.*[12] In contrast to the settlement of the bride-debt, which is an obligation of the lineage segment as a whole, the payment of the *ashibyèya* is the responsibility of the would-be husband, and his father and elder brothers. The *ashibyèya* is not a genetricial payment; it does not entitle the bride-receivers to the offspring of the bride. That right is only guaranteed by returning another woman to the bride-givers. The *ashibyèya* is not a fixed sum and the equivalent in cash – in particular of the personal services – is hard to rate, it ranges from approximately 15,000 francs CFA to 30,000 francs CFA when the personal services are not included. (1000 francs CFA = 20 French francs = approx. $ 4.50.) The most important material elements of the *ashibyèya* are the harvest products and the *kurubi*[13] money which are given to the prospective mother-in-law every year at the end of *Ramadân* and which she spends little by little on the trousseau of her daughter. The quantity of harvest products and the amount of *kurubi* money depend on the age of the girl, but also on the outcome of the harvest.[14] In addition, a man helps his prospective father-in-law in the fields and organizes work-parties for his benefit.

Quite as important, however, are the immaterial elements of the *ashibyèa.* A suitor should make regular visits to the girl's parents, do his utmost to please them in all ways possible, and emphatically show them respect and gratitude. Neglect or inability to make the required gifts may be overlooked if a man shows respect to his future parents-in-law, but material gifts can never compensate for a lack of respect. It is primarily disrespect which may cause parents to break off an engagement and marry their daughter to someone else. This is, however, an exceptional occurrence.

Restitution of marriage prestations

If a woman refuses to marry her fiancé or a married woman elopes with her lover, a claim for restitution of the marriage prestations is considered highly improper. The *ashibyèya* is aimed at establishing and maintaining a good relationship between a man and the parents of his future wife and is not considered payment for the woman or her procreative capacity. Restitution of the marriage prestations would disrupt the relations between a husband (or fiancé) and his (future) family-in-law. If a woman abandons her husband or fiancé, the best he can do is to wait patiently for his parents-in-law to offer him another girl as compensation. This will probably happen, provided that the elopement was not a result of his own behaviour. A man will only claim return of the *ashibyéya* from his parents-in-law if he is convinced that they have caused or abetted their daughter's behaviour. In that case, the relationship between a man and his (future) parents-in-law will be beyond redemption anyhow. Since the *ashibyèya* is given personally to the girl's father and mother, a claim of restitution is addressed only to them, not to the woman's lineage as a whole.

If the *ashibyèya* is claimed back, this is usually intended as a show of anger against the lover, not the (future) parents-in-law. A man who elopes with the wife or betrothed of another man may nowadays be legally forced to pay the latter a considerable sum of money, in part by way of indemnification for the *ashibyèya* he had paid to the family of the woman, at least 25,000 francs CFA if the case is treated by the Paramount Chief and between 5,000 and 10,000 francs CFA if his rival has gone to the *Tribunal Coutumier de Ire Instance* (see below).

Even after he has indemnified the husband (or fiancé), a lover is not assured of the normal relations entailed by marriage with the family of the woman. According to Anufò norms, a woman can only be given in marriage once and any second marriage is her own affair. Her parents will say they have nothing to do with the second man, whom they do not know (i.e. they do not recognize him as the husband of their daughter). Moreover if the parents of the woman were too ready to accept their daughter's lover as her husband, this would be an insult to the first husband (fiancé), and he would suspect them of having instigated or abetted their daughter to leave him. The lover will, nonetheless, do his best to come to good terms with his wife's parents, especially when he has children with her (thinking of their rights in their *na-awuru*, their mother's patrilineage). If he bides his time, there will come a point when greetings and presents will be accepted; and if he never overlooks an occasion to prove his good intentions, he will eventually be accepted, the more so after the first husband has been indemnified by him. Apart from the indemnification to the first husband, he will thus have to pay a lot of money for presents to his wife's parents, not to mention the presents he gave to his wife when she became his lover in order to prove his love. A marriage resulting from a love affair is generally very expensive.

It sometimes happens that a man confronted with everything he will have to pay for (indemnification of the husband (fiancé) for the *ashibyèya;* presents to the parents of the woman; and presents to keep his lover with him) retires from the whole affair, leaving the woman in a somewhat awkward position. Should the woman still refuse to return to her first husband, she can only return to her parents. The husband who cannot claim from the lover and does not want to claim from the parents of his ex-wife is left without indemnification. As a solution to cases like this, the Court of the Paramount Chief nowadays usually puts indemnification of the *ashibyèya* on the head of the woman: the moment she starts a love affair with someone, this man will be obliged to pay the *ashibyèya* back to her first husband (fiancé).

THE LAW IN ACTION

Disputes concerning the exchange of women, refusal to marry, and claims for the restitution of marriage prestations occur frequently. When not informally disposed of, such claims can be brought both in the *Tribunal Coutumier de Ire Instance*, and in the Court of the Paramount Chief of the Anufòm.

The *Tribunal Coutumier de Ire Instance* was set up under the 'Loi relative à l'Organisation Judiciaire' of the 12th of June 1961.[15] It is thus an official court. It is staffed with an African lawyer (trained in French law) known as the 'Juge de Paix', advised by two African assessors whose opinions are not binding on the Juge de Paix. The competence of the Tribunal is restricted to civil matters[16] *('en matière civile et commerciale')* and to minor criminal cases which the Juge de Paix tries without assessors. In general the territorial jurisdiction of a *Tribunal Coutumier de Ire Instance* is limited to one *circonscription.* In Sansanné-Mango the *Tribunal Coutumier de Ire Instance* commenced its duties in October 1965.[17]

The Court of the Paramount Chief of the Anufòm is the highest traditional judicial institution. The present Paramount Chief, Na Tyaba Tyekura, was officially so designated by the Togolese government on 6 December 1963, after being elected to that function by the Anufòm. As in the case of other traditional authorities[18] the Paramount Chief is, as far as the government is concerned, only a local civil servant, and not, as in the opinion of the Anufòm, a 'judge'. Local chiefs are not recognized as 'courts' in section 1 of the abovementioned law of 1961. The judicial competence of traditional chiefs in Togo is still based on two decrees issued during Franch colonial rule.[19] According to these decrees the Paramount Chief is only authorized to *conciliate* people, and only in civil matters. In practice the Paramount Chief does not restrict himself either to conciliation or to civil matters, frequently handling (among other things) accusations of witchcraft[20] and theft. Although the local government in Sansanné-Mango condones this exercise of unrecognized jurisdiction by the Paramount Chief, it keeps a close watch on all his activites. The Chief himself is very well aware of this fact. During his service as head of a canton, and from 1963 onwards as Paramount Chief, he has learned what the local government will leave to him and what not.

Despite the high rate of litigation of marital disputes at both courts, it is clear that many such disputes are handled initially and often conclusively at lower traditional levels, e.g., by lineage-, village-, canton-, or ward-heads. In this article we restrict ourselves to the *Tribunal Coutumier de Ire Instance* and the Court of the Paramount Chief, although we observed and recorded on tape many dispute settlements by these lower institutions.[21]

The Juge de Paix and the Paramount Chief have differing viewpoints concerning the exchange of women, divorce, and the restitution of marriage prestations. These differences may be attributable to the different cultural backgrounds, educations and positions of the Juge de Paix and the Paramount Chief; the first represents 'modern' and mostly western law (which in official and educated circles is also regarded as 'progressive'), while his traditional counterpart, the Paramount Chief, represents traditional rules and values. This does not mean that in his decisions the Paramount Chief ignores rapidly changing ideas about an institution like marriage, such as the fact that nowadays a woman cannot be forced to marry a man whom she does not want. On the other hand, in certain situations the Juge de Paix must apply customary law, and certainly cannot act in utter disregard of traditional ideas. Nonetheless there is a tension between the jurisdiction of the *Tribunal Coutumier de Ire Instance*, which is directed by the central government to introduce new institutions, and the conservatism of the Paramount Chief. Consequently the two legal institutions are more or less competitive with each other. Since both are available to men and women who are looking for a favourable disposition of their disputes, there is an excellent opportunity for many a litigant to play off these institutions against each other. At the same time, for the Chief and the Juge de Paix, litigants are to some extent the means of their competition with each other: thus every case is potentially an affair of four parties engaged in mutual manipulation. At any event, the Juge de Paix and the Chief must always each take account of the existence and views of the other in rendering the decisions.[22]

We shall illustrate the different views of the *Tribunal Coutumier de Ire Instance* and the Paramount Chief concerning the exchange of women, divorce and marriage prestations, by presenting two cases. The first is based on a record of the *Tribunal Coutumier de Ire Instance*, amplified from our own knowledge of Anufò society. The second was tried several times by the Court of the Paramount Chief, and observed by us.

Case 1: The Tribunal Coutumier de Ire Instance (1968)

In August 1968 a young girl of 18 years, Nabara, sued her father's sister Awu for attempting to force her to marry one Yombo, to whom she had been given in marriage by her father before he died. Nabara refused, however, to marry her fiance Yombo, because she preferred her lover Takpye, by whom she was pregnant (we do not know whether Nabara refused Yombo before Takpye had made her pregnant, or only afterwards). Nabara had been entrusted to Awu after the death of her father. The record refers to Awu as the 'tutrice' (i.e., the guardian) of Nabara.[23] Before the Tribunal appeared Nabara, her father's sister Awu, Nabara's fiancé Yombo and her lover Yakpye.

The facts appear, from the record, to have been as follows: Several years ago Nabara was given in marriage to Yombo. He started with the *ashibyèya* and for several years he paid the *kurubi* money to his mother-in-law (first to Nabara's own mother, but after her death to Awu). However, before the marriage was contracted both parents-in-law died. During the betrothal Nabara had taken a lover, Takpye, and after her father's death she refused to marry Yombo and eloped with Takpye. Her family however, insisted that Nabara should marry Yombo, as her father had wished. They forced her to come back and to cut off her relationship with Takpye. Awu in particular was opposed to her 'daughter's' refusal to marry Yombo, because she, as she said, had 'the responsibility to carry out her brother's wish'. This was an important indication that Awu feared retribution from her deceased brother.[24] The Juge de Paix did not pay much attention to her fear, though Awu expressed it more than once.

The discussion between the Tribunal and the litigants was very brief, except in connection with Yombo's calculation of the total amount of the marriage prestations. 'After long hesitation and calculation,' as the report says, 'I [Yombo] fix the *ashibyèya* at *82,000* francs CFA.'

On account of the clarity with which his views concerning the bride-exchange system and the restitution of the marriage prestations are set forth, we quote at length from the opinion of the Juge de Paix:[25]

that the customary rule [i.e., that a father gives his daughter in marriage] had its origin in a patriarchial society heavily dominated by the cult of the ancestors;

that the paternalistic power of the family-head, so provided, is excessive;

that the family constituted the basic unit of traditional society;

that it is composed of all those who are descendants of a common ancestor;

that it protects and subjects;

that such a rule is dictated by concern for the protection of the family against every undesirable intrusion;

but considering that the system has been very markedly changed over time because of various circumstances, in particular the intermingling of ethnic groups and the rural exodus;

that lovers have succeeded in making girls pregnant, despite traditions;

that thus the social structure is transforming itself;

that one witnesses the liberalisation of institutions and the simplification of certain formalities;

that this current of innovation exists in all societies;

that henceforth the society is going to be more individualistic;

that nowadays the wife lives alone with her husband and often far from her family;

that it is important, in these conditions, that the spouses know each other;

that this implies and requires the consent of the girl;

that the obligation of the girl to marry the man to whom she has been assigned, and the ensuing compulsion are contrary to public order;

such practices should not be legitimized because they involve a serious abridgment of the freedom of marriage;

that they instead incite girls to engage in illicit unions with their lovers;

that it is therefore fitting in order to facilitate marriage and to make sexual relations moral, to renounce this customary rule;

that therefore it is appropriate to grant the petition and to uphold the petitioner in her refusal to marry her fiancé and in her choice of her lover as her future husband ...

The Tribunal thus pronounced the betrothal between Nabara and Yombo illegal because it considered the Anufo system whereby the girl is given in marriage by her father (or family head) as against the fundamental right of every person freely to choose his or her spouse. This fundamental right is a rule of public order (*'ordre public'*) and therefore any compelled marriage is considered to be illegal. Nabara was held under no obligation to marry Yombo, and free to marry her lover if she wished. Her lover was, however, obliged to pay 20,000 francs CFA as indemnification to Yombo.[26]

There is no information in the record about the way in which Takpye was to pay Yombo, nor the date by which the payment had to be made, nor how Yombo might execute the award of the Tribunal. We do not know whether Yombo was able to execute the award but we found no evidence in the records of the Tribunal between 1968 and 1973 of any suit by Yombo against Takpye for non-payment.

Case 2: The Court of the Paramount Chief

This case appeared three times in the Court of the Paramount Chief between May-June of 1971.[27] The relationship of the litigants to each other is as follows:

Diagram 5

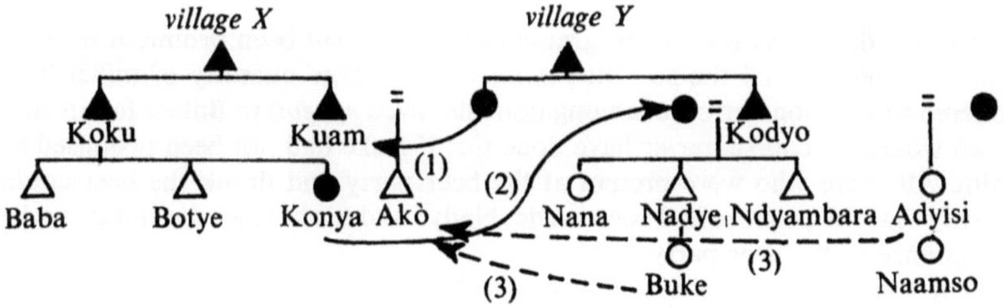

Akò, an old man of about sixty from the village X, is the son of an elder sister of Kodyo, from the village Y. The marriage between Kodyo's sister and Akò's father Kuam (from the village X) entitled Kodyo's lineage to a woman from Kuam's lineage. Kuam gave a younger (classificatory) sister of Akò, called Konya, to Kodyo, who married her. Before his death, Kodyo promised Akò his own daughter Adyisi. She is Akò's MBD and a marriage with her would be a preferential one. Akò had already begun to fulfill his *ashibyèya* duties, but when Adyisi had grown up, she refused to marry him because, like several other men in his lineage, he is blind. Kodyo understood quite well that he could not force Adyisi to marry Akò. He offered Akò to refund the *ashibyèya* rendered to him and Adyisi's mother, but Akò waved his offer away and expressed the hope for a second girl from Kodyo's lineage, if not for himself, then for his son. Kodyo promised to look for another girl in his lineage and Akò continued paying the *ashibyèya*, not to Kodyo, who had died in the meantime, but to Kodyo's sons Nadye and Ndyambara.

After some time, Kodyo's lineage promised to give Buke, Nadye's daughter, to Akò's lineage. Buke had been brought up by her father's sister Nana, because Nana herself had no daughters. As Buke reached the age to marry, she too refused to marry Akò or any man from his lineage, because of the blindness in Akò's lineage.

Before her betrothal Buke ran away with a lover. She then appeared before the Tribunal, accusing her lineage of forcing her to marry the old man Akò. As in Case 1, the Tribunal declared the betrothal illegal, and Buke's request for freedom to marry the man she liked was upheld. Her lover, however, was ordered to pay compensation to Akò. After this trial Buke had a miscarrage and her lover – a clerk at the local administration – abandoned her, probably because he did not want to pay the compensation to Akò. Buke took refuge in Northern Ghana with a new lover.

When Akò heard that Buke too had refused to marry him, he was furious and decided to sue Nadye, Nana, and Ndyambara at the Court of the Paramount Chief.

During the first session Nadye and Ndyambara denied doggedly that they knew anything about the promise of Buke to Akò. They rejected every responsibility, saying that Nana, their elder sister, had been the guardian of Buke. They knew, however, that the Court could not accept this defence, for a woman is never entitled to marry off her adopted child without permission of the girl's father.

In fact, the Court took it for granted that Buke had been promised to Akò, for Akò had offered the so-called *nashi* beer (a large quantity of millet beer offered to sanction betrothal among non-islamized *ngyem*) to Buke's family and Akò would, of course, never have done this if Buke had not been promised to him. All those who were present at the beer party and drank the beer could testify that the promise had been made, Nadye and his brother did not deny the occurence of the beer party.

The Chief's Court held Nadye responsible, as he was Kodyo's eldest living son. He was given the choice between keeping his father's promise or compensating Akò with 35,000 francs CFA. This was 10,000 francs CFA more than the usual amount, but after all Akò had rendered the *ashibyèya* twice.

Nadye, however, objected that not he, but his elder sister Nana had received the *ashibyèya*. This defence was rejected by the Court, which stated that he and his brother Ndyambara were responsible for paying the compensation and that Buke would remain in the custody of the Court until Nadye promised to give another girl to Akò, or paid the 35,000 francs CFA.

Again Nadye protested, saying that a man of Akò's lineage had recently eloped with Naamsò, daughter of Adyisi. He maintained that this elopement should offset the debt from Kodyo's lineage to Akò. Although Akò did not deny this claim the Court did not go into the matter, probably on account of the fact that the elopement was too recent to be sure whether Naamsò would marry her lover or not.

Partly as a result of pressure by the Chief, who argued that a good relationship between cross-cousins (as Nadye and Akò are) is preferable to a selfish orientation towards seeking the maximum gain from oneself, the bitterness between Akò and Nadye appeared to subside considerably in the last session, even though Nadye had not yet been able to keep his promise to pay a small part of the 35,000 francs CFA to Akò. Both men were already inclined to compromise. This endeavor was facilitated by the fact that Naamsò was still living with her lover in Akò's lineage.

DISCUSSION

Considering the traditional views and attitudes of the Anufò, one is puzzled to see both the *Tribunal Coutumier de Ire Instance* and the Court of the Paramount Chief upholding and even encouraging claims for recovery of the *ashibyèya*. Yet there are some remarkable and interesting differences between the views of the Tribunal and the Court of the Paramount Chief.

(1) As the Anufò system of bride-exchange is considered to be against public order the *Tribunal Coutumier* will declare a betrothal or marriage void when the woman sues her fiancé, her husband, or her parents for forcing her into an unwanted marriage. The Court, seeing that nowadays a woman cannot be forced to marry her fiancé or to stay with her husband against her will, accepts factual separation between a man and his wife or fiancée, but this does not necessarily imply disruption of the relationship between the two lineages.

(2) The Tribunal indemnifies the fiancé or husband for his loss on the basis of an actual calculation of the value of the *ashibyèya* payments he made. The Court upholds the outburst of anger by the fiancé or husband against the lover who has stolen his bride. In 1963, after the installation of the present Paramount Chief Na Tyaba Tyekura, a standard award of 25,000 francs CFA has been allowed as a kind of retaliation against the lover. That amount, however, is in fact approximately the same as is usually paid as *ashibyèya*. The Court does not requires an exact calculation of the marriage prestations and considers it immaterial whether or not the eloping wife had born children. According to the members of the Court the standard award is meant as a preventive measure against the increase of elopements.

(3) The Tribunal requires that the indemnity be paid by the lover, the parents of the woman, or even the woman herself. The Court usually exacts its fixed award not from the parents of the woman, nor from the woman herself, but from her lover.

(4) The Tribunal does not take past and future bride-exchange into consideration. If possible the Court takes account of and encourages continuation of the bride-exchange relationship. It does its best to maintain relations between the two lineages, often referring to promises made

by the ancestors (thus implicitly referring to the importance of not provoking their anger).

In admitting claims for the restitution of the marriage prestations, both courts differ from the view that is still widely held by Anufòm, that restitution of the *ashibyèya* is an unwise and incorrect (if not impossible) action. In the traditional view the only possible compensation would be another woman given by the parents of the eloped wife, but as such a claim would never be supported by the *Tribunal Coutumier de Ire Instance*, with its pronounced ideas on freedom of marriage, an alternative compension is sought and found even by the rather tradition-oriented Chief's Court in a monetary award which is approximately equivalent to the value of the *ashibyèya* paid to the woman's parents during the period of betrothal.

The Chief's Court does not speak explicitly of divorce, but it does accept the fact that a woman is opposed to an arranged marriage, a view which formerly would hardly have been tolerated once a marriage had been concluded. Here we may find some influence of the *Tribunal Coutumier de Ire Instance*.

By contrast, the idea that a husband should be compensated is explicitly accepted by the Chief's Court, but in that Court the choice is left to the husband whether he prefers to claim a sum of money or to wait patiently for the woman's parents to compensate the loss by giving him a second woman in marriage. As the Chief's Court is well aware of the fact that a claim for restitution of the *ashibyèya* from the wife's parents will disrupt the relations between a man and his in-laws, this court never encourages a man to claim his *ashibyèya* back. Should he nevertheless choose to claim what is commonly called his 'sufferings', his claim is hardly ever directed towards his parents-in-law (from whom he still may receive another bride), but in most if not all cases against the man who eloped with his wife. Recovering the *ashibyèya* from one's wife's lover is not in the first place an attempt to be indemnified for the loss, but mainly an act of revenge by the husband and of punishment by the Chief's Court. As an act of revenge it is compared by the Anufòm to the armed pursuit of a lover by the woman's husband in the past. As punishment by the Chief's Court it replaces the punishment of a man who eloped with another man's wife and is meant to have a preventive value.

By upholding a claim for recovery of the marriage prestations the Chief's Court is introducing a new element into Anufò family law, though it knows this to be contrary to traditional Anufò ideas. The innovation has taken place supposedly through the influence of the Tribunal, which has introduced two non-traditional elements, firstly the dissolution of marriage and secondly the restitution of the marriage payments.

Restitution of arranged marriages has been well received by a segment of Anufòm society – there was a very popular song about the justice of the Tribunal to the effect that the Juge de Paix had freed the women and girls. Disputes concerning such marriages are the subject of the great majority of cases tried by the Tribunal and they are often accompanied by a counter-request for restitution of the *ashibyèya* by the husband. But the idea of claiming the marriage prestations, considered by the *Tribunal Coutumier* as a rightful one, is not acceptable to all Anufòm, particularly not when the claim is directed against the parents-in-law.

NOTES

1. The Anufòm, or Tyokossi (Chokosi, Chakosi and Tschokossi), as they are called by the administration and other surrounding ethnic groups, are practically unknown in ethnographic literature. Some German articles at the beginning of the 20th century can be mentioned:

R. Asmis 'Die Stammersrechte der Bezirke Sansanne-Mangu'. *Zeitschrift für vergleichende Rechtswissenschaft*, 1219:78–89.

R. Fisch, *Nord-Togo und seine westliche Nachbarschaft* (Basel, 1911).

von Thierry, *Deutsches Kolonial Blatt*, Band 1899(10): 16.

Freiherr von Seefried, 'Betrage zur Geschichte des Manguvolkes in Togo', *Zeitschrift für Ethnologie*, 1913:421–35.

Graf von Zech, 'Land und Leute en der Nordwest Grenze von Togo', *Mitteilungen des deutschen Schutzgebieten*, 1904, Heft 17: 107–35.

More recently the Anufòm are mentioned by:

Neh. Levtzion, *Muslim Chiefs in West Africa, a study of Islam in the Middle Volta Basin in the pre-colonial period* (Oxford, 1968);

– *Islam in Africa* (J. Kritzeck and W.H. Lewis, eds., New York, 1969) 301.

I. Wilks, 'A note on the chronology and origins of the Gonja Kings', *Ghana Notes & Queries*, 1966, No. 8.

Kwame Ahrin, ed., *The papers of George Ekem Ferguson, a Fanti official of the government of the Gold Coast*, 1890–1897, (African Social Research Documents, No. 7, Cambridge, 1974).

E.A.B. van Rouveroy van Nieuwaal, 'The Tyokossi or Anufòm', *Yearbook of the Foundation for Scientific Research for the Tropics* (The Hague, 1971).

– *Essai sur quelques aspects du droit matrimonial chez les Anufòm*, *Mededelingen No. 10* (Afrika-Studiecentrum, Leiden, 1973).

– *Mbambim, un chef de famille d'Ayikpèrè* (Afrika-Studiecentrum, Leiden, 1973). *Musulmans à Mango* (Afrika-Studiecentrum, Leiden, 1974).

– *Sherea, la justice coutumière à la cour du chef supérieur à N'zara*, (Afrika-Studiecentrum, Leiden, 1975); forthcoming in: *Recueil Penant*, vol. 752, 1975.

– The Plot of the Sophisticated Son-in-Law, Disparity between Old and New Ways of Establishing Rights over Land in N'zara, North Togo', *Kroniek van Afrika*, (1) 1973: 47–60.

Diana Rey-Hulman: "Les dépendants des maîtres Tyokossi pendant la période précoloniale', in: *L'esclavage en Afrique* précoloniale (Cl. Meillassoux, ed., Paris. 1975), 297–320.

For discussion of the Anufò language:

U. Hintze, 'Die sprachliche Stellung des Anufò (Chokosi), ein Betrag zur Gliederung der Akansprachen'. *Mitteilungen Insitut für Orientforschung*, vol. 1, 1953: 151.

R. P. A. Prost, *La langue des Anufòm de Sansanné-Mango* (Documents Linguistiques, No. 3, 1958, Université de Dakar, Sénégal).

J. M. Stewart, 'Akan history: some linguistic evidence', *Ghana Notes & Queries*, 1966, No. 8.

2. In 1974 the Anufòm renamed the town N'zara. In this article, however, we shall refer to the town by its former name for the sake of convenience.
3. See for discussion of the term *donzo:* Youssouf Cissé, 'Note sur les sociétés des chasseurs', *Journal de la Société des Africanistes*, 1964; and M. Delafosse, *La langue mandinque*, vol. 2 Paris, 1955: 470.
4. The terms for these are *awuru adya* and *tí adya*, *adya* meaning marriage, and *tí*, far away.
5. The terms for these are *tò bara kari* and *kye bara*, respectively.
6. The obligation to return a woman to the bridge-givers is called *barankatò: bara*= woman; *n*=*ni* suffix which indicates that it concerns *this* woman *(bara ni)* who will be given in marriage as a discharge of a debt; *katò*=*kari tò* and *kari*=debt; *tò*=*to* pay, thus *tò kari:* to pay a debt.
7. *Na*=term for FF, FM, MF, MM and all parents two or more generations older than ego. *Na-awuru* is always used for the patrilineage of the mother's father's father. The man's own lineage is referred to as *shi-awuru* (*shi*=father).
8. *Bara*=woman.
9. Ayikpèrè is a village of about 400 inhabitants, mostly Anufòm, near the border with Ghana and about 30 miles south-west of Sansanné-Mango. Since January, 1972 it has been situated in the newly created National Wild Park.
10. See above, note 9.
11. These mourning ceremonies are believed to be required by one's ancestors, and neglect of them may be punished by illness or death. He who acts against the will of an ancestor (especially his own mother or father) runs the risk to be called to account by his deceased parents. He can be tried by the ancestors in a so-called *ashyèngu dyòrè*, i.e., a judgment (= *dyòrè:* word, judgment) under the earth (=*ashyè*). The outcome of this ancestral trial may be, if the living man or woman is found to be guilty by the dead, a *samandò*, punishment or curse.
12. The term *ashibyèya* is derived from the kinship term *shibyè*, for a male affine; it indicates:
    1) the affinal relatives as a group;
    2) the duties and obligations towards affinal relatives.
13. The *kurubi* feast is celebrated on the 27 th of *Ramadân*, the night in which the Koran is said to have descended from Heaven. The *kurubi* money is not given on the *kurubi* day itself, but usually some weeks or even several months later. The amount varies from 500 francs CFA to 5,000 or even 10,000 francs CFA, depending on the age of the girl.

    For a rating of marriage payments see my 'Essay sur quelques aspects du droit matrimonial chez les Anufòm', Afrika-Studiecentrum, *Mededelingen No. 10*, 1973: 46.
14. If the mother of the girl considers the amount paid by the future son-in-law insufficient to buy her daughter's trousseau, she may try to delay the marriage for another year or two. In doing so, she takes the risk that her grown-up daughter will run away with another man and she may then even find herself accused of deliberately

giving her daughter the opportunity to run away.

15. See J.D. Laloum, *Manuel du Juge de Paix* (Lomé, 1963), 124.
16. '[E]n matière civile, et commerciale.'
17. See, for the relation between modern and customary law and the judicial organisation in Togo, E.A.B. van Rouveroy van Nieuwaal, 'Droit Moderne et droit coutumier Togo,' *Receuil Penant*, No. 747, 1975: 5–19.
18. See, for a detailed discussion of the lower traditional authorities, E.A.B. van Rouveroy van Nieuwaal, 'La justice coutumière au Nord-Togo', *Receuil Penant*, No. 752, 1976.
19. *Journal Officiel du Togo*, No. 1145, 2 October 1949; *Journal Officiel du Togo*, No. 59–121, August 1959.
20. Compare Michael J. Lowy, 'The Fetishes Are There: The Management of Sorcery in an Urban Ghanaian Town', *Kroniek van Afrika*, Vol. 1, 1975: 38.
21. See E. A. B. van Rouveroy van Nieuwaal, 'Law, women and dispute settlement in a West African society', Ph. D. thesis, University of Leiden, the Netherlands (forthcoming).
22. Compare R.E.S. Tanner, *The Selective Use of Legal Systems in East Africa* (Uppsala, 1970).
23. If a woman is childless or bears only sons, one of her brothers will frequently entrust a daughter to her for education and to help her 'sweep her court-yard'. However, this guardianship–*atari*–does not entitle the woman to marry off her pupil without the permission of the father, although she may of course suggest someone as a fiancé to her brother. Marriage prestations would be made to the girl's guardian only after deliberation between the fiancé, the girl's parents (or, if they are deceased, their successors), and the guardian.
24. See note 11.
25. [Q]ue la disposition de la coutume se concevait dans une société de type patriarcal fortement dominé par le culte des anciens;

    que la puissance paternelle, celle du chef de famille, y est excessive;

    que la famille constituait la cellule de base de la société traditionelle;

    qu'elle est formée de tous ceux qui se rattachent à un ancêtre commun;

    qu'elle protège et assujettit;

    qu'une telle disposition est dictée par le souci de protection de la famille contre toute intrusion indésirable;

    mais attendu que le système a été très sensiblement altére au cours des ages a cause de multiple circonstances notamment la compénétration des groupes ethniques et l'exode rural; que des amants sont arrivés à mettre enceintes des jeunes filles au mépris des traditions;

    qu'ainsi la structure sociale se transforme;

    qu'on assiste à la libéralisation des institutions et à la simplification de certaines formalités;

    que ce courant novateur se rencontre dans toutes les sociétés;

    que désormais seule l'épouse vit avec son conjoint et bien souvent loin de la famille;

    attendu qu'il importe dans ces conditions que les epoux se connaissent;

    que cela implique et exige le consentement de la jeune fille;

    que l'obligation pour la jeune fille d'épouser tel homme déterminé et la contrainte subséquente sont contraires aux règles d'ordre public;

    de telles pratiques ne sauraient être consacrées parce que portant une atteinte grave à la liberté du marriage;

    qu'elles incitent plutôt les jeunes filles à s'engager dans une union illégitime avec leurs amants;

    qu'il convient donc pour faciliter le mariage et moraliser les relations sexuelles de renocer à cette disposition de la coutume;

que c'est le cas dès lors de faire droit à la demande et de donner acte à la demanderesse de son refus d'épouser son fiancé et de son choix de son amant comme future époux ...

26. In the records of the *Tribunal Coutumier de Ire Instance* the marriage prestations are referred to as '*dot*'. Although the word means in French 'dowry', it is commonly used by the Tribunal to indicate the *ashibyèya.*
27. All three court sessions were recorded on tape and transcribed and translated in full.

Judicial manipulation of customary family law in Tanzania* 6

AKILAGPA SAWYERR
University of Ghana

INTRODUCTION

One of the striking features of the legal situation in Tanzania, and in other African states, is the phenomenon of legal pluralism – that is, the accommodation within the national legal system of a variety of bodies of law, customary, religious, and English-inspired, applicable under specified conditions to the different ethnic, religious, and racial groups. This phenomenon, and the manner in which it has been approached by both legislature and courts, has received much attention from writers on the African legal scene.[1] The only justification for adding to this literature yet again is a feeling that it is possible and necessary to approach the entire question of legal pluralism from a fresh angle.[2]

The general approach to date has been to consider the legislative or judge-made rules provided for the guidance of judges dealing with problems of 'internal conflict of laws', to argue for this or that interpretation of the rules, and sometimes to evaluate the general effectiveness of the scheme for the resolution of such conflicts. The alternative approach we here advocate would look to the basic causes of such variation as exists between the different bodies of law operating within the country, their relation one to another, and the general direction of motion of the whole complex under the pressure of the objective conditions in which the legal system operates. This calls for an examination of among other matters, the basic economic

* This paper reworks material used in the preparation of an article entitled 'Customary Law in the High Court of Tanganyika', published in the *Eastern Africa Law Review*, Vol. 6, 1973, pp. 265–284.

and political forces at work in the society, the institutions for the administration of the country, and their relation to those forces. It is essential that any such examination be informed by a sound understanding of the historical processes behind the development of those forces and those institutions.

This paper represents a tentative application of this approach to the study of the position of customary law in Tanzania. It begins with a sketch of the context of pluralism and an indication of some of the basic tendencies in the development of Tanzanian society. This leads into a discussion of the position and role of the superior courts within the described processes. Against this background, some High Court decisions in the area of family law are discussed in order to show the relationship between the objective position of the Court and the pattern of its decisions.

THE CONTEXT OF PLURALISM AND THE POSITION OF THE SUPERIOR COURTS

The indigenous peoples of Tanzania consist of a variety of linguistic groups. In addition to the majority Bantu peoples, there are small groups of Khoisan, Cushitic, and Nilotic peoples. These groups are in turn subdivided into smaller groups. In terms of economic activity these peoples range from relatively settled agriculturalists, through nomadic pasturalists, to the essentially hunter/gatherer Kindinga. (Sutton 1969; Taylor 1963). This variety is reflected in differing patterns of family relations, control, and enjoyment of land and other property, and processes for the adjustment of competing claims and redress of grievances.

These complexities were compounded by the presence and influence of Arab, Indian, and European invaders, traders, and settlers. This entailed more than an addition to the ethnic and racial mix, for it introduced the Islamic, Hindu, and Christian religions into the situation.

The impression of cultural diversity given by this description of the Tanzanian scene has provided the foundation upon which the formal structure of the judicial and legal system has, since the beginning of colonial rule, been built. Thus the main determinants of the appropriate court to hear a case and the law to be applied were supposed to be the race or ethnic origin, or sometimes religion, of the parties to the suit. This impression, it need hardly be stated, did not conform in full to the reality of the basic forces within society and therefore constituted a predictably fragile foundation for the legal superstructure (Sawyerr 1971, 1974).

A better indication of the significance of the forms of the legal superstructure and, in particular, the place of customary law within it, can be obtained by an analysis of the objective position of the superior courts and their relation to the economic forces at play in society in colonial and post-colonial Tanzania. A brief outline of such an analysis is sufficient for our purpose.

The dominant factor throughout this period has been colonialism. For over sixty years Tanzania was under the political and economic control first of Germany, then of the United Kingdom. This involved the treatment of the Tanzanian economy, like all other colonial economies, as an adjunct to the economy of the metropolitan power (Johnstone 1918; Lugard). In specific terms the leading sectors of the local economy were increasingly geared to production for the world capitalist market, and the consumption of the products of the metropolitan economy.

This led to significant transformations in the economic and social conditions in the country. The imposition of territory-wide administrative control, tenuous though it was at the edges, and the introduction and expansion of the cash economy, had the effect of drawing hitherto relatively isolated groups within an increasingly territory-wide economy. This centripetal tendency was aided by the general improvement of communications. The upshot of these developments was the growth of relatively modern urban centres and plantations, which constituted the conduits that linked the local economy to the world market (Frank 1967; Stephens 1968; Szentes, 1971; Parker 1972; Beckford 1972; Rodney 1972; Seidman 1972). These centres at the same time provided bases from which novel and sophisticated patterns of life and economic activity spread to the rest of the country.

It was primarily to promote and service these modernising sectors of the economy and thereby to facilitate the economic exploitation of the colony that English law and the system of superior courts, like all other major colonial arrangements, were introduced. For, in spite of all the mystifying euphemisms used to describe and justify the colonial enterprise, all implying a mission to civilise and Christianise the natives (Cameron 1939), the prime concern of the colonial power and the interests it represented was to so transform the economy and administer the territory as to fit it most effectively into the world capitalist system. It followed from this that the superior courts, as instruments of colonial policy, stood for policies in important ways antithetical to the traditional patterns of economic activity and social relations.

This was and, as will appear below, remains, the basic contradiction in colonial and post-colonial Tanzania. For the cultural diversity we noted earlier counted for very little. As against the forces introduced by colonialism as an economic phenomenon, all traditional society (whatever its superstructural form) was subject to basic transformation. In this contradiction between the basis of the superior courts and the social conditions of indigenous society lay the objective basis for judicial control over customary law, irrespective of the ethnic or religious groups concerned.

The attainment of political independence has brought little change in the basic position of the superior courts in relation to traditional society and therefore to customary law. To be sure, a number of important political and economic factors have emerged, among them:

(a) the removal of direct external political influence through the substitution of a national for a colonial administration;
(b) the adoption of a socialist path of development by the national government;
(c) the localization of the judiciary; and
(d) the increase in knowledge about traditional society and greater emphasis by the central government on the development of the whole country and of all the people.

Whilst these new factors have a bearing on the specific policies that move the courts (Sawyerr 1969: 33–34) they do not affect the basic position of the superior courts, which still remains that of an institution of central authority concerned with *national* policy. Simply put, the superior courts stand in relation to customary law rather as the central government does to traditional forms of economic and social organisation. To the extent that the central government, colonial or post-colonial, seeks to transform traditional organisations, to that extent will the superior courts tend to control the application of customary law. This, we would suggest, is the objective basis for superior court control today over the application of customary law. And it not only explains why such control has survived the removal of the formal statutory authority for it, but also why its exercise, as some of the cases discussed below show, seems more vigorous now than ever before (Sawyerr 1969: 32).

CUSTOMARY FAMILY LAW IN COURT

The superior courts have always exercised a discretion to refuse application of any rule of customary law considered 'repugnant to justice and morality'. This was the broad formula under which control over the application of customary law was exercised. Having explored in detail elsewhere the range of techniques employed by the court (Sawyerr 1973a) we can here only provide a summary.

Under the rules of evidence customary law has always had to be established in the superior courts by 'experts' in customary law, and, more recently, by reference to books of authority and other sources satisfactory to the court. The very nature of customary law as an unrecorded, ever-developing law, ensures that there is always room for doubt about the exact content of a particular rule. So whenever the parties disagree about the rule, the court has considerable freedom to accept whichever it considers the better of alternative formulations. This provided the opportunity for the most regular exercise of judicial control over the application of customary law.

A second, more direct, form of control is exercised by the court in the process of 'modernising' the applicable rule. Here there is no dispute as to the content of the rule, no suggestion that it is repugnant or immoral. The third and most direct form of control is the outright rejection of a custom as being 'repugnant to justice and morality'.[3]

When we come to a consideration of what constitutes 'modernity' or 'justice and morality', the yardsticks by which customary rules are purportedly measured, the cases are most instructive. For in the area of customary family law, the cases reveal something of a judicial bias towards the nuclear family of husband-wife-children at the expense of the wider traditional family, and the encouragement of individual as against communal ownership of property.

It is generally recognised that an outstanding feature of traditional society is the extent of the subordination of the particular rights of the individual to those of the various groups to which he belongs – nuclear family, extended family, and clan. (Memo No. 2, 2; Schneider 1970: 49). In consequence, membership of a group such as the family *ipso facto*, and entirely apart from the volition of the individual, imposes upon him many obligations to other members of the family and entitles him to a host of rights in return. It is this network of rights and obligations attaching to membership of a family that characterises the traditional social arrangements. And it is by undermining the links established by this network that the courts reveal their bias against traditional family and property relations.

To demonstrate this we examine a few illustrative cases, beginning with one in which the claims of the extended family were discounted in favour of the nuclear family In *Mazuguewa d/o Chilennu v. Mwango s/o Chilennu*, [(1969) H.C.D. 182] the respondent claimed from his half-sister the portion of the bridewealth paid on the marriage of the latter's daughter (his niece) to which he was entitled under Gogo law. He was successful in both the Primary and the District Courts. But in the High Court his claim was rejected. The technical ground was that the suit had been brought against the wrong party, the mother instead of the father of the bride as required by the Law of Persons. But to forestall a reinstitution of the suit against the father, the court took the opportunity to pronounce on the substantive question. In rejecting as unreasonable and contrary to the spirit of modern times the Gogo custom allocating a fixed share of the dowry to the maternal uncle, the judge observed that the latter may have contributed nothing to the upbringing of the girl. Instead of the customary arrangement, he would have the father do the distribution on the basis of *agreement* with his relatives. He concluded, '(W)hen benefits are to be shared, this can be done with regard to the degree with which attention and assistance have been given in the past, *not merely on the strength of the relationship itself*' (my italics).

Here we find the court disapproving the ascription of rights among members of the wider family 'on the strength of the relationship itself', i.e., on the basis of 'status', in favour of their acquisition by specific actions and agreement. This puts the property relations of family members on an entirely different footing, tending to nullify the obligations that spring from the relationship of nuclear to the extended family, and which bind the whole together.

In similar vein was the case of *Abdallah Salimu v. Ramadhani Shemodoe*, [(1968) H.C.D. 129]. The appellant there argued that his obligation to maintain his child was subject to Sambaa customary law, which required only the award of *mtonge* – one cow – an argument which was supported by the village elders who testified before the court. Whilst recognizing this customary obligation to provide for the maintenance of a child, the court substituted for the customary *mtonge* a substantial amount of money based on a realistic assessment of the cost of maintaining and educating a child under existing conditions. As the judge put it:

> '*Mtonge* might have been a very good custom ... when it came into operation, but I think that must have been a very long time ago, when a cow would have a very high value .... It is abundantly clear that no parent could bring up a child to age seventeen ... on the [value of one cow]. What must be done is to face the facts as they are, rather than take shelter under an old customary practice.'

Which is to say that the customary obligation owed by a person to house, feed, clothe, and educate the child of a relative, which makes it unnecessary for the parent to give him more than a token of acknowledgement, is outdated.[4]

More instructive than all these cases are those in which a customary practice is attacked explicitly on the basis of infringement of 'individual rights of property'. The old case of *Gwao bin Kilimo v. Kisunda bin Ifuti* [(1938) 1 T.L.R. (R.) 403], is a good one to start with. Mange, a government clerk, was convicted and punished for converting to his own use money belonging to the respondent. The latter then brought this action to recover the money, and, having obtained judgment, sought to attach the property of the appellant, father of Mange. The issue was whether the attachment of the father's property was proper.

The respondent relied on the customs of the Wanyaturu. The evidence, although confused and often conflicting, established that according to Nyaturu custom where a father failed to make voluntary compensation for cattle stolen by his son he could in some cases be compelled to do so (Schneider 1970; 92). This evidence the learned judge found weak support for the respondent's claim. But, assuming the custom established, he would still have rejected it, he said, as being repugnant to British ideas of justice. He went on:

'Is it just according to our ideas to take away a man's property in order to compensate a party who has suffered injury at the hands of the man's son, the son being of full age and fully responsible in law for his own actions? .... It is against general ideas of justice that a man should suffer ... directly either in person or in property for some wrong which he has not done himself ...'

This statement is striking for a number of reasons. To begin with, the first sentence begs the question whether the son was 'fully responsible *in law*' for the act complained of. Which law? That was the very question posed by respondent's reliance on Nyaturu law, for under that law the son was *not* directly and exclusively responsible. The judge's statement, without addressing this question, assumes that the son's responsibility was initially determinable under the received English law.

Secondly, even if one were to concede the controlling force of English ideas in such a situation, it just was not true that it was against those ideas for a person to answer in a civil action for the wrongs of another. For a very long time a husband was liable at common law for the torts of his wife, and still today the common law doctrine of vicarious liability belies the judge's assertion. Again, vicarious liability under criminal statutes was not unknown in colonial Tanganyika.[5]

Finally, the statement reflects the judge's failure to consider the asserted customary law within its social, economic, and legal context. If it could be shown, for instance, that the herd allegedly owned by the father, the subject-matter of the suit, was family property in the sense that it was built up by contributions of the father's family past and present, would a rule that cattle from it could be used in meeting the obligations of other members of the family be unjust or repugnant to morality? Perhaps this argument was not put to the court and the judge's knowledge of customary relations was not such as to make him sensitive to this possibility.

It is possible to dismiss this statement as one more instance of a judge overgeneralising through ignorance. But such a view misses what we would suggest is the true significance of the statement and of the whole decision: namely, the unwillingness of the court to accept the notion inherent in the asserted custom that a person's property is not his 'private property' to the extent that it may be used to meet a range of obligations wider than those which English law would consider strictly his. The judge's action must then be seen as a judicial attempt to impose notions of a private property on a society still communally-oriented.

In a more recent case, *Masero Mwita v. Rioba Masero* [(1969) H.C.D. 199] a Kuria son sued to compel his father to provide cattle to enable him to get married, as was their custom. This the father refused to do because of an earlier dispute with the son. The latter enlisted the help of the clan elders to persuade the father. When this failed, he brought an action in the Primary Court. That court, and the District Court on appeal, upheld his claim and ordered the father to meet his customary obligations. In subsequently reversing these decisions and denying that the father was under any legal obligation, the High Court judge said:

> This dispute involves a very difficult problem. And that is, how much of the recognized customary law should be enforced by the courts? It is undisputed that according to Kuria customary law the [son] has the right to claim bride price from his wealthy father and in the remote past a reluctant father could have his cattle seized by the clan elders and used for the son's bride price .... But I am of the view that this obligation, though very strongly felt by Kuria tribesmen, cannot be enforced by the courts. To do so would be dangerously encroaching on the individual rights of property.

One does not find here any reference to 'British ideas', nor even to 'natural justice and morality'. Instead this custom of the Kuria people is denied enforcement in court because it was incompatible with 'the individual rights of property'. The court in this passage thus makes explicit what we have suggested is an important factor behind many decisions rejecting the application of specific customary norms.

One could cite other instances of the High Court implicitly measuring customs according to its own notions of the 'natural order' of *property* relations. Among these would be cases in which it was held that wards were entitled to an accounting from their guardian,[6] and those in which the court refused to order property, title to which was disputed, to be partitioned among competing relatives. In *Kapasyi s/o Mwaipinga v. Mwendileo s/o Mwakyusa*, [(1968) H.C.D. 82] two relatives came to court each claiming the disputed property by inheritance. The assessors in the district court suggested that as the parties were related the dispute could be brought to an amicable solution by dividing the land equally between the two claimants. As this was consistent with Nyakyusa customary law, the magistrate accepted the suggestion and so ordered. In reversing this decision and giving judgment in favour of one of the parties, the High Court observed:

> It is clear that any customary law which dispossesses an owner would be contrary to the principles of natural justice .... The 'Solomon' ruling must be disturbed.

Here we find the court starting from a premise that the property must be owned by one or the other party, and that a resolution which produced an effect other than this, 'would (clearly) be contrary to natural justice'. This discounted the validity of the conception of property the Nyakyusa practice asserted in the case, namely that as the property in dispute was essentially family property, the individual members deriving title from family membership, an amicable settlement that ensured enjoyment by family members was preferable to any 'either/or'decision which in difficult cases, such as the one here, was apt to exacerbate family discord. This shows that in rejecting partition as a means of resolving the conflict as to title the court was being faithful, under the guise of natural justice, to the conception of individual ownership of property.

To round out this survey of judicial practice we consider a few cases dealing with the customary requirement of payment of bride wealth, traditionally regarded as a necessary condition for the completion of a customary marriage and the acquisition by the groom of all the attributes of a husband and father. Important among the social functions of the payment of bridewealth has been that of drawing the wider kin of the bride and groom into the marriage almost as participants, certainly as witnesses. This was intended to help ensure to the union of the immediate parties the stability that comes from a wide base of social approbation and concern, and to the larger family the reinforcement of mutual bonds of cooperation and solidarity. To support all this, the non-payment of bridewealth was visited with a host of sanctions. The ultimate sanction was in some societies the right of the wife's family to demand the return of their daughter or sister, together with any children born of the union, at any time. Short of this, the husband could be denied custody of the children upon separation or the death of the mother. On the other hand, where full bridewealth had been paid, the husband was entitled not only to his wife, but also to custody of all children born to her, whether by him or by someone else, whether born while they were living together or separate. Further, upon his death, especially if the marriage had been childless, other members of his family were in some societies entitled to take his widow in marriage.

There are many cases dealing with the court's treatment of these traditional incidents of payment or non-payment of bridewealth.[7] A few will illustrate our position. In *Loijurusi v. Ndiinga* [(1971) H.C.D. 331], the respondent took his sister and her children away from her husband, the appellant, 'in order to exact payment of bride-price' from the latter. This was rejected by the Primary Court, but upheld by the District Court as being in accord with Masai customary law. In the High Court respondent's action was condemned as 'clearly inequitable and contrary to public policy', and it was observed that it was time the courts put a stop to any custom which gave the respondent such a right. The reason for the court's reaction was the threat posed by the respondent's action to the welfare of 'the appellant, his wife and their offspring' – the nuclear family. Not even the wider family was to be allowed to interfere with the this unit, which is described as 'the fabric of the entire society'. Here the court leans in favour of the nuclear family and against the claims of the wider family.

As has been noted one of the important consequences of the payment of bridewealth was traditionally to consign exclusively to the groom the productive capacity of the wife, so that he was entitled to claim as his all children born to his wife, until such time as his bridewealth or an appropriate proportion of it had been refunded to him. Thus even if he and his wife should separate, he continued to be entitled to the custody of any children born to her no matter how long after the separation, and no matter that she was known to be cohabiting with another man, who also claimed the children.[8] The colonial courts were torn in two on this question. On the one hand this custom was so ingrained in people's minds and tied in with the entire patrilineal system that the courts were loath to tamper with it. On the other hand, they were heavily influenced by the principle that the welfare of the children should be the prime, if not the sole, determinant of the parent into whose custody they were to be given. Thus the customary right of the legal father to custody was held not repugnant to natural justice or morality, and therefore enforceable.[9] It was early recognised, however, that one of the main purposes of custody claims was the assertion of customary rights in respect of the children, particularly the right to bridewealth payments due on the marriage of daughters. In several cases the courts separated the question of customary 'proprietary' rights from that of physical custody, with the result that while the legal father was held entitled to collect bridewealth payments when the time came for daughters to be married, his right to physical custody was made to depend upon what would best serve the interests of the children.[10]

Rule 175 of the Law of Persons in 1963 restated the customary law that children born in lawful wedlock belonged to the legal father. For some time this seemed to have been quite firmly followed by the courts. In *Makafu Nyamrunda v. Muga Okanda* [(1968) H.C.D. 83] a man sued for custody of his two children. When his marriage to their mother was dissolved, the latter kept the children and took them to live with her second husband. It was established that while the plaintiff was poor and still single, the defendant had remarried a wealthy man who was looking after the children. The district court awarded custody to the defendant because 'the first thing to be considered (was) the welfare of the children'. On appeal the High Court acknowledging this principle and accepting the evidence of the relative material circumstances of the claimants, reversed the district court, and awarded custody to the plaintiff on the grounds that as father he had under Rule 175 an absolute right to custody of his children.[11] This position has been upheld even in cases where the evidence showed beyond a doubt that the legal husband could not be the natural father of the children.[12]

This 'absolute' right of the father has in several cases been rejected outright in favour of the welfare of the children.[13] But in many more cases the questions of physical custody and entitlement to customary rights, especially bridewealth payments, have again been separated.[14] The case of *Waryoba d/o Katara v. Kirimi s/o Wagari* [(1969) H.C.D. 6] provides a clear illustration of what may well be the trend of the near future. Upon the dissolution of the marriage of Kirimi and Waryoba, the latter sought the custody of their only child. This claim was rejected by both the Primary Court and the District Court on the ground that as father Kirimi was entitled to custody. On appeal Saidi, J., in awarding custody to the mother said:

> The judgments of both courts below are ... right in pronouncing the respondent the father of the child but I think they did not properly take into account the welfare of the child itself. As the facts are I am firmly of the view that the welfare of this child will be more secure if it remains in its mother's custody than in its father's custody ....

'The respondent is declared the father of the child and will have the right in due course to arrange the marriage of the child and to receive the bride price ....

This principle that the welfare of the child counts for more than the customary right of the father to custody, as distinct from other rights, is one more instance of the courts leaning in favour of the individual member of the family as against the family. For in this the court tends to discount the rights and duties ascribed to members of the family as such, and looks primarily to the interests of a member as an individual. While the principle is not as yet unequivocally accepted by the courts there is little doubt that it is the trend of the future.

Among other examples of bias towards the particular rights of the individual we may mention the insistence that a widow may refuse to be 'inherited' by a relation of her deceased husband,[15] and the tendency to reject or modify rules barring females from inheriting certain types of property.[16]

CONCLUDING REMARKS

It should be noted that in speaking of this bias against the traditional family system, it is not intended to present a picture of a uniform and unrelenting judicial assault on the traditional family. Three qualifications are called for. First, the force with which this bias has operated has depended in large measure upon the extent to which the custom in question was considered offensive to the court's notion of morality, and detrimental to accepted policy objectives. Secondly, this in turn depended upon the clarity with which the policy was perceived and the extent of the threat posed by the custom to specific interests protected by that policy. Thus a custom which offended the moral sense of the court would be tolerated if it was seen as posing no direct threat to important interests of the central authority. Such was the case with the institution of polygamy. The colonial courts were never comfortable with it, frequently describing it in the most perjorative terms, and sometimes denying polygamous marriages the usual attributes of a civil marriage (Sawyerr 1967: 128–30). But they never moved directly against it. Similarly tolerated were such institutions as marriage between two women[17] and the inheritance of a woman as wife by relations of her deceased husband.[18] On the other hand customs which could not be considered morally offensive but which threatened important interests were apt to be struck down. The cases of *Gwao bin Kilimo* and *Masero Mwita*, discussed above, provide examples.

In the third place, customs that were enforced at one time either because they ran counter to no established policy or because their impact on important interests was negligible, were at other times differently treated because of differences in the factors that ensured their enforcement. Thus for a long time customs restricting inheritance of property by females were tolerated, to such an extent that they were reproduced in the Law of Persons (G.N. 436 of 1963). But of late many judges have refused to enforce them, boldly explaining away the clear terms of the relevant provisions.

It may be suggested that this trend is not the result simply of an increase in the court's disapproval of such 'outdated' customary practices. It is more the result of the extension of the area of concern of the courts. The concern of the colonial officials was essentially focussed on administration for the benefit of the modern sectors of the territory and the success of the colonial enterprise. Today central policy in Tanzania is more broadly gauged, taking in the welfare of all the people of the country (cf. the Arusha Declaration). In consequence the concerns of the courts have also expanded, moving to touch customs and practices that colonial courts left untouched because of their more limited concern (Cameron 1937: 22–24; Liebenow 1971: 88, 138–46; Sawyerr 1969: 30–32).

In summary of our survey, we merely restate the theme that has been running through our discussion: *to the extent that a bias in judicial orientation is discernible, it has been towards the encouragement of individual as against communal ownership of property, and the promotion of the nuclear family of husband-wife-children at the expense of the wider traditional family.*

To maintain faith with our starting point, a final observation is in order. It is the case that the induction of Tanzania into the world capitalist system and the consequent introduction and expansion of the money economy led to such changes in the pre-existing economic formations as to set up, or at any rate accelerate dramatically, a trend away from emphasis on the communal towards the individualistic, and from the extended towards the immediate family. The objective function of the judicial system as we have noted was to reinforce this trend. Thus in their bias towards 'individualism', the courts were not acting capriciously, but in accord with their objective function in the system.

NOTES

1. See, e.g., E. Guttman, 'The Reception of Common Law in the Sudan', 6 I.C.L.Q 401 (1957); F.A.R. Bennion, *Constitutional Law of Ghana* (London: Butterworth, 1962), Chap. 12; B.O. Nwabueze, *The Machinery of Justice in Nigeria* (London: Butterworth, 1963); P. Contini, 'Integration of Legal Systems in the Somali Republic', 16 I.C.L.Q. 1088 (1967); A.N. Allott, *New Essays in African Law* (London: Butterworth 1970), Pt II.
2. My earlier contributions are listed in the bibliography.
3. For discussion of case law supporting these observations on techniques of control, see Sawyerr 1974a, notes 9–24 and accompanying text.
4. See also *Eliatosha Elisamia v. Theofio Josia*, (1960) Digest 178; *Juma Kisuda v. Hema Mjie*, (1969) H.C.D. 188; contra, *Murisho v. Halima* (1971) H.C.D. 256.
5. See, e.g., *Alimohmed Osman v. R.* (1952) 1 T.L.R. (R). 391.
6. *Shija Kadasa v. Mahuyi Kadasa*, (1961) Digest 208.
7. Though it may create a civil debt recoverable by action from the groom, non-payment of bridewealth is no longer fatal to the validity of a customary marriage: Law of Persons (G.N. 436 of 1963) R. 5; Law of Marriage Act, 1971 (Act No. 5) s. 41(a). This of course does not affect our discussion since other consequences of non-payment under customary law remain untouched by the statutory changes.
8. E.g., *Shija Maziku v. Mpemba Nzunya*, (1969) H.C.D. 4.
9. *Maranya Chacha v. Muhabe d/o Wambura* (1952) Dig. 36; *Jospeh Makirai Nyaiseti v. Chacha Musioni* (1952) Dig. 37.
10. *Enock Majani Mutoni v. Bakari Kibogoti* (1956) Dig. 103; *Mtatiro Mwita v. Robi Mwita* (1963) Dig. 243.
11. See also *Mohamed Hamisi v. Salum Alli* (1967) H.C.D. 169; *Matinde d/o Rukonge v. Mwita Mayntumutura* (1968) H.C.D. 4; *Shija Mzaiku v. Mpemba Nzunya* (1969) H.C.D. 4.
12. *Shija Maziku v. Mpemba Nzunya* (above); In *Magunda v. Komea* (1972) H.C.D. 17, the legal father's claim was bolstered by the fact that the court pronounced the general conduct of the mother '*contra bonos mores*'.
13. E.g., *Adam Kharid v. Amina Rajabu* (1968) H.C.D. 405; *Bakari v. Bakari* (1971 H.C.D. 170.
14. E.g., *Makende s/o Kisunte* (1969) H.C.D. 5; *Waryoba d/o Katara v. Kirimi s/o Wangari* (1969) H.C.D. 6; *Ng'washi Kamwezi v. Bungo Kulaba* (1969) H.C.D. 267.
15. See, e.g., *Juma Kisuda v. Hema Mjic*, (1969) H.C.D. 188, and *Mkitiri v. Mtanyi*, (1972) H.C.D. 7.
16. *Saidini d/o Angovi v. Saiboko Mlemba* (1960) Dig. 205; *Ndewawiosia d/o Ndeamtzo v. Imanuel s/o Malasi* (1968) H.C.D. 127.
17. E.g., *Kirisa s/o Kitentera v. Patiri d/o Magesa*, (1968) H.C.D. 254.
18. See cases cited *supra*, n. 15.

Economic consequences of divorce: a case study of some judicial decisions in Lagos 7

A.B. KASUNMU
University of Lagos

The decision to write a paper under the title above was provoked by the following observations of Adewale Thompson, J., in *Akinsemoyin* v. *Akinsemoyin:*

> ... the history of maintenance in England is different from the history here. We have merely inherited a statutory provision based on the customs of the people of England, which are not only unknown in this country but are in contradistinction to our own. The English man who receives Dowry from his wife's family has got a pecuniary benefit from the marriage; part of which the law permits him to return on the dissolution of the union. The Nigerian man is not so blessed. He pays *donation propter nuptias* and in some parts this fee is so exhorbitant that it savours of tax. Anthropologists call it Bride price. Now, it will be ridiculous and indeed unreasonable to expect a man who has gone into all that expense in order to get married to be overburdened with maintenance for the woman unless there are exceptional circumstances warranting it (1971 N.M.L.R. 272 at 275).

No attempt will be made at this stage to comment on the correctness of the above observations, but anyone familiar with the trend of judicial decisions in Nigeria, particularly in the field of family law, would notice the concern of the courts over the uncritical application in Nigeria of concepts derived from English law without due regard being given to the social realities in the country. Judicial pronouncements on the relevance of adultery as a ground for divorce in Nigeria and also on the importance to be attached to it in divorce petitions are but a few illustrations of this concern by the courts. In *Adedoyin v. Adedoyin*, the view was expressed that:

In Nigeria as in many other countries monogamy in the sense of the union for life of one man and woman to the exclusion of all others is a phenomenon which is so rare. The [Matrimonial Causes] Decree expects some amount of tolerance though not heroic virtue on the part of spouses in matters of extra-marital sexual intercourse or adultery (HD/9/72).

In yet another case, the same judge (Odesanya, J.) noted that 'a husband who is guilty of adultery can find life intolerable with a wife who has also committed adultery. In fact, social reality in Nigeria is such that husbands often find life intolerable with their wives even when they themselves flourish in adultery openly' *(Labode v. Labode* [1972]*)*.

The attitude of an English judge in a similar situation has been ably summarised by Bagnall, J., in *Ash v. Ash:*

... a flirtatious husband can reasonably be expected to live with a wife who is equally susceptible to the attractions of the other sex; and if each is equally bad, at any rate in similar respects, each can reasonably be expected to live with the other. ([1972] Fam. 135 at 140E).

As far back as 1963, some concern was also expressed on the relevance in Nigeria of English rules relating to the maintenance of divorced wives, where Udo Udoma, J. (as he then was) remarked that:

It is almost unprecedented in this country for a wife having divorced her husband to turn round and seek maintenance from the same husband. The very idea of maintaining a wife after divorce appears to me to be foreign to the African conception of marriage and divorce. A situation like the present cries aloud for distinct Nigerian rules (WD/19/61 [unreported]).

These observations were made in the knowledge that under customary law, there was no statutory provision for maintenance of divorced wives. An attempt was made in 1965 by a female member of the then Eastern House of Assembly to introduce legislation dealing with the maintenance of women married under customary law but the proposals did not proceed beyond the Bill stage due to the dissolution of that legislative body.

Since the promulgation of the 1970 Matrimonial Causes Decree, much time in divorce proceedings in Nigerian courts has been devoted to resolving custody and maintenance claims, a situation similar to that depicted by *Jackson* which prompted his observation that 'divorce has become less about divorce and more about money'.[1] This paper therefore seeks to examine through an analysis of some decided cases the attitude of judges in the Lagos High Court on the question of maintenance of divorced wives. Has the court been influenced in its interpretation of the statutory provision on maintenance under the 1970 Matrimonial Causes Decree by the fact that the concept of maintenance is alien to Nigerian society? How far is it possible to achieve what Udoma, J. referred to as 'distinct Nigerian rules' on maintenance while at the same time making it possible for one to meet one's obligations to one's extended family?

Although this paper deals mainly with the problem of maintaining a divorced wife, it is necessary to make some general observations on two other related problems. First, unlike the case of maintaining a divorced wife, not much controversy surrounds the question of whether or not a child of the marriage should be maintained after dissolution of the marriage. It is very rare to find a case where the man does not readily accept that responsibility, although the amount payable might still be vigorously contested. The few cases where some sort of objection has been raised to the question of maintaining a child of the marriage arose because of the definition now given to the expression 'children of the marriage'. Section 69 of the Matrimonial Causes Decree defines that expression as follows:

> (a) any child adopted since the marriage by the husband and wife or by either of them with the consent of the other;
> (b) any child of the husband and wife born before the marriage, whether legitimated by the marriage or not; and
> (c) any child of either the husband or wife (including an illegitimate child of either of them and a child adopted by either of them) if, at the relevant time, the child was ordinarily a member of the household of the husband and wife, so however that a child of the husband and wife (including a child born before the marriage, whether legitimated by the marriage or not) who has been adopted by another person or other persons shall be deemed not to be a child of the marriage; ....

There is thus a ready acceptance of financial responsibility only in respect of a natural child. *Asomugha v. Asomugha* (M/139/72) is a very good illustration of the resistance to paying maintenance in respect of children qualifying as a child of the marriage under section 69(c).

In determining the amount to be awarded to children of the marriage, the decided cases all seem to proceed on the assumption that the husband has been or should be primarily responsible for looking after the home, at least financially. This however is an assumption which does not often accord with reality. It is common practice particularly with newly married young couples for both of them to make some sort of financial contribution – even if on an unequal basis – to the running of the home. Of the over fifty cases examined by the writer, only in one – *Olufuwa v. Olufuwa* (WD/39/71) – was any specific reference made to the duty of the wife to share in the maintenance of the children. I suspect that the allusion to this duty in that case was due to the fact that the wife was not only earning more than the husband but was also largely providing for the family out of her income.

MAINTENANCE OF DIVORCED WIVES

The relevant statutory provision on the power of the court to order maintenance is section 70 of the Matrimonial Causes Decree:

(1) Subject to this section, the court may, in proceedings with respect to the maintenance of a party to a marriage, or of children of the marriage, other than proceedings for an order for maintenance pending the disposal of proceedings, make such order as it thinks proper, having regard to the means, earning capacity and conduct of the parties to the marriage and all other relevant circumstances.

(2) Subject to this section and to rules of court, the court may, in proceedings for an order for the maintenance of a party to a marriage, or of children of the marriage, pending the disposal of proceedings, make such order as it thinks proper, having regard to the means, earning capacity and conduct of the parties to the marriage and all other relevant circumstances ....

Although the above provisions technically make it possible for a divorced husband to ask for financial support from his ex-wife, in no case has such a request been made, not even in *Olufuwa* where the wife was earning more than the husband. Various reasons[2] have been advanced in favour of the wife's support right from the husband. It is said to be based on the fact that, at common law, a husband was entitled to his wife's earnings and most of her personal property in addition to the pleasure of her company and services in the home. Also canvassed is the argument that it is based on the fact that a wife's position at common law is like that of a chattel. We have also seen above that Adewale Thompson, J., in *Akinsemoyin's* case tried to link the support right of wives with the question of dowry, but this it is submitted seems rather far-fetched, particularly as the payment of dowry to the husband is not as widespread as was imagined by the learned judge.

Section 70 merely sets out in skeleton form the factors to be considered by the court first in deciding whether or not a divorced wife should be maintained, and secondly on the quantum of the award. Since these provisions are stated in broad terms, trial courts do exercise wide discretion – probably wider than in any other branch of the law – in applying the provisions of that section. The exercise of this discretion has led not only to some apparent inconsistencies but also to the introduction of subjective factors in the adjudication process. An analysis of a few of the decided cases supports this observation.

In *Arinye v. Arinye* (HD/30/71), the marriage was dissolved on a cross-petition by the wife based on desertion. She is an Inspector of Police while the husband is a Captain in the Army – both of them according to the trial judge (Savage, J.) 'are earning good salaries'. The wife's salary as disclosed in her affidavit of means shows that she was earning N 2,000 a year. Rejecting her claim for maintenance the learned judge commented:

The powers of the court with regard to the maintenance of a party to a marriage, or of the children of the marriage are discretionary, and in the exercise of this discretion regard being had to the means and earning capacity of the parties to the marriage, and to all the circumstances of this case, it is my view that the only award that ought to be made is one of maintenance of the children.

Apart from the fact that she was earning 'a good salary', and was also innocent of any wrongdoing, it is not clear what 'the circumstances of this case' are.

The petitioning wife was more fortunate before Lambo, J., in *Segun v. Segun* (WD/73/72), when she claimed maintenance pending the hearing of a divorce. Here she was earning N 4,412 per annum as against the husband's salary of N 5,270 per annum. The evidence before the court further revealed that her expenditure every month was well above her monthly salary – a fact that is capable of many interpretations. Emphasising again the discretion of the court on whether or not to award maintenance, Lambo, J., stated as follows:

A close scrutiny of the details of the applicant's income and expenditure reveals that her standard of living has not shown any downward trend since the parties separated. Furthermore, I have no details of what the applicant used to enjoy which has now been denied her by reason of their separation. Bearing in mind that the court has an unfettered discretion in these matters I propose to award the Applicant alimony of £ 10 per month '*pendente lite*'.

At the end of the scale is *Smith v. Smith* (HD/4/72) where the wife's earning cannot by any standard be said to be good. She was on a salary of N 1,010 per annum as against her husband's salary of N 4,992 per annum. It is not clear from the judgment on what grounds the marriage was dissolved, apart from the finding that the marriage has broken down. Explaining his reasons for not granting maintenance, Adeeipe, J., declared that the respondent wife 'is only 38, attractive, and has every chance of getting married again'.

Judicial inconsistency arising from the exercise of discretion in the area of maintenance awards is most prominent when the quantum of award in these cases is considered. Most of the judgments examined by the writer are unreasoned in the sense that the courts do not articulate the basis on which the quantum of award is arrived at. Such an unreasoned exercise of discretion is very difficult to upset on appeal. Appellate courts are invariably very reluctant to upset judgements of trial courts on the exercise of judicial discretion, and the observations of Barry, J., in the Australian case of *Atkinson v. Atkinson* ([1969] 13 F.L.R. 322) are equally applicable in Nigeria:

> As it has not been shown that the trial judge acted upon a wrong principle, or that he mistakenly gave weight to extraneous or irrelevant matters, or failed to give weight or sufficient weight to relevant considerations, or made a mistake as to the facts, the strong presumption in favour of the correctness of the decision under appeal must prevail unless the judgment and its consequences have been shown to be so plainly unreasonable and unjust that in the interests of justice it is imperative for this Court to interfere .... It is, however, a grave step for an appellate court to stigmatize as plainly unjust and unreasonable the exercise of discretion by a competent trial judge where no error of law or of fact invalidating his decision can be found.

Acting on this principle, the Supreme Court had no difficulty in reversing the decision in *Olu-Ibukun v. Olu- Ibukun* (S.C. 200/73 in [1974] 2 S.C. 41) where the trial judge instead of discussing the principles governing maintenance awards under Section 70 of the Matrimonial Causes Decree devoted much tine to discussing the common law principles governing the award of alimony *pendente lite.*

Curiously enough, it is in the exercise of their discretionary powers that the courts have and could further develop what Udò-Udoma, J., referred to as 'distinct Nigerian rules' on the law relating to maintenance of wives following dissolution of the marriage. Regrettably however, the over-reliance of Nigerian courts on English cases has slowed down this process. There is for instance the uncritical application[3] of the old practice of the English courts of giving the wife a maintenance award that will bring her income up to one-fifth of the joint income of the spouses. In fact, in *Enahoro v. Enahoro* (WD/78/72) the trial judge refused to order any maintenance in favour of the wife simply because the husband's income was not known and that this was essential for an application of the one-fifth rule! Why must it be one-fifth and not less having regard to the financial commitments imposed on Nigerians by the extended family system in Nigeria? One recalls here the lament of Sowemimo, J. ,(as he then was) in *Giwa v. Giwa* (WD/40/67), a case dealing with a maintenance award against the husband who is also responsible for maintaining his brothers and other jobless relations:

The unfortunate thing with regard to Nigerians contracting marriage under either the English Laws or the local Marriage Act is that those laws do not take into consideration the 'extended family' responsibilities of either the husband, or wife as the case may be. The result has been that those English cases cited cannot be of much assistance if one has to take into consideration what is the accepted practice amongst the Yorubas as regards their attitude with regard to responsibility of their families having regard to the extent of the meaning of that term.

Perhaps the best way of illustrating the challenge before the courts is to consider decisions where attempts have been made either to escape paying maintenance or to have the quantum awarded reduced on the grounds of other obligations to the extended family. It is common knowledge as alluded to in *Giwa's* case that in Nigeria, unlike in England and other western countries, one's obligations to the extended family are very difficult to avoid. This is more so having regard to the general level of poverty. Since a majority of those who marry under the Marriage Act are generally in the higher income group, they fall within the group most often looked to for financial support.

In *Dawodu v. Dawodu* (M/258/73), there was a claim by the divorced wife for an increase in the maintenance award made to her and the child of the marriage. One of the reasons given against the increase by the husband was the fact that he had to support his aged mother. Dealing with this, Odesanya, J., observed thus:

If the monthly maintenance is to be increased it can only be at the expense of the mother. In Nigeria one owes one's parents some moral but not legal obligation to assist with their maintenance. One's parents' claim can of course not rank higher than that of one's wife and children. Parents' claim is not legally enforceable whereas that of the wife is legally enforceable as well as that of one's children. Still I think social realities would persuade a Nigerian court to take into account the moral obligation one owes one's unemployed parents in this matter. Of course if one can speak of priorities in this matter I must emphasise that the Nigerian husband's primary obligation is to his wife and his children. The claim of the parents should not be ignored although it is founded on a moral obligation. If the parents have no independent or other means of subsistence then their claim cannot be ignored. In the circumstance I am unable to increase at the expense of the respondent's mother the maintenance now paid to the wife.

More complex however are the issues raised in *Ibironke v. Ibironke* (M/16/66). The court had to decide what the husband's disposable income was before assessing the quantum of maintenance to be given to the wife. It was contended on the husband's behalf that expenses incurred on the child begotten by another woman during the subsistence of the marriage were expenses which could be subtracted from his income before arriving at his disposable income. Cited in support of this contention was the irrelevant English case of *Williams v. Williams* ([1964] 3 All E.R. 526) where expenses incurred by a husband on a child or children of his first marriage were treated as expenses properly deductable from his income before assessing his liability for maintenance. Rejecting the husband's contention, Taylor, C.J., held that the husband's duty to his wife comes before any duty to an offspring of an adulterous union during the course of the marriage to the applicant. To hold otherwise the judge remarked 'would result in incompatibility and put a premium on adultery'.

Another area for the exercise of judicial discretion is in deciding whether or not the nature of the financial support should be by way of periodic payment or lump sum or property settlement. The choice as to the form of support is important when one thinks of the problems of enforcing maintenance awards of a periodic nature. The problem of enforcement is perhaps the most difficult and frustrating aspect of the law of maintenance. In almost all the decided cases examined, the award is often in the nature of periodic sums to the wife and children since lump sum payments are only possible where the party condemned to pay maintenance has substantial assets. The result is that instead of the decree terminating a marriage bringing an end to the unhappy and strained relationship between the parties, it is often the beginning of endless litigation to enforce periodic maintenance awards and in some cases custody rights.

Eyo v. Eyo (WD/95/72) seems to be the only case out of all those examined in which the court could have ordered a lump sum payment in lieu of periodic payments. The husband's gross income in that case was stated to be N 26,460.00 and the judge believed that he was earning much more than that. In addition, the trial judge found that 'he has substantial amount in Banks here and in other parts of the world'. Instead of making a lump sum grant, the court awarded N 400 a month as maintenance. There is also the odd case of *Okigbo v. Okigbo* (WD/13/72) where in addition to a maintenance of N 60 a month given to the three children of the marriage, the husband agreed to settle property on the wife for life, the reversion going to the children of the marriage.

It is difficult without further empirical study to say precisely why the default rate is very high in complying with court orders on maintenance but one has the feeling that one reason for this might be that the amounts awarded by the courts are sometimes unreasonably high and oftentimes beyond the means of the party in default. This of course is in addition to the fact that maintaining a divorced wife is alien to Nigerian ideas. The making of a realistic award first presupposes that the true income of the parties is known. Most of the awards are made on the basis of disputed, unreliable and sometimes unknown salaries. In *Enahoro v. Enahoro*, for example, Adefarasin, J., remarked that the wife's allegation that the husband's salary was about N 10,000 per annum 'seems to [him] to be guess work and unreliable'. It was as a result of this that no award of maintenance was made in favour of the wife as earlier explained. None-theless, the judge was able to award N 90 per month as maintenance for the three children.

Another case in point is *Eyo's* case already mentioned above. In two affidavits of means filed within one month of each other, the husband's declared gross income rose from N 14,400 per annum to N 26,460 per annum. Commenting on this, Taylor, C.J., said:

> It is most regrettable that the two affidavits violently contradict each other ....
>
> When one looks at the whole of the affidavit of the respondent and when one takes into account the evidence which he gave in court during cross-examination, there is not the slightest doubt that the respondent is not being completely frank with this Court in either of these affidavits.

The two cases discussed above related to self-employed persons, but the difficulty of establishing a person's income is not confined to such persons and could also arise with persons in salaried employment especially if there is an allegation to the effect that such a person is deriving income from other sources. In *Akpabot v. Akpabot* (WD/104/72), the judge remarked that there was a general denial by the husband that his income was N 9,000. However, the very stiff award made in favour of the wife in that case would suggest that the judge rejected the husband's denial, for how else could one justify an award of N 250 a month out of a salary of N 500 per month (the maximum salary the husband could have been earning as a Senior Research Fellow in one of the Nigerian Universities).

The Appendix attached to this paper represents an attempt to relate the respective financial positions of the spouses both before and after the award. The award by the court, in addition to the amounts shown in the Appendix also imposes upon the husband, the duty to pay the school fees of the children of the marriage in addition to all hospital bills. Where children are in boarding schools, one would normally expect a reduction in the amount awarded to the mother in favour of that child; but in none of the cases is this reflected. For example, in *Enahoro's* case, one of the children was said to be in a boarding school in the United Kingdom and yet the maintenance given to the mother in respect of that child was the same as that of the other two children.

CONCLUSION

So long as marriages are contracted under the Marriage Act, it seems that the courts have no alternative but to apply the provisions of the Matrimonial Causes Decree relating to maintenance. What has been advocated above is that the court in the exercise of its discretionary powers should attempt to relate these statutory provisions to the social and economic factors prevailing in Nigeria. The basic question however still remains unanswered – and this is, should maintenance be awarded to a divorced wife and if so, what factors should the legislature take into account in deciding whether to make an award and the amount to be awarded?

The judges in both *Akinsemoyin* and *Coker*, though critical about the wholesale importation of English law on this topic, are prepared to award maintenance in certain cases. Udo Udoma, J., feels that 'a wife ought not to be left destitute for having divorced her husband on justifiable grounds'. While the exceptional cirumstances justifying an award as instanced by Thompson, J., would be 'the inability of the woman to fend for herself owing to ill health or mental infirmity or an over-powering barrage of adverse circumstances, leading to abject impoverishment'.

It has been suggested in some quarters that all that is necessary is support for the children of the marriage and that the divorced wife should be left to fend for herself. After all, that is the position under customary law. This suggestion is not only short-sighted but could also be faulted on other grounds. If the children of the marriage are supported, the likelihood is that the divorced wife will spend whatever sum is awarded on herself rather than on the children. A non-support rule might also be unfair to the wife. For example, in more than one half of the cases analysed above, the parties got married in England, It is usual among this group to find that the wife would at one stage have been the bread-winner mainly to allow the husband to concentrate on his studies full-time. Having thus invested heavily on the husband, is it fair that the man should be allowed to walk out on her without some sort of financial support? *Adeoye v. Adeoye* (WD/75/72), is typical of such cases although the wife in that case was not a Nigerian. She holds the M.A. Degree in the History of Arts in Poland and the respondent her husband qualified as a doctor in Poland. She gave evidence that after their marriage they lived in her flat in Poland and that when they were about to come to Nigeria she sold all the furniture in her flat and all her property in order that they might both have enough money to pay their passage to Nigeria. They were married in May 1971 and things started to fall apart in December 1971 – just three months after their arrival in Nigeria. Taylor, C.J., was moved by all these factors in making what the writer believes to be a punitive award having regard to the husband's salary. He remarked that it is the duty of the husband, having brought 'this lady so far away from home as a result of which as I said earlier she had to sell her furniture, etc., to meet their joint passages to Nigeria, to maintain her in a befitting manner'. One cannot also but look sympathetically at the claim for maintenance in *Eyo v. Eyo.* The husband in an attempt either to avoid paying maintenance or at least to have the sum reduced contended that the wife was lazy and would not take any job. The wife had no qualification for any job, and further alleged that she did not complete her educational training in the United Kingdom owing to her pregnancy by the husband. It is factors like this that provoked the remarks of the trial judge in the American case of *Doyle v. Doyle*[4] to the effect that if a woman has contributed indirectly to her husband's career and helped to increase his substance, she may rightfully be regarded as entitled to his gain.

Accepting in principle the concept of a support right for divorced wives, the necessary limits to such support must reflect the values in the society. There is first the question of whether a woman whose conduct was responsible for the break-down of the marriage should be given a support right irrespective of her contribution to the 'making' of the husband. In view of the Nigerian attitude to adultery by wives, Nigerian courts should be reluctant to award maintenance to a wife guilty of adultery. It might well be that they should act differently if the divorce was on grounds other than adultery. By some sort of coincidence, the cases examined seem to fall into this pattern. In both *Irinoye v. Irinoye* (HD/60/71), and *Oseni v. Oseni* (HD/2/72), where the marriages were dissolved on the grounds of the wife's adultery, no award for maintenance was made, while in *D'Almeida v. D'Almeida* (WD/47/72), and *Akpabot v. Akpabot*, such awards were made. The award in *D'Almeida* was made despite the judge's remarks as to the wife's attitude to this marriage and it would seem to marriage in general. She had had three marriages and the longest that anyone has lasted is two years.

Secondly, there is as yet no serious discussion in any of the decided cases as to what the law relating to the support of divorced wives should seek to achieve in a Nigerian or African setting. The Decree only imposes on the Courts the duty to make 'such order as it thinks proper' having regard to the years of the parties, their capacity and conduct and all other relevant circumstances. Nigerian courts in carrying out this mandate have relied to a large extent on English cases even though the statutory provisions of the two countries are differently worded. Section 25 of the 1973 English Matrimonial Causes Act requires an English court to exercise its power to grant maintenance with the aim of placing 'the parties, so far as it is practicable and, having regard to their conduct, just to do so, in the financial position in which they would have been if the marriage had not broken down and each had properly discharged his or her financial obligations and responsibilities towards the other'.

In short, the declared aim of an award of maintenance by an English court is to see that the wife's standard of living does not fall below what it was during the marriage. But should this also be the aim of the award of maintenance in Nigeria? The courts seem to be suggesting that the answer is in the affirmative. This has resulted in the high awards made in some of the cases listed in the Appendix. In *Akpabot's* cast for instance, a specific award was made for the employment of a maid presumably because the wife was used to the services of maids and stewards when she was in the matrimonial home. Similarly in *Somorin v. Somorin* (HD/48/72), the question was raised as to whether or not it was proper to allocate a special sum to rent in a support award. The Supreme Court had in an earlier case – *Balogun v. Balogun* ([1969] 1 All N.L. R. 349) – indicated that that question was a substantial issue of law which could be raised on appeal.

The trial judge in *Somorin* took the view that, in fixing maintenance in Lagos, it is realistic to regard accommodation as an important item and to allocate a special sum for this. He declared:

> In allocating a definite sum of money to rent, I tried to ensure that the accommodation of the two children would be reasonably good or not fall too much below the standard they were accustomed to when they were in their parents matrimonial home from which the applicant wrongly ejected his wife ... it will be wrong to lower the standard of living of the wife and the two children ....

The writer is not necessarily suggesting that a maintenance award should be limited only to support for food and clothing. What is being seriously challenged is the assumption that the aim of an award of maintenance should be to enable the wife to enjoy the same level of comfort she had before the dissolution of the marriage. The emphasis should be more on need. The award of N 200 per month to the wife in *Ibukun* was not as a result of her need but to keep up the image the husband has made of her (the wife of a U.N. Chief of Mission, a showpiece to women not only in Nigeria but in Kenya where the husband was serving!) The approach of the court might also have been responsible for the demand by the wife in *Eyo* (who admittedly was unemployed) that her husband should be made to buy her a car as part of her entitlement to maintenance.

A discussion on the support right of divorced wives will be incomplete without a short reference to the present controversy as to whether or not a suit for maintenance simpliciter is maintainable in Nigerian courts without its being coupled with a request for any other relief. Prior to the promulgation of the 1970 Matrimonial Causes Decree, such petitions were freely entertained by the courts despite convincing arguments to the contrary by text writers.[5] It was argued then that Nigerian courts have jurisdiction to order maintenance if such request is ancillary to a petition for divorce, nullity, judicial separation, and the like. That if the request is not within the above category, then the courts have no jurisdiction.

Whether or not the above contention still holds after 1970 has arisen in such cases as *Esua v. Esua* (unreported) *Akinwunmi v. Akinwunmi* (m/66/70), and *Adekoya v. Adekoya* (m/100/72). With the exception of *Adekoya*, the cases support the contention that under the 1970 Decree, an action for maintenance is sustainable without being coupled with any other request. The reasoning in some of the cases in favour of this contention is, however, difficult to support. Adefarasin, J., (as he then was), for example, sought support from section 112 of the Decree which provides that the Chief Justice could make rules as to practice and procedure and that in the absence of such rules, the rules of court in force before the Decree – that is English rules – should apply. He concluded from this that since such actions are maintainable in England and were in Nigeria before the Decree (a point which is also debatable), then it is still maintainable in Nigeria by virtue of section 112. We have argued elsewhere[6] that this argument is erroneous and that the rules relating to maintenance are not rules of practice and procedure but rules of substantive law.

It is clear beyond doubt that the jurisdiction conferred on the courts by virtue of section 2 of the Decree is in respect of 'matrimonial causes' as defined by section 114. That term means:

a) proceedings for a decree of dissolution of marriage; nullity of marriage; judicial separation; restitution of conjugal rights or jactitation of marriage.
b) proceedings for a declaration of the validity of the dissolution or annulment of a marriage by decree or otherwise or of a decree of judicial separation, or for a declaration of the continued operation of a decree of judicial separation, or for an order discharging a decree of judicial separation.
c) proceedings with respect to the maintenance of a party to the proceedings, settlements, damages in respect of adultery, the custody or guardianship of infant children of the marriage, or the maintenance,

welfare, advancement, or education of children of the marriage, *being proceedings in relation to concurrent ,pending or completed proceedings of the kind referred to in paragraph (a) or (b) above, including proceedings of such a kind pending at, or completed before, the commencement of this Decree.*

The underlined provisions above therefore emphasise the point that a maintenance claim should be maintainable only if coupled with proceedings under paragraph (a) or (b).

From the analysis of the decided cases, it seems to me that we are still a long way from achieving our desired goal – the formulation of 'distinct Nigerian rules' on the maintenance of divorced wives. To reach this objective, *trial* courts must shake off the excessive reliance on English cases and be more forthcoming in formulating rules that have bearing to conditions in Nigeria. I have deliberately put the emphasis on 'trial courts' since very few of the cases on matrimonial causes go on appeal to the Supreme Court.

NOTES

1. Jackson, *Matrimonial Finance and Taxation*, 1972, v.
2. M.G. Paulsen (1956), 'Support rights and duties between husband and wife', Vanderbilt Law Review Vol. 9, No. 4: 709.
3. *Shokunbi v. Shokunbi* IK/28WD/73; *Ibukun v. Ibukun* WD/32/72.
4. 158 N.Y.S. 2d 909 at 912 (1957).
5. Kasunmu and Salacuse, *Nigerian Family Law*. Ch. 1; Adesanya, *The Nigerian Matrimonial Causes Decree*, Ch. 1.
6. Kasunmu, *The Matrimonial Causes Decree*, 1970, Vol. 2 102, *The Nigerian Journal of Contemporary Law*.

Appendix

Cases	Husband's monthly salary	Wife's monthly salary	Monthly award to wife and/or children	New income after award Husband	Wife
Adeoye v. Adeoye	N 270	N 100	N 100 to wife	N 170	N 200
Akpabot v. Akpabot	N 750 (disputed)	Nil	N 250 to wife and 3 children	N 500	N 250
Okigbo v. Okigbo	unknown but N 4000 anticipated	N 250	N 60 plus property settlement to wife and 3 children	?	N 310 plus settlement
Shokunbi v. Shokunbi	N 130	N 43	N 10 to wife	N 120	N 53
Adeleye v. Adeleye	N 575	N 188	N 220 to wife and 4 children	N 355	N 408
Somorin v. Somorin	N 500	N 166	N 125 to wife and 2 children	N 375	N 291
Ibukun v. Ibukun reversed on appeal.	N 833	N 164	N 272 to wife and 3 children	N 561	N 446
Jegede v. Jegede	N 334	N 84	N 50 to wife and 3 children	N 283	N 134
Osiname v. Osiname	N 334	N 102	N 55 to wife and 1 child	N 279	N 177
Eyo v. Eyo	N 2204	N Nil	N 400 to wife	N 1804	N 400

Problems of creation and dissolution of customary marriages in Nigeria

8

OKAY ACHIKE
University of Nigeria, Enugu

INTRODUCTION

Under the Nigerian legal system two forms of marriage exist side by side: marriage under customary law,[1] and marriage celebrated in accordance with the Marriage Act (popularly referred to as Ordinance Marriage). These two forms of marriage trace their origins from separate legal systems, the indigenous and the 'received' legal system. This paper seeks to examine legal problems connected with the creation and dissolution of customary marriages in Nigeria.

Customary marriages are potentially polygamous. In spite of the fact that Christianity is widely practised in Nigeria by educated and uneducated alike, polygamy has survived and continues to enjoy social acceptance. Thus, while Nigerian Christians may enter the monogamous form of marriage many thereafter resort to plurality of 'wives' in the belief (gravely misconceived) that they are entitled to marry another wife under customary law, during the existence of a statutory marriage.

It is widely recognised that there is no single system of customary law marriage prescribed in Nigeria or even within any of its twelve states. Any assumption of uniformity of customary marriage law is untenable,[2] although this assumption was made by some colonial administrators and judges.[3] For example, Verity, C.J., delivering the judgment of the West African Court of Appeal, observed that:

> Although the principles of native law and custom to which we have referred are, in the specific instances cited, applicable expressly to the law and custom of the Gold Coast they are nevertheless equally applicable as general principles to the

law and custom of Nigeria, a departure from which can only be justified if it is established by evidence that the native law and custom in any particular area differs from the general principle.[4]

It is trite that there are very numerous ethnic groupings in Nigeria and that these groups differ in language, mode of life, and in traditional cultural and social systems. As in other African States the customary rules of marriage in Nigeria are as diverse as these ethnic groups. It is impossible in a brief paper such as this to examine the rules of each system of customary law on the topics under discussion. However, these customary law systems exhibit similarities rather than diversity of basic concepts and principles; it is these similarities that will be highlighted.

WHAT IS CUSTOMARY MARRIAGE?

What constitutes a customary marriage has not been defined under any Act or law, and those unfamiliar with customary law have had difficulty in grasping its nature. Hence, Osborne, C.J., confessed:

The consideration of the law of native marriage is beset from the start with great difficulty. The sexual relations are viewed from such totally different standpoints by Europeans and natives of West Africa, that it is hard for the European to understand native ideas on the subject.[5]

Considerable concern at widespread ignorance on the subject of customary marriages was observed by Dundas:

It is regretted that Europeans have not given sufficient consideration to this subject – in fact, we are apt to regard native marriage as a commercial transaction. So long as we speak of 'purchasing wives' we shall probably continue to think of matrimony among natives as a matter of sale and barter.[6]

It will promote clarity if an attempt is made at identifying what is comprehended by the term customary marriage. In traditional Nigerian society, a customary union is not merely an agreement between the two spouses it is also a union of two families.[7] This at once distinguished a customary marriage from a Christian type of marriage. Hence traditionally the necessary overtures in bringing about a customary union and the consent to it are the preserve of the parents of the prospective spouses. Often the girl was married at birth since child marriage was permissible. Even where the male has attained the age of puberty or manhood, in some parts of the country it is traditional for his parents to choose a wife for him. Therefore traditionally the spouses to the proposed marriage have no official role in the arrangement of their marriage.

Although the traditional practice is still followed, the prospective spouses are today very vocal in the choice. This development has some statutory recognition as infant betrothal is now prohibted in many parts of the country, with the result that a marriage, or promised offers of marriage, between or in respect of persons either of whom is under the age of sixteen shall be void.[8] The effect of this provision and the influence of western notions of courtship is that the role of parents in the arrangement of, and sealing of, customary unions is today almost wholly advisory.

CREATION OF CUSTOMARY MARRIAGE

Like a marriage under the statute, the fact of being married under customary law cannot be implied by mere conduct. In his famous work on Yoruba law, Ward said[9]:

> Why does the average native rarely fail to carry out the prevailing ceremony when taking a bride? It would seem that in the eyes of the people there it constitutes an essential part of the wedding. People speak of a woman acquired without the customary ceremonies as a 'lover', a concubine in other words.

This observation on the Yoruba custom represents the general attitude of the various communities in Nigeria. In practice, the formalities and principles prescribed by a particular locality are given effect unless they have been abrogated by reason of being 'repugnant to natural justice, equity, and good conscience'.

ESSENTIAL ELEMENTS OF CUSTOMARY MARRIAGE

Parental consent

In traditional society two essential elements must be shown in order to create a valid customary marriage. The first element comprises the parental consent. Such consent will be presumed when the parents of the two spouses successfully negotiated the proposed union. It is necessary, however, to distinguish between the bride's parental consent with regard to her first marriage and her subsequent ones. While the parental consent is a legal requirement in the first marriage, it does not appear that such a requirement is recognised as mandatory with respect to subsequent ones. Today there is also the requirement for actual agreement of the man and the woman immediately concerned.

A point that calls for examination is whether the consent of bridegroom's parents is an essential requirement of a valid customary marriage. Traditionally the groom's parents or family had to give their consent but it was common practice for a man to marry without first obtaining such consent. The consent of the groom's parents or family remains today a purely social requirement and has never been regarded as a legal essential to his marriage. This view prevails in the Southern part of Nigeria and it appears to be in accord with the practice in the Northern group of States, for while the several declarations of native law and custom of Northern Nigeria expressly provide that parental consent of the bride is a legal essential to a valid marriage yet there is no such requirement with regard to the bridegroom.[10]

Payment of bridewealth

The second requirement for constituting a valid customary marriage is the presentation of bridewealth,[11] the payment in cash or in kind made by the bridegroom in respect of the customary marriage to the family of the bride. The acceptance of bridewealth before the families of the two parties affords a further confirmation that the prior consent to the proposed marriage or that of the parties thereto (in modern times) was obtained. We need hardly stress that bridewealth does not represent the purchase of the bride. In common parlance it is generally said that 'no bridewealth no marriage', under customary law. The payment of bridewealth and its acceptance in respect of the proposed marriage seals up the customary union and the bride cannot negotiate a future marriage while this deposit remains unrefunded. All other subsequent ceremonies, such as the giving away of the bride to the bridegroom constitute evidence of the proposed marriage.[12] These subsidiary or evidential requirements may be relied on to prove the existence of a binding marriage particularly as neither the fulfilment of the chief elements nor the marriage itself required to be evidenced in writing.

The amount of money or goods presented as bridewealth varies from place to place. The education, beauty, family background of the bride as well as the affluence of the bridegroom and his position in society are factors which influence the negotiations over bridewealth. In some communities, such as these found in Onitsha, Calabar, the Rivers States, and the Northern States, the value of bridewealth is comparatively low. But among the Ibos bridewealth has been known to reach several hundreds of pounds. In most communites bridewealth is fixed by agreement.[13] The payment of high bridewealth in the former Eastern Nigeria (now East Cyntrali Rivers, and South-Eastern States) led to the passing of the Limitation of Bridewealth Law, 1956 by which the sum of N 60 (£ 30) was prescribed as the highest amount for bridewealth throughout these three states.[14] Similar measures were adopted in the western,[15] midwestern states and so also in the northern group of States.[16]

These provisions were welcomed throughout Nigeria, but they have nonetheless been widely flouted. Undoubtedly there is difficulty in enforcing them since the settlement of bridewealth is a private concern of the families involved. Perhaps the only part of these provisions that has proved practicable and successful is that which provides that on the dissolution of the customary marriage the bridewealth refundable should not exceed the maximum amount prescribed by the statute. It is interesting to note that gifts to the bride such as clothing or money or incidental expenses made pursuant to the marriage are not regarded as part of the bridewealth; consequently on no account are such gifts and expenses recoverable.[17]

Traditionally, it was always difficult to distinguish bridewealth from gifts and expenses. This led a husband seeking a divorce to prefer that the issue of refundable bridewealth be put to the appropriate customary panel (i.e., the families of the husband and wife) rather than dealt with in proceedings before the ordinary courts. If the issue of refund of bridewealth is handled extrajudicially, it is possible to recover almost all the bridewealth paid against receiving the lesser sum prescribed by statute. In many cases husbands have refused to accept the refund of bridewealth on the ground that the amount offered was completely at variance with the amount actually paid. Traditionally, where the amount paid by way of bridewealth is seriously disputed, the party challenging it may be called upon to take oath upon a *juju*.[18] It may be noted that the practice is to hand the bridewealth to the bride's father or his representative through a middleman, a key witness as to the amount of bridewealth actually paid, and which must be refunded on the dissolution of a marriage.

We have emphasized the importance of bridewealth as the element which validates the customary marriage. A nominal amount paid as representing the bridewealth suffices to seal a valid customary marriage. It is of no moment that the bridegroom has neglected or refused to pay the balance. Any amount that remains outstanding is viewed as an actionable debt. Traditionally, where the balance of bridewealth has been in arrears for a considerable period, the parents of the bride may entice their daughter to return home until the balance has been satisfied.

As we have observed, bridewealth may be paid in kind. It may consist partly of farm products such as Yams, Cassava, Kola nuts, palm produce, sheep, cows, goats, etc., and partly of farm labour to be rendered by the bridegroom either personally or by those hired by him. In either case it is difficult to ascertain the point at which the amount agreed as bridewealth can be said to have been completely satisfied by payment in kind. This has given rise to the saying that the bridewealth payable cannot at any time be claimed to have been completely discharged. Furthermore, the fact that bridewealth has not been exhaustively paid is seen as preserving the tie between the families of the spouses. One result is that where the bridegroom is affluent his financial assistances to the family of his wife subsists throughout the period of their marriage.

Whose personal customary law controls payment of bridewealth?

One point which must be mentioned is that the payment of bridewealth often raises inter-personal conflicts of customary law, where the proposed union is between people from two different customary law systems. The current view is that the customary law system of the bride controls the amount of bridewealth to be paid while that of the bridegroom's ,we shall see later, controls the amount of bridewealth refundable at the dissolution of the marriage.[19]

DISSOLUTION OF CUSTOMARY MARRIAGE

Extra-judicial divorce

The dissolution of customary marriage may be either extra-judicial or judicial. Under customary law no ground for divorce need be alleged or shown by the spouse wishing to terminate the marriage; it is enough for either the husband or wife to call off the marriage unilaterally at his or her whim. It is however, imperative to bring this decision to the knowledge of the other spouse. This may be done by telling the other spouse or by some overt act. For example, the quitting of the matrimonial home by the wife with all her personal effects or the husband throwing out one or more of the wife's personal effects will suffice. Observing the simplicity attached to the dissolution of customary marriages, a witness in *Re Sapara* said:' a woman is like this hat, if one man drops it, another may pick it up'.[20]

Although the extra-judicial process of divorce is relatively easy, mere separation by the spouses does not constitute a valid dissolution of the marriage. The mere fact that the wife leaves the matrimonial home will not necessarily be construed as a termination of the union. Such a desertion must be accompanied by a positive declaration or overt acts referable to a clear intention of terminating the union for good. The case of *Chawers v. Hannah & Johnson*[21] is illustrative. The plaintiff's wife, Hannah, deserted him and lived with the defendant. The lower courts held the consequence of her act was that she became the wife of the defendant. On appeal, Graham Paul, J. rejected this finding and said:

If the suggestion is that there is a native custom by which a wife who commits adultery, *because* of the adultery becomes automatically the wife of the adulterer, I have two comments to make:
1. There is no evidence of such a custom.
2. Such custom is one which the courts will not be prepared to give judical sanction to, under section 20 of the Supreme Court Ordinance.[22]

There can also be a non-judicial consensual divorce. This is an important way in which customary marriage differs from marriage under the Marriage Act. The extra-judicial dissolution of customary marriages whether unilaterally or mutually is not only recognised today in many parts of Nigeria but it is very much preferred on grounds of cheapness, relative ease ,and lack of publicity.[23]

The validiity of this mode of dissolution has, however, been doubted in some quarters. In *Re Sapara* where a Lagos Chief testified as to the relative ease and simplicity of dissolution of customary marriage, Osborne C.J., commented:

Native marriage is not a capital knot which is loosely tied and can be untied by the man at will. I do not believe that this is, or ever has been the native custom, and even if it were, it is repugnant in the last degree to natural justice.[24]

It is difficult to appreciate the repugnancy test evoked by the learned Chief Justice in reaching this conclusion. While such dissolution is unacceptable to Western laws, or even marriage celebrated under the Marriage Act of Nigeria, it is hard to comprehend why the standards of dissolution of Christian monogamous marriage should be used to gauge the propriety of forms of dissolution found in other societies. Rejecting the view of Osborne, C.J., two learned authors have commented as follows:[25]

To hold that it is repugnant to natural justice would mean that, at least for now, people married under customary law in Lagos could not be divorced since there are not customary courts in Lagos. The superior courts have no original jurisdiction in the dissolution of marriages under customary law.

Its critics would want it abolished for the reason that it reduces customary marriage to a contract of convenience. In fact, one would respectfully submit that that is what marriages ought to be. Neither spouse ought to be compelled by the protracted formalities of courts of law to continue for a day longer with a marriage contract which the parties thereto are satisfied had broken down irretrievably.

Judicial divorce

A customary marriage may also be dissolved by judicial process, either unilaterally or by the mutual consent of the spouses. The dissolution of customary marriages in Nigeria is generally a matter within the competence of customary courts for they have 'unlimited jurisdiction in matrimonial causes and matters between persons married under customary law'.[26]

It is interesting to note that in both the Western and Mid-Western states of Nigeria, the 1958 Adoptive Bye-Laws had affected a considerable degree of integration with marriage under the Marriage Act by providing expressly for specific grounds for dissolution of customary marriage.[27] A question which has agitated many minds is whether this provision has by implication abolished dissolution by extra-judicial process, and if it has not been abolished, whether these prescribed grounds for dissolution of customary marriage must be adhered to even when a marriage is being dissolved by extra-judicial process. With regard to the first problem raised, the view that dissolution of customary marriage by extra-judicial process in these two States survives predominates. With regard to founding a dissolution of customary marriage upon any of the statutorily prescribed grounds when the dissolution is being effected extrajudicially, the current view is that the statutory grounds for divorce are wholly inapplicable to such extra-judicial dissolution. It has been argued that since the extra-judicial divorce is a creature of customary law and not statute, if it was the intention of the legislature to abrogate customary law rights, such a statutory provision ought to be expressed and not inferred by implication.[28]

PROBLEMS UPON DISSOLUTION OF MARRIAGE

Extra-judicial dissolution

As we have observed, a customary marriage may be dissolved by extra-judicial process. This raises both evidential and legal problems. In some cases, the proof of divorce may be difficult since there are no records from which the fact of the dissolution can be ascertained.[29] In other cases, legal problems may arise as to the moment in point of time the marriage may be said to have been terminated extra-judicially.

Refund of bridewealth

Since the payment of bridewealth constitutes an integral part of a valid marriage, its refund on the termination of the marriage is equally a matter of importance. Traditionally, the effective date of dissolution of marriage is the date of the refund of the bridewealth.[30]

Under some systems of customary law, particularly among the Ibos, bridewealth is generally only refundable when the wife remarries. This, however, does not preclude a wealthy wife from refunding the bridewealth immediately she has deserted her husband, particularly when she wants to to have children out of wedlock. In most systems of customary law, refund of bridewealth is not conditional on the husband being the innocent spouse; but under some systems, if the husband is the guilty partner, or initiates divorce proceeding he is barred from recovering the bridewealth.

The point on which serious legal battles have been fought is the question of the amount of bridewealth refundable on the dissolution of the marriage. In some areas the amount refundable is fixed.[31] In most places the general rule is that the amount refundable must tally with the amount actually paid. This approach creates some problem since there are today statutory limitations placed on the amount of bridewealth payable or refundable,[32] and on no account will the court in computing this amount include ante-nuptial gifts. The operation of the statutory limitations inhibits husbands from initiating divorce by judicial process. In practice, many husbands prefer divorce by the nonjudicial process under which the wife can be compelled to refund the amount which the husband paid. Such an approach enables a husband to defeat the statutory limitation at the risk of incurring the penalty prescribed by law.[33]

Under most customary law systems, the bridewealth is refunded *en bloc*, but in others bridewealth may be refunded by instalment. The latter mode of refund creates some problems for it is far from being clear at what point of time the marriage may be said to have been dissolved. Is it when the first instalment or some appreciable number of instalments, or the final installment is paid? Unlike the partial deposit of bridewealth which preserves the proposed customary marriage, the better view is that a partial refund of bridewealth is not enough to terminate the marriage.

In some areas, the amount of bridewealth refundable diminishes, regard being given to circumstances such as the duration of the marriage and the number of children born to it. Thus, in *Okalude v. Onama*[34] the husband instituted an action for refund of bridewealth claiming the sum of N 120 (£ 60), but the court awarded only N 20 (£10) holding that under Yoruba custom the amount of bridewealth refundable decreases as the marriage endures.[35]

Refund of bridewealth and inter-personal conflicts of law

The prevalance of different systems of customary law inevitably creates inter-personal conflicts of law. Such problems arise where one party to a dispute is a stranger in the locality where the dispute arises, or where both are temporary residents. The various provisions in many areas in Nigeria are designed to accommodate conflicts between the personal laws of the parties and the law of the place in which the adjudicating court is situated, but the present state of the law leaves much to be desired. In the Eastern States of Nigeria, for example, the Customary Courts Law, 1963, provides that the court shall administer:

> the law prevailing in the area of the jurisdiction of the court or binding between the parties ....[36]

This provision is capable of being both vague and unjust, as is shown by a simple illustration. Suppose A from Onitsha (Ibo) marries B from Udi and at the time of the proposed dissolution of the marriage both reside at Oba (a town situated in the Ibo area of East Central State of Nigeria). Which customary law system governs the issue of refundable brideweatlh? First, there is no one customary law binding between A and B since their customary laws on this point are different. Secondly, the law prevailing in the area of the jurisdiction of the court has never been allowed to control the dissolution of a marriage of parties who are not natives of that area. To apply Udi customary law will produce an unjust result defeating the ordinary expectations of both parties.

Although as a general rule the customary law of the woman governs the amount of bridewealth payable whether the parties are from the same area or not, it is still an open question which customary law controls the refund of bridewealth in a situation where both parties belong to different customary law areas. Some people take the view that since the amount of bridewealth refundable must correspond with the amount paid, the customary law of the woman governs the amount of refundable bridewealth. Others however hold the view that since the wife's subsequent life after marriage is governed by the husband's customary law, that law of necessity governs every incident of the marriage and therefore the amount of refundable bridewealth.

Neither of these two views is specifically prescribed under any of the prevailing laws. Each spouse will, in the matter of refund of bridewealth, prefer that which is more favourable; the husband would prefer an arrangement whereby he should be refunded the amount he paid (the statutory limitation notwithstanding), while the wife would invariably welcome the system of customary law which prescribes a diminution of refundable bridewealth. It is submitted that it would not matter which of the competing approaches prevails. So long as the prevailing law is specifically defined (and in this connection both views seem reasonable and just) it would clarify the situation and avoid the expense of litigation.

Refund of bridewealth where customary marriage is superceded by statutory marriage

It is fashionable today in Nigeria for parties who have contracted a customary marriage to follow it up by celebrating another marriage under the Marriage Act. This is permissible under the law, and it is provided in some areas that the statutory marriage supercedes the prior customary union. It has been argued that there is no reason why a subsequent statutory marriage should take precedence over an earlier customary marriage celebrated by the same parties.[37] Whether the pride of place is to be accorded to the one or the other must depend on the intention of the parties. Be that as it may, the English case of *Ohochuku v. Ohochuku*[38] is authority for the proposition that the dissolution of a statutory marriage does not have the automatic effect of dissolving the prior customary marriage between the same parties. There are two Nigerian Christians who had earlier married in accordance with customary law in Nigeria followed by a second marriage in London. On the wife's petition for divorce based on the husband's cruelty, Wrangham, J., pronounced a *decree nisi* to dissolve not the Nigerian marriage but the marriage in London. This decision is clearly supportable. The reason for this decision should not be dimissed as being that English law has no machinery for dissolving customary unions, because in Nigeria in a petition suit such as the *Ohochuku* case the High Court would have jurisdiction only to dissolve the statutory marriage. In other words, the current belief is that the dissolution of a statutory marriage leaves the customary union intact. It follows that the customary union which subsists after the dissolution of the statutory marriage may be effectively dissolved only upon the refund of bridewealth and under the circumstances and conditions we had earlier examined.

It is clear that many of the rules operating in respect of the amount of bridewealth payable or refundable call for re-examination since they are manifestly unsuitable in present Nigerian society. The unsettled rules involving inter-personal conflicts of law with regard to the refund of bridewealth call for new legislative provisions.

CONCLUSION

(i) As we have observed, the traditional element of parental consent to customary marriage is gradually being supplanted by personal consent of the parties. The impact of Western values, and the current drive towards prohibiting child-betrothal, under which marriage becomes a matter of the individuals concerned, will call for a redefinition of the customary law marriage.

(ii) So far as bridewealth is concerned, it is submitted that presentation should no longer constitute an essential requirement for the formation of a customary marriage.

(iii) Certainty would be achieved by insisting on compulsory registration of *all* customary marriages. Furthermore, each local authority charged with the responsibility for registration of customary marriages should be required to issue a marriage certificate to the parties upon the registration of the marriage.

(iv) One would urge the retention of the extra-judicial process of dissolution but with the proviso that upon such dissolution it should be registered and a certificate issued to the parties.

(v) If bridewealth ceased to be an integral part of marriage, as we have urged, the vexed problem of evaluating the amount refundable would fall away. Where bridewealth continues to be presented, the modern legislative trend of limiting bridewealth and the amount refundable should continue, and a well defined reducing scale should be introduced by delegated legislation (i.e., bye-laws) for each customary law area where the custom of reduction in bridewealth on dissolution is recognised.

NOTES

1. For the purposes of this paper the term customary law does not include Moslem law.
2. For the debates which have surrounded this issue see Allott, *Essays on African Law* (1960), pp. 55–64.
3. See my paper titled 'Some aspects of African customary law of contract', presented at the Workshop on African Indigenous Laws, under the auspices of the Institute of African Studies of the University of Nigeria, Nsukka, Nigeria, 6th–9th August, 1974.
4. *Awgu v. Neziana* 12 W.A.C.A. 450, p. 451. For the views of text writers on this point, see T.O. Elias, *Nature of African Customary Law*, p. 3; C. Dundas *Native Laws of some Bantu Tribes of East Africa* (1921), 51 J.R.A.I.P. 21.7.
5. *In Re Sapara* (1911), Renner Rep. 605 at 606.
6. *African Marriage Survey*, parts 1 and 2, p. 291.
7. This appears to be the position under Ashanti customary law in Ghana, See R.S. Rattray, *Ashanti Land and Constitution* (1920), p. 26.
8. E.g., see Age of Marriage Law, Cap. 6, *Laws of Eastern Nigeria* (1963), s. 3(1). It provides that no person under the age of 16 years can enter into a valid customary marriage.
9. Yoruba Husband and Wife Code (1938), p. 15.
10. For examples of the various declarations of native law and custom of Northern Nigeria, see N.A.L.N. 63 of 1959, N.A.L.N. 52 of 1960, and N.A.L.N. 9 of 1964.
11. The word 'dowry' is a misnomer. It is used in Nigeria to show a payment of money or money's worth made by the bridegroom to the family of the bride.
12. *Okpanum v. Okpanum* (1972), Vol. 2, pt. 11 E.C.S.L.R. 561, p. 563.
13. But in some communities such as in Onitsha (bridewealth is N40) the bridewealth is pre-fixed by society.
14. Limitation of Dowry Law, *Laws of Eastern Nigeria (1963)*, S. 3.
15. Western Nigerian Marriage Divorce and Custody of children Adoptive Bye-Laws Order 1958, W.R.L.N. 456 of 1958. This law has force in the mid-western state of Nigeria.
16. There are various declarations in operation in various parts of Northern group of States.
17. *Ossai Okaludo v. John Omama* (1960) W.R.N.L.R. 149.
18. The belief was that the person taking the oath was under a duty to speak the truth and it was strongly believed that he would be killed by the gods of the *juju* if he perjured.
19. The proposition follows from what appears to be the system in all customary marriages observed by the writer. It will, however, be appreciated that the incidents of customary marriages have neither featured prominently in legal literature nor have they attracted much litigation as such issues are invariably settled out of court by the village elders. But with the present legislative provisions, such as The Marriage, Divorce and Custody of Children Adoptive By-Laws Order 1958 (Western Region Legal Notice 456 of 1958) which applies in parts of Lagos, Western and

Mid-Western States of Nigeria which prescribes a standard bridewealth of N20; The Limitation of Dowry Law 1956 (Cap. 76 Laws of Eastern Nigeria 1963) which fixes the ceiling for bridewealth at N60 for the East Central, South Eastern and Rivers States of Nigeria, the declaration of customary law marriage in Biu, Borgu, Idoma which fixes the bridewealth at N30, the issue under reference admits of little argument today. The effect of these statutory provisions and declarations is that bridewealth within each state is uniform and whoever wants to marry a girl from another State must do so in strict compliance with the law of that State.

20. (1911) R.G.C.R. 603, p. 613.
21. (1935) 12 N.L.R. 4.
22. (1935) 12 N.L.R. 4, at p. 5.
23. *Alavo v. Tunwase* (1946), 18 N.L.R. 88. Extra-judicial process of diverce has now been abolished in certain parts of the northern states of Nigeria; See the N.A.L.R. 149 of 1955, S. 9 and N.A.L.R. 63 of 1959.
24. (1911) Ren 605 at p. 613. See, also, *Oladele & Ors v. Akinshola & Anor*, AB/7/63 (unreported).
25. Kasunmu & Salacuse, *Nigerian Family Law* (1966), p. 175.
26. For example, see Customary Courts Law for Western & Midwestern Nigeria S 18(2). Similar provisions exist for other States in Nigeria except in the East Central State of Nigeria, where the customary courts have been abolished and their jurisdiction is exercised by the High and Magistrates Courts.
27. These grounds, some of which include desertion, leprosy, neglect, are much wider than the grounds under Matrimonial Causes Decree of 1970, S. 15.
28. See Kasunmu and Salacuse. *Nigerian Family Law*, pp. 174–5.
29. That appeared to have been the dilemma which confronted the court in *Oladele & Ors v. Akinshola & Anor*, AB/7/63 (unreported).
30. This view appears to have been exploded in *Edet v. Essien* (1932), 11 N.L.R. 47; the issue in this case however was one of custody, and not legitimacy.
31. E.g., at Onitsha, although the amount of bridewealth payable is N40 or £20, the amount refundable is fixed at N34 or £17.
32. Limitation of Bridewealth Law, *Laws of Eastern Nigeria (1963)*, S. 5 the Declaration of Idoma Native Marriage Law & Custom Order 1959, S.12(2), N.A.L.N. 63 of 1959.
33. To the knowledge of the present writer, no one has been prosecuted for infringing these statutory limitations even though they are widely flouted.
34. (1960) W.N.L.R. 149.
35. For conditions and circumstances under which refundable bridewealth decreases in Western State of Nigeria, see Western Region Marriage, Divorce and Custody of Children Adoptive Bye-Laws, W.R.L.N. 456 of 1958, and a similar provision among the Tiv people, see N.R.L.N. 149 of 1955. Query: Is there a time when the bridewealth will completely vanish by process of reduction?
36. Cap. 32 Laws of Eastern Nigeria (1963), S. 23 (a). A similar provision in the Northern States is provided under S. 20 (a) of Cap. 78, Laws of Northern Nigeria (1963). Section 20(3) of Customary Courts Law of Western Nigeria, Cap 31 makes a similar provision for western and mid-western Nigeria.
37. This view is favoured by Dr. T. O. Elias, *The Nigerian Legal System* (1963), p. 294.
38. (1960) 1 All E.R. 253.

The effect of marriage on the status of children in Ghana 9

W.C. EKOW DANIELS
University of Ghana

INTRODUCTION

It has been a time-honoured principle of Ghanaian Customary Law that the status of a child is determined by the type of the extended family into which he is born rather than by the fact of his being born in lawful wedlock. This is not peculiar to Ghana. It is one of general application in most countries in Africa. As a result of his studies of the laws in Africa, Driberg (1934) wrote as follows:

> Every individual is born into a certain status relative to all other members of his community. It is not a personal status as it might be in an individualistic society, and does not imply rank, but reciprocal obligations and benefits which he incurs as a member of the Community. All his conduct is conditioned by his status which is not a permanent one but changes with age and experience and may be affected by the decease of relatives and the inheritance of new responsibilities (Driberg 1934:230.251).

The learned author's observation has been subjected to criticisms by some writers on African jurisprudence. He might have gone too far in matters of detail; but by and large his main proposition that status thus acquired is relative and that it could be enlarged or diminished on the occurrence of certain events such as on marriage remains valid.

The truth of the matter is that the common law concept of legitimacy was introduced into the Ghana legal system as a result of the British Colonial policy. Barely a hundred years ago, the Colonial Legislature enacted the Supreme Court Ordinance (No. 4 of 1876) which provided *inter alia* that the common law in force in England should be applied by the courts in so far as the local circumstances permitted. Again in 1884, the concept of monogamous marriage was given statutory effect by the enactment of a Marriage Ordinance (Cap. 127 1951 Rev.), which provided an alternative method of contracting marriages in Ghana. By providing a machinery for the legitimation of children born before the intermarriage of their parents under the Ordinance, that enactment categorised by implication children born out of wedlock as illegitimate for the purpose of inheritance. Section 49 of the Ordinance provides as follows:

> Any child born before the intermarriage of his parents under this Ordinance and not procreated in adultery shall on such intermarriage be deemed the lawful issue of a marriage under this Ordinance, and shall be entitled to the same rights and privileges and his property shall in case of intestacy be subject to the same incidents as though his parents had been at the date of his birth married under this Ordinance.

Thus on a strict interpretation of this section, it would appear that it goes beyond the provision of a machinery for the legitimation of the children of parents married under the Ordinance.The following inferences can be drawn from the provisions of the section:

(a) A marries B under customary law and has children by her. On the dissolution of the customary law marriage A subsequently marries X under the Ordinance. On a literal interpretation of section 49 the children of the customary law marriage could not be legitimated for the purposes of inheritance under the Ordinance. They could not be deemed to be the lawful children of the father now married under the Ordinance. This was the view held by the Divisional Courts until it was exploded by the Court of Appeal in *Coleman v. Shang* (See below).

(b) A child born to a man before he marries another woman under the provisions of the Marriage Ordinance cannot be deemed to be the lawful issue of a marriage under it. Koranteng-Addow, J., in *In re Blankson-Hemans* ([1973] 1 G.L.R. 464 at 468) was even prepared to go further. To him, such a child cannot be legitimate in the eyes of the law. With respect his view is erroneous. (See *Yaotey v. Quaye* [1961] G.L.R. Pt. II 573).

(c) Finally, a child born to either spouse of an Ordinance marriage with a man or woman who is not the one married to him or her during the subsistence of that marriage is not a legitimate child and cannot be legitimated ever for the purposes of the Ordinance.

For the purposes of inheritance under the Ordinance, children belonging to categories (a) to (c) inclusive were for a long time deemed to be illegitimate until *Coleman v. Shang* reversed that judicial trend.

The introduction of the concept of legitimacy at Common Law in Ghana was never understood to have displaced the customary law principle regarding the determination of the status of children. The English Common Law was declared to extend to Ghana in so far as the local circumstances permitted. In other words the judges whose duty it was to apply the laws were given ample discretionary powers to mould all the laws imported to Ghana in order to suit our local circumstances. Two judicial dicta may be cited to illustrate the manner in which the courts were expected to deal with the application of imported legal theories. They both relate to the question of legitimacy. The first is taken from the Nigerian case of *Re Sapara* ([1911] Ren. 605 at 606) where Osborne, C.J., made the following remark:

> Again in English law, marriage is necessary to legitimise offspring of two persons, such offspring, if illegitimate, having no right of inheritance; but under native law a child's right of succession to his father's property can be legalised by his mere acknowledgement of paternity, without the necessity of any form of marriage between the parents. Consequently, the legal importance of the marriage ceremony is not nearly so great under native law as it is under the law of England.

Secondly, a declaration on the same lines as the one just cited was made by Lord Phillimore when delivering the opinion of the Judicial Committee of the Privy Council, then the final appellate court for all the former British Colonies in the case of *Khoo Hou Leong v. Khoo Kean Kwee* ([1926] A.C. 529 at 543). His Lordship said:

> In deciding upon a case where the customs and the laws are so different from British ideas a court may do well to recollect that it is a possible jural conception that a child may be legitimate, though its parents were not and could not be legitimately married.

Unfortunately our courts did not follow the guidelines contained in these sound judicial pronouncements until 1959. Ghana had attained her independence for two years and judges had become aware of the need to foster the progressive development of our laws. In the celebrated case of *Coleman v. Shang* ([1959] G.L.R. 390, 405) the Ghana Court of Appeal gave the quietus to the old principles of law that had been applied by our courts to determine questions of legitimacy for the purposes of succession under the Marriage Ordinance. Van Lare J.A., who delivered the unanimous judgment the Court of Appeal observed thus:

> Until now in this country, the opinion which the Divisional Courts have followed is that if a native who had married under the Marriage Ordinance

dies intestate no consideration is given to entitlement in the distribution of his estate either to any widow, other than a widow of a marriage under Ordinance, or to any issue of the deceased of a marriage other than a marriage under the Ordinance. All such persons, that is to say the widow in respect of a lawful marriage according to native customary law, or the children of such marriage born legitimate according to the law of the domicile (which is native custom), have been so far considered to fall out [side], and therefore to be excluded from consideration as to distribution. It is this opinion which we are, in this judgment, anxious more than anything else to declare to be erroneous in the light of recent decisions by the Privy Council.

Since the decision in *Coleman v. Shang* the view of the need to separate questions of legitimacy from those of the means by which legitimacy is acquired has prevailed. In other words if a person is legitimate by the system of customary law that applies to him, then he is to be regarded as legitimate for all purposes.

The present position of the law may be recapitulated thus: Save that a child procreated in adultery during the subsistence of an Ordinance marriage may be deemed to be illegitimate as far as the Ordinance is concerned, a child's status is determined not by the common law concept of legitimacy to which the customary law attaches little or no importance, but by the personal law which governs his relationship with the ethnic grouping to which he belongs. His status within his family is considered to be his most fundamental asset.

The expression 'family' in the Ghanaian context calls for an explanatory comment. Various definitions have been given of that term. Under English law the family which is generally restricted to a husband, his wife and children, has been termed a word of a most loose and flexible description; a popular and not a technical expression (see *Green v. Marsden* 1 W.R. 512, 513; *Burt. v. Hellyas* L.R. 14 Eq. 160).

English law has consistently refrained from giving a definition to that word. It has also refused to recognise the family in whatever form as a legal entity. Sir Leslie Scarman, one time Chairman of the English Law Commission writing in *The Listener* (1970) expressed an opinion that it would be utterly wrong and contrary to the spirit of English law to recognise the family as a legal person. English law notions about the family system just recounted appear to be diametrically opposed to Ghanaian ideas. I do not venture to hazard an opinion as to which system is better. In the present legal system of Ghana the extended family is recognised as a legal entity whilst the nuclear family comprising a man, his wife or wives and children is given lesser legal recognition.

Families in Ghana are either matrilineal (e.g., the Akan of Southern

Ghana) or patrilineal (e.g., the Ewe of Eastern Ghana). A matrilineal family comprises all persons male and female who are lineally descended from a common ancestress. A patrilineal family consists of all those persons male and female who are considered to have descended in the direct male line from a common ancestor (Ollennu 1962: 140; cf. Allott 1960).

A child born to a woman who belongs to the matrilineal system becomes a member of her matrilineal family whether that child was born out of wedlock, as an issue of customary law marriage or as an issue of an Ordinance (monogamous) marriage. If the child is a daughter she is regarded as being the potential ancestress of a future matrilineal family. A child born to a woman belonging to the patrilineal system is considered to be a member of his father's family if he is born as issue of a customary or Ordinance marriage.

The family system as outlined is proving inadequate to resolve the membership of a child whose mother is patrilineal whilst the father is a member of the matrilineal system and *vice versa.* The matter becomes more intractable in the case of a child born to a Ghanaian father and an expatriate woman. I am not aware of any decision in our courts in which the issue has been satisfactorily resolved. In the absence of legislation common sense must be the guiding principle in the solution of such a problem. The problem however is a real one and in my respectful opinion, neither the legislature nor the courts can regard the question as academic for much longer.

In the foregoing analysis I have tried to establish the fact that the question whether a child was born in wedlock or otherwise does not affect his membership of his family. It has also been suggested that a child's status within his family has hitherto been accorded more recognition than his status as a child of a marriage. I think it will be fairly accurate for me to state that in the Ghanaian context the most important aspect of a child's status is his status within his family. A child called legally an infant, is defined by section 32 of the Interpretation Act, 1960, as someone who has not attained the age of 21 years. In this paper I use the word child without restriction as to age. I now wish to examine the status of a child as a member of his family before considering the effect, if any, which that marriage has on his legal position.

STATUS AS A MEMBER OF THE FAMILY

The centre of the social system in Ghana observed Rattray (1929) 'is not the king or chief or clan or tribe or even the individual; it is the family'.

Status as a member of a family is all important. Membership of a family carries with it certain legal rights and duties. It confers the right to enjoy equally with all other members the fruits of any family property, and on reaching adulthood it confers the right to sit in or be represented at family meetings where decisions are taken regarding the family. Members of the family are also under a duty to contribute towards the payment of family debts. They are also under a duty to comply with the lawful directions of the head of family.

The family, in the traditional customary law sense, is the most important single entity in Ghanaian society. It can own, acquire, and dispose of property. It can through its properly elected head sue and be sued. Membership of a family in most cases ensures that no child, albeit an orphan, is left destitute or homeless. A member of a family has a right to reside in a family house and to be maintained by the family. Membership of a family is not severed as a result of marriage. The traditional concept of marriage is that it is not just a union of 'this man' and 'this woman'; it is the union of 'the family of this man' and 'the family of this woman'. In *Yaotey v. Quaye* ([1961] G.L.R. (Pt. II) 573 at 579) Ollennu, J., as he then was, observed that the union of the families carries with it certain incidents:

> For example, it confers upon the family of the man a right to call upon the wife or her family, in certain eventualities, to perform certain customary rites and imposes an obligation upon the wife and her family to perform these rites; and *vice versa*.

As soon as the marriage of a member of a family to a woman is terminated by divorce or death the member is taken back fully into the family. Status as a member of a family is acquired either by birth or by adoption. It lasts until the connection is terminated by adoption or by the rare event of the severing of the family ties between a membei and the family.

STATUS AS A CHILD OF A MARRIAGE

Does marriage affect the status of a child begotten by that union? If the answer to this question is in the affirmative, then it may also be pertinent to ascertain the extent to which it does. There are three ways of contracting a marriage in Ghana. It may be contracted (a) under customary law, (b) in accordance with the rites of Mohammedan law, and (c) under the provisions of the Marriage Ordinance. Customary and Mohammedan marriages are polygamous in nature, while marriage under the Ordinance is monogamous in character. In the eyes of the law all the three types of marriage are given equal recognition.

If the main purpose of marriage were to accord the children of that union the status of legitimacy, one would have been inclined to suggest that since it has been established that in Ghana the status of a person as a child of his father with one exception does not depend upon a valid marriage of his parents, then marriage has no bearing on the status of children. (An illegitimate child is the child which a spouse, married under the Marriage Ordinance, has during the subsistence of the said marriage with a person other than his spouse by the marriage under the Ordinance). Fortunately marriage is still regarded by Ghanaians as an important social institution. Writing on kinship and marriage among the Ashanti, Meyer Fortes (1950) observed as follows:

> The general rule that a child is considered by law to be the offspring of its pater prevails in Ashanti, but the ideal is that pater and genitor should be the same person.

This statement applies with equal force to all the other communities in Ghana. Regardless of the family system in Ghana a father in a properly contracted marriage is not a mere figure head. It is true that in the olden days an Akan father did not have much control over his children. For example he could not pawn his child without the authority of his child's maternal uncle. Times have changed. The law recognises the legal relationship which exists between a father and a son. Subject to the laws of the land, a father possesses a right to name his child. He has the right to its custody. He can discipline his child. He is entitled to be consulted when his son is desirous of acquiring a bride. His consent must be sought before his daughter is married. In return for all these rights, a father is required by law to maintain and support all his children. If a father wilfully neglects to provide or contribute towards the reasonable maintenance of his children an application can be made to the court on their behalf for an order of maintenance.

The children during minority are also expected to render general services to their parents. They can be called upon to assist the father in the carrying out of the duties of his station in life, e.g., farming or business, without any hope of financial remuneration. In the event of the death of the father, difficult questions crop up with regard to the right to maintenance. If the father was a member of a matrilineal family, on a strict interpretation of the rules of customary law, the surviving children have no right of inheritance to the estate of their deceased father. Children of a patrilineal family are however allowed a share in their father's estate. The anomalous position is still with us. The courts have however through a process of judicial legislation, minimised the hardship suffered by the surviving children of a matrilineal household. It has been held that the responsibility of a father to maintain his children passes on to the customary law successor in the event of the death intestate of the father. Thus in *Manu v. Kuma* ([1963] 1 G.L.R. 464 at 469) van Lare J.S.C., in reading the judgment of the former Supreme Court stated the new approach thus:

> We consider that the responsibility of a successor to maintain and train the child of his predecessor is a legal one, and the right enuring therefrom to the child is different in nature from a right to succeed to or have a share in the estate of his deceased father.

What is the position with regard to the children whose parents are married under the Ordinance? As I have already indicated the Marriage Ordinance passed in 1884 was designed to encourage Ghanaians to discard the existing traditional polygamous system of marriage as well as to foster the growth of the concept of the nuclear family. Towards these objectives certain provisions are inserted in the marriage legislation which have the effect of enhancing the status of the parties to that marriage as well as that of their offsprings. Regardless of the proprietary inducements offered by that legislation, the greater majority of Ghanaians are still married under customary law. The beneficial effect of the Ordinance is felt only on the death intestate of either party to that marriage. By section 48 of the Ordinance, it is provided that where a Ghanaian contracts a monogamous marriage under it and later dies intestate, leaving a widow or husband or any issue of such marriage, two-thirds of his property shall devolve on the widow and children of that marriage, and the remaining one-third shall devolve on the family of the deceased intestate.

With the exception of the statutory right conferred on children of an Ordinance marriage there is no distinction regarding the rights and duties of a father towards his children and vice versa.

STATUS OF CHILDREN BORN OUT OF WEDLOCK

Customary law recognises the difference between concubinage and the institution of marriage. According to Sarbah, a woman living with a man as concubine, mistress, or friend, is not encouraged in the eyes of customary law. Recently Koranteng-Addow, J., in *Re Blankson-Hemans* has had occasion to reiterate this view of the law with these words:

> For all I know, even though a polygamous society, the customary law of Ghana puts a high premium on and encourages people to contract marriages. Concubinage is frowned upon.

In the case of a patrilineal family a child born to a woman either in concubinage or out of wedlock will become a member of his father's family only if his father acknowledges paternity. Acknowledgement of paternity is necessary for the purposes of succession to the estate of the father in the event of his death. Such a child whose paternity is not acknowledged would still be considered as the lawful issue of his mother.

In a matrilineal system acknowledgement of paternity by the father is necessary to enable a child born out of wedlock to rank with the other lawful issue of the father, e.g., for purposes of maintenance and support.

Without the performance of an act of acknowledgement of paternity the family of the mother may consider themselves entitled to deny the father a right to the child's custody. In the case of *Awortwi v. Nwansu* ([1969] C.C 31), Aboagye, J., in refusing an application for custody by a putative father observed as follows:

> By the Akan custom it is only the legitimate child which belongs to the father and in respect thereof he is entitled to custody; for a child born through immoral association does not belong to its natural father. Such a child belongs to its mother or its mother's family; for as the Akan saying goes, '*Okronfo nni ba*' (meaning literally, that 'a thief has no child').

According to Kludze (1973) the patrilineal Ewe group also regard the father of a child of an extra-marital association as a thief who is not entitled to 'own the products of a farm'.

An extramarital offspring of a spouse married under the Ordinance is an example of a child who bears the brand of 'illegitimate child' on his forehead when questions of succession to property are at stake. The fate of such a child still hangs in the balance. The law has often been cruel to him. It is to be hoped that the Law Reform Commission will soon consider the plight of such children who are not in any way to be held answerable for the actions of their genitors. Hitherto the question of the financial assistance that can be awarded to children of unmarried mothers has been fixed by the Maintenance of Children Act (Act 297). It is much smaller than the amount the courts in their discretion can award for the maintenance of children of regular marriages. The Law Reform Commission has proposed uniform treatement for all children in need of financial provision for their maintenance and support.

CONCLUSION

From time immemorial our laws have recognised the extended family as the most important single social entity. The family has been accorded immense proprietory powers and privileges with respect to succession to the self-acquired property of a deceased member. The stress of modern ways of life has nevertheless demonstrated the need for a change of the law in in favour of the members of a nuclear family. Recent legislation has thus endeavoured to develop the concept of the nuclear family at the expense of the proprietory rights of the extended family, especially the succession rights of children of matrilineal groupings. Under the Wills Act (Act 360) for example, the only dependants who can apply to the court for reasonable financial provision out of the estate of a deceased testator are his father, mother, spouse or children under 18 years. This trend is forward looking and one hopes that it will not be reversed. We have to agree with Sir Leslie Scarman that 'the family exists for human beings and not human beings for the family'.

The choice of law dilemma in Lesotho: some criteria for decision making in family law

10

SEBASTIAN POULTER
University of Southampton

1. INTRODUCTION

The purpose of this paper is to explore the basis upon which family matters involving Basotho fall to be governed by the customary law on the one hand or the received common law on the other. This will naturally necessitate a consideration of the position of those couples who have chosen to marry according to civil rites; currently there are around 2750 civil ceremonies each year, representing probably about one third of all the marriages contracted in the country annually.

Although at present Lesotho can hardly be described as a state in the throes of very rapid change, it is clear that political independence, an expansion in commerce, the development of a few industries and greater educational opportunities are thrusting more and more Basotho into what might be called the 'modern' sector of society. As this number increases so will the need for clear and well established rules as to the circumstances in which one or other of the two legal systems will be held by the courts to be applicable to the facts of a given case. People will then be in a position to appreciate the significance which the law attaches to particular acts and will be able to arrange their affairs accordingly, if they so wish.

Unfortunately criteria for making a choice of law have, for the most part, neither been enacted by the legislature nor worked out judicially by the courts. Of necessity, therefore, the analysis which follows must be somewhat speculative, concentrating on laying down some general considerations and leaving over for another occasion their detailed application to specific questions.

While the discussion is directed specifically to the situation in Lesotho, the choice of law dilemma pervades nearly every legal system in Africa. It is therefore hoped that some of the suggestions made in this paper may contribute to a greater understanding of similar problems in other countries and of the solutions which are available.

2. A DUAL SYSTEM OF LAWS

Part of the colonial legacy which Britain bequeathed to Lesotho on independence was the dual system of law which had been established at the end of the last century. Proclamation 2B of 1884 had provided for the continuation in force of both the customary law (Sesotho law) and the Roman-Dutch common law which had been introduced during the period of rule by the Cape Colony from 1871 to 1883. The modern version of the relevant provision, section 2 of the General Law Proclamation, spells out the current position in the following terms:

> In all suits, actions, or proceedings, civil or criminal the law to be administered shall as nearly as the circumstances of the country will permit be the same as the law for the time being in force in the Colony of the Cape of Good Hope: Provided, however, that in all suits, actions, or proceedings in any Court to which all of the parties are Africans, and in all suits, actions, or proceedings whatsoever before any Basuto Court, African law [i.e., customary law] may be administered ....

It will be noticed that the received law is referred to as the 'law for the time being in force' in the Cape Colony. In 1884 this undoubtedly meant the Roman-Dutch law but the proper construction to be placed on these words today is far from settled. *Prima facie*, the words 'for the time being in force' would seem to indicate the living law as it is administered at the present time in the Cape. However, the Cape Colony, as such, disappeared with the Union of the various South African colonies in 1910. Since then the geographical area of the former Cape Colony has been known as the Cape Province of the Union (and now Republic) of South Africa.

The various possible approaches to this question have been extensively reviewed by the present writer elsewhere (Palmer and Poulter 1972) and it is sufficient here to reiterate that it seems probable, if rather unfortunate, that broadly speaking the current South African common law as administered in the Cape Province constitutes the modern common law of Lesotho.

3. GENERAL CONSIDERATIONS IN THE CHOICE OF LAW

(a) The jurisdiction of the courts

Inevitably the choice of law will depend to some extent on which court hears the dispute in question. The lower-level customary courts known as the 'Basotho Courts'[1] do not have jurisdiction to administer the common law,[2] they can only apply a very limited range of statutes and they can only apply customary law in so far as it is not repugnant to justice or morality.[3] Thus the fact that a plaintiff has instituted proceedings in a Basotho Court virtually amounts to an election on his part to have his case decided according to Sesotho law and he cannot complain if he discovers afterwards that he would have done better by commencing an action at common law in a subordinate court. However, the choice of court by the plaintiff does not similarly bind the defendant who can apply to the president of the court for the case to be transferred. If a president considers that the matter ought properly to be determined in terms of the common law he is bound to decline jurisdiction and transfer the case to a subordinate (magistrate's) court.[4] In addition, the Basotho Courts have been barred by statute from hearing any cases in connection with civil marriages except insofar as the case concerns the payment, return or disposal of *bohali* (bridewealth).[5]

The subordinate courts, on the other hand, generally restrict themselves to the common law and a magistrate has the power to transfer an action to a Local or Central Court if he is of the view that it would more conveniently be dealt with there.[6] However, the High Court has a very broad discretion since the General Law Proclamation merely says that where all the parties are Africans, African (i.e., customary) law 'may' be administered and there is no power to transfer cases to the Basotho Courts.[7]

(b) Statutory direction as to the law applicable

Apart from the legislative provisions setting out the jurisdiction of the courts there are only two statutory enactments (both in the field of inheritance) specifying that one system rather than the other should apply in a given set of circumstances. This minimal interference with the discretion of the courts is a rare phenomenon in Africa and very many decisions from different parts of the continent on internal conflicts of laws problems will be found to turn on particular statutory guidelines or prescriptions and are thus of little relevance to the lawyer in Lesotho.

The two statutory provisions referred to are section 3(b) of the Administration of Estates Proclamation[8] and section 2 of the Intestate Succession Proclamation.[9] The former proclamation introduced into Lesotho an English-style system of executorship and winding up of estates and section 3(b) declares that the proclamation is not to apply to the estates of Africans which will continue to be 'administered'[10] according to the customary law. Then there follows a proviso with a true colonial ring to it:

> ... provided that such law and custom shall not apply to the estates of Africans who have been shown to the satisfaction of the Master [of the High Court] to have abandoned tribal custom and adopted a European mode of life and who, if married, have married under European law.

The Intestate Succession Proclamation was introduced to confer rights of inheritance upon a surviving spouse on intestacy which were not available at common law and there was a similar provision that it was only to operate in circumstances where the Administration of Estates Proclamation applied.

The phrasing of the proviso just quoted is obviously absurdly paternalistic,[11] but while it remains on the statute book some attempt must be made to interpret it. Presumably the reference to a 'European mode of life' means European in the South African sense of 'white' rather than its true meaning. The expression 'tribal custom' also comes from South Africa and since it has offensive overtones it is not used in current parlance in Lesotho today, but in *Mokorosi's* case[12] Roper, J., held that it signified the customary way of life of a Mosotho 'tribesman' and went on:

> The next matter for consideration is the meaning of the phrase 'to have abandoned tribal custom and adopted a European mode of life'. This does not seem to contemplate two separate and distinct acts or processes, namely one act or process of abandonment of tribal custom and another act or process of adoption of a European mode of life. The adoption of one mode of life and the abandonment of another is all one process. The idea underlying the phrase is that the person concerned has forsaken one mode of life in favour of another.

Taking the decision in this case together with the judgments of the High Court and Court of Appeal in the recent case of *Hoohlo v. Hoohlo*[13] it seems that the following fourteen factors are regarded by the judiciary as individual indications of the fact that a Mosotho has 'abandoned tribal custom and adopted a European of life':

(i) living in one of the 'towns'[14] rather than in the countryside where a person is directly under the control and authority of a chief or headman;

(ii) not being in receipt of any ploughing or grazing rights in the countryside from a chief or headman;[15]
(iii) earning one's living from employment in the professions, commerce, industry, or government service;[16]
(iv) ownership of a motor vehicle;
(v) the wearing of 'European' clothes;
(vi) possessing a savings or other account at a bank;
(vii) ownership of life insurance policies;
(viii) adherence to the Christian faith;
(ix) marriage both of oneself and of one's children according to civil rites involving a commitment to monogamy;
(x) the education of one's children in government or mission schools and not at an initiation school;
(xi) sleeping on a bed rather than a mat;
(xii) eating one's meals with one's family rather than the husband eating separately;
(xiii) consulting attorneys about various matters including the drawing up of a will;
(xiv) the execution of a will in which the bequests do not follow the usual pattern of inheritance under Sesotho law.

On the assumption that today Lesotho courts will see their task under the Proclamation as one of trying to decide whether the deceased's style of life was predominantly modern or predominantly traditional, how far are the criteria listed above relevant or helpful?

First, there are a growing number of Basotho who rightly regard themselves as living in the modern sector of society who have two residences – one in the town where they work and another in the countryside where they farm or have their family homes. The fact that if they are to have any ploughing or grazing rights these must emanate from a chief or headman to whom they will owe allegiance would not seem to be of great importance. In *Mokorosi's* case the deceased had loaned out his cattle to people who had grazing rights, and ploughed on a partnership basis with people who had been allocated arable land and yet was held to have 'adopted a European mode of life'. An interesting question is whether a chief or headman could himself be regarded as having 'abandoned tribal custom and adopted a European mode of life'. Education and wealth have enabled some chiefs to lead a very modern style of life and it would be unrealistic to maintain that their possession of a traditional office and status automatically bars them from qualifying under the Proclamation.

Secondly, if employment in the modern sector in an urban or semi-urban setting is held to be a factor, what conclusions are to be drawn about the 60–65% of Basotho men who spend their lives as migrant labourers, taking employment on short contracts in South Africa in the mines, industries and commerce? Is this a European mode of life when the 'Europeans' in South Africa are unwilling to undertake the menial and unskilled tasks which are the lot of nearly all Basotho employees? Presumably not. Spells of migrant labour must be regarded as having become, through very frequent occurrence over a long period, an integral feature of Sesotho custom.

Thirdly, caution must be exercised in judging a man on the basis of the clothes he wears. For many years now most Basotho have worn clothes reflecting a mixture of modern and traditional styles. Some of the most traditional Basotho of the older generation are still to be found wearing the army greatcoats which were issued to them during the 2nd World War. On the other hand, colourful modern versions of the traditional Basotho blanket are often worn by government ministers, civil servants and the like, particularly on special occasions.

Fourthly, adherence to the Christian faith would seem, of itself, to give little indication of a modern style of life. At the last census the proportion of professing Christians was as high as 82%. On the other hand, it seems that only about a third of all couples actually choose to marry in church. Perhaps regular attendance at church or the possession of some office in the congregation would provide more positive proof of 'modernity'.

Finally, not only is a civil marriage on the part of the deceased treated as an indication of his adoption of a European mode of life, it is actually a precondition for the application of the Administration of Estates Proclamation since it forms an integral part of the proviso in section 3(b). If the deceased's marriage was a customary one his estate can only be administered under customary law. Since a man's marriage may have occurred more than half a century before his death, during which time his life-style may have undergone very considerable changes, this provision appears to be unduly restrictive and is clearly ripe for repeal.

(c) The exercise of discretion by the courts

Apart, then, from the two proclamations on inheritance and the statutory restrictions on the jurisdiction of the Basotho Courts, a very broad discretion has been conferred on the judiciary in choosing which is the appropriate law to resolve disputes between Basotho. On what principles should this discretion be exercised?

Probably the only accurate generalisation about existing practice is to say that the courts have hitherto made no attempt to formulate any guiding precepts or rules. Almost invariably the judges have come forward with sweeping assertions that one or other of the systems applies to the particular case, unsupported by even a vestige of reasoning.[17] Alternatively they have been totally unaware that they were called upon to make a choice at all.[18]

It would appear that in the family law sphere there are essentially only three possible grounds on which a choice can be made between the systems.

First, the choice can be made by reference to a specific event which can be interpreted as an adherence (express or implied) to one system or the other. In family law the obvious event of this nature is a marriage. The rule can thus be propounded that family matters which are connected with marriage should be determined by applying the law under which the marriage itself was contracted. This approach has the great merits of simplicity, predictability and certainty and it has been accepted by various writers as reflecting the general position in Anglophone Africa.[19] It has also been adopted in many cases by the Lesotho courts.[20]

While this test is admirably suited to the resolution of matters intimately bound up with the actual contracting of a marriage (such as compliance with formalities, grounds for annulment, the capacity to take further wives and the legitimacy of children) because it coincides with the normal intentions and expectations of the parties, it works less well in relation to more disconnected issues. It begins to appear rather unreal and artificial when applied mechanically to such questions as the property relations of the spouses (both during the marriage and on its dissolution by death or divorce), the grounds for divorce, the status of a widow, parental rights and duties in respect of their children and so on. Here the link between the issue before the court and the nature of the marriage ceremony, which may have taken place many years earlier, is very tenuous. Furthermore one should bear in mind the reasons why Basotho select one ceremony or the other. The conflicts problems almost always arise out of a civil marriage and it is as well to appreciate why about a third of all couples choose to have a church wedding. Partly it is because of the religious beliefs of the spouses and their parents, partly because it is a fashionable thing to do and partly because the marriage certificate will provide satisfactory evidence of the status of matrimony to the various South African authorities and employers. In the main the spouses have no desire that their relationship should be governed exclusively by rules of the received law. They accept, obviously, that the marriage is monogamous and that they must have complied with the proper formalities, but they do not, in the vast majority of cases, regard themselves as having stepped outside the customary law for all purposes connected with their married lives. Therefore to apply the received law to them automatically and indiscriminately is to sacrifice the normal expectations of the people involved for the sake of simplicity in judicial administration.

The conclusion to be drawn from this brief examination of the 'law of the marriage' test is that it is appropriate for handling *some* of the conflicts issues that may arise but is by no means suited to all of them.

The second possible basis for choosing between the systems is that propounded by Schreiner, J.A., in the South African case of *Ex parte Minister of Native Affairs: In re Yako v. Beyi.*[21] Mr. Justice Schreiner joined the Lesotho Court of Appeal after his retirement from the South African bench but in this particular case he was considering how a choice between the customary law and the common law should be made by the courts of native commissioners in South Africa, upon whom a wide discretion had been conferred.[22] He reached the conclusion that the primary desideratum was 'an equitable decision between the parties' and that the native commissioner had to determine which system of law it would be 'fairest' to apply:

> the native commissioner must ... pay principal regard to the facts of the case before him since the dominant consideration is his own reasoned view as to the best system of law to apply to reach a just decision between the parties.[23]

This test successfully avoids the rigidity of the 'law of the marriage' approach, but its very flexibility brings certain dangers in its wake. Each judge is free to impose his own version of what is just and equitable, concentrating on the particular case in hand. There is no suggestion that any principles should be established through the doctrine of precedent. At the present time this may perhaps be too great a risk. The criteria surely need, if possible, to be more susceptible to a clear and consistent articulation than those proposed and some objective factors require to be built into the process of choice. This, it is thought, can to a large extent be achieved by the third approach.

This is the 'style of life' test in terms of which the choice is made on the basis of the type of lifestyle followed by the persons involved. It has the advantage of selecting the law which most nearly approximates to the general social values, beliefs, circumstances, and needs of the members of a particular family and which should therefore correspond quite closely with their intentions and expectations. The concept is a reasonably flexible one enabling a court to place special emphasis on certain matters which are peculiarly relevant to the point at issue, such as the public opinion in the social group in which the family moves and the nature of any property in dispute or contract entered into.[24] It is obviously wide enough to encompass the type of marriage which the spouses have entered into, but it does not allow this to be decisive in the way it was under the first test. Subject to the reservations expressed earlier, the various criteria set out above in relation to the *statutory* 'mode of life' test in certain inheritance questions can be equally useful here. In whatever circumstances they are used, they will, of course, each have to be weighed carefully in relation to the individual dispute and obviously cannot be applied in a sweeping 'all or nothing' fashion.

The strongest judicial statement endorsing the style of life test is to be found in the judgment of Schreiner, J. A., in *Khatala v. Khatala.*[25] He took the view that where parties to a civil marriage had also married customarily and had followed a customary way of life, their property relations should be governed by Sesotho law.

It is my belief that in the present state of affairs in Lesotho this test is the most appropriate one to solve many of the difficult choice of law questions in family law. One of the reasons for its special value in this field is that the lifestyles of the persons involved in a family dispute will very often be the same. Where, however, they are not, intractable problems are likely to arise which seem at present only susceptible to resolution by a wide judicial discretion under the second test, i.e., by the court seeking to do what is just and equitable in all the circumstances. The outstanding instances of this sort of situation are likely to be in relation to breach of engagement, seduction and abduction cases, adultery, and the death action.[26]

4. DUAL MARRIAGES

It may be helpful in this connection to examine briefly the phenomenon of dual marriages where the spouses have married one another both under the received law and under customary law.

At present about 600 dual marriages occur each year, representing some 22% of civil marriages contracted in the country annually. These are the figures for situations where the first marriage, a customary one, is followed by a civil ceremony – almost always in church. The extent of *these* dual marriages is known because the registered marriage certificate describes the parties as having previously been married by Sesotho custom rather than as bachelor and spinster. Figures are not available for dual marriages which take place in the reverse order because Sesotho marriages are not required to be registered, but it is thought that dual marriages of this type are rather rare. This is because the bride's parents may experience considerable difficulty in obtaining any *bohali* if the civil marriage occurs first; the bridegroom's family may regard this marriage as the sole marriage and refuse to undertake the obligations of a customary marriage.

What is the juridical nature of the normal dual marriage?

The first possibility is that Lesotho follows the South African approach in terms of which the civil marriage always predominates, overriding and absorbing a prior customary marriage.[27] Duncan has taken this view in his book,[28] but it is totally unacceptable. The reason for the South African stance is that customary marriages are given very limited recognition in that country anyway, being designated mere 'customary unions'. In Lesotho both types of marriage are equally valid and there is no authority, either statutory or judicial, for holding that a civil marriage literally cancels out a customary marriage.

A second possibility is that the marriage which takes place *first* is the only valid marriage, the second ceremony amounting to no more than a blessing or confirmation of the status created by the first ceremony. There is judicial support for such an approach in two East African cases, *Rattansey v. Rattansey*[29] and *Ayoob v. Ayoob*.[30] In both, the spouses had first contracted a civil marriage and then gone through an Islamic ceremony of marriage. In both cases the courts held that the second Islamic 'marriage' was completely devoid of legal effect because the parties were already man and wife.[31] The religious ceremony did not convert their relationship into one under Islamic law.

If the underlying principle of these East African authorities were to be adopted in Lesotho then the normal type of dual marriage would, in law, be nothing more than a customary marriage. The religious ceremony would merely have served to consecrate the existing marriage, not to supersede it or change its nature. What significance would this have? In the first place, it would mean that the Basotho Courts possessed jurisdiction over the marriage.[32] Secondly, the husband would not be barred from taking a second wife under customary law. Thirdly, the parties would not qualify to have their estates administered under the inheritance proclamations because they were not married 'under European law'. All these conclusions are so surprising that there must be the strongest doubts whether this can be the correct approach in Lesotho. The last consequence would mean that, through an oversight, the recent decisions of both the High Court and the

Court of Appeal in *Hoohlo v. Hoohlo*[33] were wrong. The deceased's wedding in an Anglican church had been preceded by a customary marriage in which *bohali* was transferred. The Court of Appeal declared that the deceased was 'unquestionably' married under European law and this would seem to have been a perfectly accurate statement of the legal position.

The third possibility is the opposite of the one just discussed, namely that the second ceremony is the vital one because it has converted the nature of the marriage from one type to another. Thus in the normal dual marriage in Lesotho the civil marriage would supersede and replace the customary marriage, not because of its intrinsic superiority (as under the first approach) but because it came later in time and had different consequences. This process of 'conversion' was recognised by the English courts in a number of cases prior to the enactment of the Matrimonial Proceedings (Polygamous Marriages) Act in 1972 in an endeavour to circumvent the decision in *Hyde v. Hyde*[34] under which they were compelled to deny matrimonial relief to parties to polygamous marriages. They were therefore prepared to hold that a marriage which was potentially polygamous in its inception had become monogamous if the spouses had entered into a second monogamous marriage.[35] This approach was clearly the product of very special circumstances and was specifically rejected by Spry, J. A., in *Ayoob's* case[36] when considering the position in Kenya.

The fourth possibility – and the one advocated by the present writer – is that the true essence of a dual marriage is to be found both in its name and in the realities of the situation. The parties have clearly manifested an intention to marry under *both* systems and therefore *both* marriages must be regarded as subsisting side by side. Instead of adopting a *negative* attitude in terms of which one of the marriages is treated as overridden, subsumed or of no significance, a *positive* approach is needed which will give life and meaning to the fruitful merging of the two cultures.

Are there any serious obstacles to this way of looking at the matter? This depends on how important it is to be able to solve a conflicts problem by reference to a single 'law of the marriage'. It has already been explained that the 'law of the marriage' test is only appropriate to govern a very small number of questions, most of which are intimately bound up with the actual contracting of the marriage. The vast majority of legal issues in relation to the family are far too remotely connected with the actual ceremony to be usefully governed by this test. Indeed the problems surrounding the juridical nature of dual marriages merely serve to emphasise the absurdity of expecting that test to provide an all-embracing panacea for choice of law questions. For if the 'law of the marriage' is to be meaningful in relation to dual marriages one of the marriages must be held to have superseded the other in terms of one of the three approaches outlined above. Yet all of these have been shown to be both illogical and inappropriate in the context of Lesotho. The limited areas in which the 'law of the marriage' test would seem to be clearly applicable are as follows:

(i) the formalities needed for a particular type of marriage must be complied with by following the law governing the contracting of that type of marriage and if the marriage is to be a dual one obviously both sets of formalities must be satisfied;

(ii) any defect recognised by only one system as sufficient to render a marriage void or voidable will operate on the marriage contracted under that system but not on any marriage under the other system;

(iii) the legitimacy of a child must be determined in the first instance by looking to the law of the marriage of its mother; it may also be regarded as legitimate *for the purposes of the other system* if, assuming the mother had married instead under that system, it would have been legitimate in terms of that system. Where there has been a dual marriage the legitimacy of the child will be determined according to the law held to be appropriate to govern the particular issue before the court, e.g., inheritance, custody, maintenance, etc.

It will be noticed that the law of the marriage test, as applied to these matters, presents no difficulties for the approach of recognising a dual marriage for what it is – two marriages subsisting side by side. But there are further positive advantages of this approach which need to be stressed. It can provide a breakthrough in the manner in which *bohali* is regarded and in answering the controversial question whether or not the husband can take a second wife.

Following the South African approach there has hitherto been a tendency in the Lesotho courts to regard *bohali* in a dual marriage as an ancillary contract attached to the civil marriage as a mere appendage.[37] The reality of the situation, of course, is that the obligation to pay *bohali* in such marriages derives from the customary marriage which subsists side by side with the civil marriage.

So far as the husband's legal capacity to marry a second wife polygamously is concerned, the clear answer is that he cannot do so. However the important point is that this is not because of any inherent superiority of monogamous marriage over polygamy or of the received law over the customary law. It can be seen as springing instead from the strength of the rules of each system so that it is this feature which resolves the conflict between them. The received law absolutely forbids polygamy once a civil marriage has been entered into. Sesotho law allows polygamy but it does not positively require it. It can therefore be argued that the weaker permissive rule has to give way in face of the mandatory prohibition.

This last interpretation of dual marriages should, it is submitted, be the one to gain acceptance by the Lesotho courts because it fulfils the intentions and expectations of the parties and because it is able to give the fullest recognition to the essential features of each type of marriage – *bohali* in the Sesotho marriage and monogamy in the civil marriage. The status of marriage is obviously created by the first ceremony, but it is modified by the second ceremony. Both marriages continue to subsist side by side and both affect the legal relationship of the parties.

NOTES

1. Their formal titles are the Local and Central Courts.
2. This would seem to make nonsense of the direction in the proviso to the General Law Proclamation that African law '*may*' be administered in the Basotho Courts. If any law at all is to be applied there (aside from the few statutes) it *must* be customary law.
3. Proc. 62 of of 1938, s.9.
4. Basotho Courts (Practice and Procedure) Rules, r. 31.
5. Central and Local Courts Proclamation, s. 8(1) (b).
6. Subordinate Courts (Amendment) Proclamation, No. 5 of 1964, s. 8(2) replacing s. 16 of the Subordinate Courts Proclamation, No. 58 of 1938.
7. *Theko v. Theko* (1963–66) H.C.T.L.R. 105 at 108.
8. Proc. 19 of 1935.
9. Proc. 2 of 1953.
10. The use of the word 'administered' causes considerable difficulty. Interpreted widely, it clearly encompasses the regulation of all matters in connection with a deceased's estate, including the devolution of property and the power to make bequests in a will. A narrow construction, on the other hand, would confine it to the mere machinery of collecting in assets, paying debts and distribution to the persons entitled under a will or the rules of intestacy. The latter interpretation was the one favoured in relation to parallel statutory provisions in the Bechuanaland Protectorate (as it then was) by the joint Court of Appeal for the former High Commission Territories in *Fraenkel v. Sechele* (1963–66) H.C.T.L.R. 70.
11. Between 1960 and 1970 there were only thirteen estates of Africans administered under the Proclamation.
12. H.C.Civ./T/4/1955.
13. C.A.Civ./A/4/1969.
14. There are no really substantial urban settlements in Lesotho. The capital Maseru has a population of 19,000 and there are eight other administrative centres but none of these has more than 6,000 inhabitants.
15. The land tenure system is based not on a concept of absolute individual ownership but upon the allocation of land rights by a hereditary chieftainship. In legal theory all land is held by the King in trust for the whole Basotho Nation.

16. Only about 7% of the male working population is currently employed in these activities within Lesotho – see *First Five Year Development Plan 1970/71–1974/75* (Maseru, 1970) p. 11.
17. See e.g., *Chokobane v. Chokobane* R.C.2/1921; *Lichaba v. Lichaba* R.C.4/1937; *Machobeng v. Mafantiri* H.C.28/1940; *Ntsinyi v. Rammoko* J.C. 268/1954; *Limo v. Matlosa* H.C.Civ./A/6/1965; *Mosoang v. Mosoang* J.C. 234/1966; *Nko v. Nko* H.C.Civ./T/3/1968; *Mosakeng v. Mosakeng* H.C.Civ./T/15/1968; *Rakhoabe v. Rakhoabe* C.A.Civ./A/5/1969.
18. See, e.g., *Maseela v. Maseela* (1954) H.C.T.L.R. 48; *Tsosane v. Tsosane* H.C.Civ.-A/6/1968.
19. See, e.g., Allott, *New Essays in African Law*, pp. 219–27 and the authorities cited there.
20. See e.g., *Nko v. Nko* H.C.Civ./T/3/1968; *Mosakeng v. Mosakeng* H.C.Civ./T/15/1968; *Nthunya v. Nthunya* H.C.Civ./T/34/1968. See also the simplistic statement of Duncan, 1960: 20 – 'If the marriage is conducted in church or in the district commissioner's office the law governing the marriage is the civil law: but if it is regulated by the families of the parties, according to tradition, then the law governing the marriage is Sotho law'.
21. 1948(1) S.A.388(A.D.).
22. Bantu Administration Act. No. 38 of 1927, s. 11(1).
23. 1948(1) S.A.388 at 397, 400–1.
24. E.g., an ante-nuptial contract.
25. (1963–66) H.C.T.L.R. 97 at 100.
26. Although this test is derived from the judgment of Schreiner J.A. in *Yako v. Beyi* I am not suggesting that the Lesotho courts follow the guidelines laid down for the native commissioners' courts in South Africa.
27. Simons, 1970: 160; *Matchika v. Mguni* 1946 N.A.C. (N. & T.) 78.
28. Duncan, 1960: 20. See also his decision as Judicial Commissioner on the jurisdiction of the Basotho Courts over dual marriages in *Tlale v. Tlale* J.C. 163/1950.
29. [1960] E.A.81.
30. [1968] E.A. 72.
31. See also the statement of Hodson L.J. in the English case of *Thynne v. Thynne* [1955] P. 272 at 304 to the effect that a second ceremony following on a valid marriage has no legal effect.
32. See Central and Local Courts Proclamation, s. 8(1) (b).
33. H.C.Civ.A/4/1969.
34. (1866) L.R.1. P. & D. 130.
35. See *Ohochuku v. Ohochuku* [1960] 1 All E.R. 253 as interpreted in *Cheni v. Cheni* [1962] 3 All E.R. 873 at 878 and in *Ali v. Ali* [1966] 1 All E.R. 664 at 669.
36. [1968] E.A. 72.
37. See e.g., *Makhele v. Rataleli* J.C. 153/1945; *Maqutu v. Hlapane* H.C.Civ.A/1/1971. For the artificial South African approach see Simons, 1970: 160, 177.

Marriage in Kwahu, Ghana* 11

WOLF BLEEK
University of Amsterdam

The Sixth International African Seminar in 1964 on 'The New Elites in Tropical Africa' (Lloyd 1966) marked the rising interest of sociologists and anthropologists in urbanized elite groups in Africa. Studies of the urban elite in Ghana deal *inter alia* with decrease of fertility, changes in family life and upbringing of children (Caldwell 1968), jointness and segregation of conjugal roles, nucleization of the extended family system (Oppong 1974) and attitudes of university students towards marriage and family size (Oppong n.d. (a) and n.d. (b); Kumekpor n.d.).

All these studies present a picture of marriage that is radically different from traditional marriage. Caldwell (1968) observed that norms as well as practices have changed considerably. The majority of his (elitist) respondents considered polygyny not to be a good thing and the practice of polygyny was found to be rather rare. The age at marriage was also rising for both men and women. Divorce seldom occurred and was almost universally condemned. Most respondents thought that their family was closer to a nuclear family than to a traditional family and in more than half of all cases husband and wife claimed that they went out together at least once a month. About 40% thought that there was 'nothing bad' about the Western family type and about 15% found 'nothing good' in large families.

Oppong (1974) describes conjugal and kin relationships among matrilineal senior civil servants in Accra. Following Bott's line of thought she

* The research was sponsored by the Institute of African Studies, University of Ghana, and the Netherlands Foundation for the Advancement of Tropical Research (WOTRO).

examines the extent to which the conjugal family is a discrete unit and the conjugal roles are joint or segregate. She analyzes the delegation of household tasks, domestic power positions, and the marital decision model. One of her conclusions is that husbands who belong to the second educated generation are more likely to have joint relationships with their wives and to have little contact with their matrikin.

While acknowledging the value of these studies we should not lose sight of the fact that they only speak about an exceptional sub-group of Ghana's population. What goes on among the elites presents but a fraction of the total picture. Ghana still has a predominantly rural population and within the cities a sharp demarcation line is drawn between the poor and the rich. There is a danger, however, that elite studies eclipse other studies oriented toward rural groups and the urban poor. In the first place social scientists tend to assume that 'the new pattern of living adopted by the wealthier residents of the towns are likely to diffuse down to the urban poor and out to the villages' (Caldwell 1968:184). If this were true, information on urban elites would definitely be more telling than rural studies. The validity of this assumption, however, has not yet been convincingly proved.

A second reason why elite studies are gaining popularity may be seen in the easy feasibility of research among elites. There is no language problem, one can work with self-administered questionnaires, and travelling can be cut down considerably. Geographical and other obstacles can further be reduced to a minimum when the sample consists of students or lecturers who reside at the same university as the researcher, as sometimes happens (e.g., Peil 1965; Caldwell 1965; Oppong n.d. (a) and n.d. (b); Kumekpor n.d.; Date-Bah n.d.). These advantages threaten to create a situation in which urban elite studies will outnumber contemporary rural oriented studies to such an extent that too little attention may be paid to the latter.

In this paper an attempt will be made to describe the position of marriage in a rural community in Ghana and to investigate whether certain changes in marriage which have been observed among the elites have 'diffused' or are likely to diffuse to the rural scene. Special attention will be given to those independent variables which, in the light of the elite studies, are most likely to promote changes in the traditional marriage system. These variables are age, education, and urban experience. A fourth variable, financial status, has been left aside as exact information on finances has not been collected. The paper focusses on types of sexual union, incidence of divorce, and jointness of conjugal relationships. Another important aspect of marriage change, filiation and residence of children, is not treated in this paper [see Bleek n.d. (b)].

1. THE SAMPLES

The original sample for this research was selected in a rather unorthodox way. There was no random selection of individuals, but instead two entire sections of a matrilineage were chosen as a sample. From these sections as many members as possible were interviewed. The aim of this approach was to gain a more complete insight into the dynamics of a lineage as a whole and to collect more reliable information about the individual members. The latter was possible by cross-checking most data through information given by members about each other. Participant observation was practised extensively.

The two sections of the lineage numbered only 76 living adult members at the time and not all of them could be included in the research. The sample is therefore rather small. Further, the selection of this particular lineage does not guarantee that it is representative of other lineages. These two disadvantages did not impair the initial aim of the study: to gain information about an arbitrary lineage, but they do render further generalization difficult. Both the smallness of the sample and the method of its selection imply that norms and conduct observed in this lineage may not occur in other lineages as well. On the other hand, we have no reason to believe that this particular lineage is atypical and we may expect that developments in this lineage occur in other Kwahu lineages as well. To confirm this we added, in a second research period, two samples of 100 men and nearly 200 women, both selected by quota sampling in the same rural town. Combined with the lineage sample, these two samples allow us to put some of our conclusions on a firmer statistical basis and to either propound or reject wider implications of our findings.

The three samples were based in a small town (4000 inhabitants) of the Kwahu Plateau, which is located 100 miles from Accra along the main road to Kumasi. The town lies about 15 miles from that main road. The Kwahu people are matrilineal like the better known Asante, and share their borders as well as most of their traditions with them. Most Kwahu are farmers, but a remarkably high proportion of them have gone into trading in Accra or some other town. It is believed that indigneous trading in the capital is almost entirely in the hands of Kwahu people. No less than 8% of all Kwahu lived in Accra during the 1960 population census. The total Kwahu population at that time numbered over 130, 000.

2. THE STATUS OF MARRIAGE

In Gibb's terminology the Kwahu are not an 'epainogamous' society, which means that the institution of marriage is not valued very highly (c.f. Gibbs 1963). To say that 'marriage is not highly valued' smacks of ethnocentrism. What criterion do we use when we speak about high or low evaluation, of marriage? How can we call the status of marriage low when after all, most Kwahu seem to enter marriage at one time or another? Looking at marriage from an emic point of view this argument sounds reasonable, but comparing Kwahu marriage with marriage in other African societies we can say without hesitation that it is not valued highly. Gibbs comes forward with a number of objective criteria which lend themselves to cross-cultural analysis. A society is 'epainogamous' when the marriage ceremony is a socially significant event, when the marital bond is not easily broken, and when conjugal rights and duties are adhered to. The structural features which in Gibb's model indicate the attachment of a high value to marriage can be summarized in two basic processes of social control: (1) the elimination of normative ambiguity through fixed conjugal rights and ceremonialization of the marriage bond; and (2) the rewarding of conformity to and the punishment of deviance from marital norms.

With respect to (1), conjugal rights and duties are ambiguous among the Kwahu. There are no strict rules as to where the wife and where the children should stay, how much the husband and how much the wife should contribute toward the upkeep of the family, how far the father's authority over the children goes and how far that of the mother's brother, who is entitled to take the children after divorce[1] and who after the death of the mother. Allocation of these rights depends on the initiative and social status of individuals rather than on clear cut rules. What is more, the marriage ceremony has little social significance. There is no public celebration as takes place on other occasions such as birth, death, and (formerly) puberty. The ceremony, which is divided into two stages, resembles the signing of a contract. The contract is sealed by the acceptance of the payments and the drinking of schnapps or palmwine. Not many people attend the function. The bride, as a rule, is not present and often the groom is absent as well. Someone acts on his behalf. This person may be his own father or a close maternal relative, but may also be a very remote relative or acquaintance who happens to be around. The meeting is not much different from the usual discussions and palavers that take place in the compound and are rounded off by the drinking of palmwine.

The amount of money involved in the payments varies from 8 to 40 cedis which is about £ 3 to £ 15, a rather low amount when we compare with payments in other African societies. The groom needs little, if any, assistance from relatives to pay this amount and, as a consequence, the marriage entails little social investment through reciprocal obligations.

Positive and negative sanctions, (2) that enforce the adherence to marriage rules are few. Sexual satisfaction can be obtained outside marriage without strong public disapproval and labour aid in the house or on the farm can be obtained from maternal relatives, particulary when a man continues to live with them after his marriage. Moreover, those who are legally married often do not enjoy all the advantages that marriage is supposed to offer. A man may receive little domestic or emotional satisfaction from his wife when she stays in a different house or goes on long journeys to visit her mother's family. He will be forced to do the household chores himself or to get domestic help from his sister or his sister's children. By the same token, a married woman may be frustrated by the fact that her husband gives little or no financial security to herself and her children, so that she has no choice other than to earn her own livelihood.

This situation is both cause and result of the fact that the institution of marriage is fragile and considered with lukewarm feelings and that many Kwahu feel more attached to their matrikin than to their conjugal partner.

However as we have seen, elite studies suggest that the status of marriage is now rising. Bonds with the extended family weaken and conjugal ties become stronger. The colourless ceremony of traditional marriage is replaced by the pomposity of a Western wedding, complete with wedding cake and bridesmaids. Divorce rates have reduced drastically and husband, wife, and children reside together. Let us investigate whether similar developments are discernable in the rural community under study.

3. TYPE OF SEXUAL UNION

Marital status

It was found that 22 (52%) of the 42 lineage members who were in their childbearing years were legally married, 8 (19%) were divorced at the time of research, 5 (12%) had never married, and 7 (17%) had a partner without having performed the required customs. We should further take into consideration that those presently divorced and those who had never married almost certainly had some kind of regular sexual relationship which was kept secret. This means that about half of the lineage had an 'illegal' relationship and half a 'legal'. We have put the term 'legal' and 'illegal' between inverted commas because the relations are not always experienced as such by the people concerned. A certain type of 'illegal' union, *mpena awadee*, for example, hardly bears any stigma of illicitness; the partners openly cohabit and behave like married people. In most cases the husband has fulfilled the first part of the marriage ceremony and people feel that the second part may follow at any time, even if it in fact never follows. It should further be observed that the distinction between married and not-married, or between legal and illegal, is more artificial than real. There is no distinct transition from being single to being married, or from an illegal to a legal union.[2] The development is an uninterrupted continuum and even close relatives may not be able to tell you someone's exact position in the continuum (c.f. van de Walle 1965:303).

The above figures suggest that marriage in the lineage has not gained the same importance that it has in elite circles. Members are little concerned about their marital status. Young men seem reluctant to enter a legalized union and try to stick to temporary unions. There is further slight evidence that female members of the lineage tend to become disenchanted with marriage and after one or more broken marriages satisfy themselves with non-legalized sexual unions (see Bleek 1975:157-68).

'Expainogamy' does not increase in any appreciable way with increase of education, as might perhaps be expected, and the influence of urban experience is difficult to assess because this experience is almost universal in the lineage (90%).

Information from and about the older generations seems to indicate that the institution of marriage is rather losing importance. The older members claim that in former times – when urban experience and education hardly played a role – customary marriage was valued more highly and alternative sexual unions were rarer than today. Even if we take these statements lightly the difference remains too big to be explained simply in terms of idealization of the past. The status of marriage seems to have fallen rather than to have risen in recent times.

Comparing the data of the lineage with those of the other two samples we meet some striking discrepancies (see Table 1).

The proportion of legally married is considerably higher among the respondents of the two larger samples. An evident conclusion would be that the lineage is atypical and that marriage in Kwahu enjoys a higher esteem than data of the lineage suggest. Another possible explanation of the

Table 1. *Marital status in three samples (percentages in brackets)*

		Lineage		Male sample		Female sample	
No partner	Widowed	–		–		1	(.6)
	Divorced	8	(19)	12	(12)	20	(11)
	Never married	5	(12)	12	(12)	6	(3)
	Legal marriage	21	(52)	69	(69)	132	(74)
	Illegal union	7	(17)	7	(7)	19	(11)
	Total	41	(100)*	100	(100)	178	(100)

* Missing observation = 1

discrepancy is that some respondents of the other two samples distorted some facts in order to become acceptable and to preclude further inquisitive questions. The latter explanation is more plausible. It was indeed discovered that during interviews in the female sample some lineage members, who happened to be included in that sample, gave misleading answers with regard to marital status, number of divorces, and knowledge and practice of birth prevention. This leads us to suspect that the actual incidence of legal marriage is lower than has been indicated in Table 1, and that more respondents were divorced or had an illegal relationship. This correction applies especially to the female sample.

In connection with this it is in order to sound a note of caution. Sociologists dealing with complex issues like marriage and divorce should not handle their information without a sense of suspicion, particulary in large-scale surveys which do not allow for personal observation and cross-checking.

In the – more reliable – male sample marital status was cross-tabulated with age, urban experience, and education. The never-married category was excluded to avoid bias towards younger age. Urban experience was shown to have no impact on marital status. With regard to education, the likelihood of being legally married decreases with the rise of educational level, althought the correlation is not quite significant ($p < .0721$; Table 2). The age factor does show a significant relationship. Among those who have not had a publicly known sexual partner the incidence of legal marriage is most common in the highest age group and least common in the lowest age group ($p. < .01$; Table 3). These correlations are remarkable in the sense that on the rural scene – in contrast to the elite – education and younger age are not associated with a more frequent compliance to marital norms but rather seem to lead to greater deviance from those norms.

It is regrettable that earlier ethnographic reports from Kwahu do not exist and reports from Asante do not contain the type of material which would enable us to look at marital status in a longer diachronic perspective. It is only on the basis of intergenerational developments within the lineage, combined with the information of Table 3 and personal communication with older informants that we cautiously suggest that the status of marriage seems to be falling rather than rising.

Table 2. *Education and marital status in the male sample (percentages in brackets)*

		Divorced*	Illegal union*	Legal marriage	Total
Education:	None/primary	1 (4)	3 (11)	23 (85)	27 (100)
	Middle school	10 (20)	1 (2)	40 (78)	51 (100)
	Beyond middle	1 (10)	3 (30)	6 (60)	10 (100)
	Total	12 (14)	7 (8)	69 (78)	88 (100)

$z = 1.47$ $p < .0721$ missing observations: 12 never married
* Combined for U-test.

Table 3. *Age and marital status in the male sample (percentages in brackets)*

	Divorced*	Illegal union*	Legal marriage	Total
Below 30	6 (19)	4 (13)	21 (68)	31 (100)
30–39	5 (20)	1 (4)	19 (76)	25 (100)
Over 40	1 (3)	2 (6)	29 (91)	32 (100)
Total	12 (14)	7 (8)	69 (78)	88 (100)

$z = 2.34$ $p < .01$ missing observations: 12 never married.
* Combined for U-test.

Another marriage survey, carried out by Pool between 1965 and 1966 among 2,700 women in Accra and 3,000 rural women in all regions of Ghana shows a similar development. There is a marked difference in the incidence of mutual consent unions between urban and rural women. Mutual consent unions are much more frequent among the urban based. The same applies, to a lower degree, to the category of divorcees. Pool's data also demonstrate that the incidence of mutual consent unions diminishes with the increase of age (Pool 1968:242).

The above information suggests strongly that urban experience, younger age and education *per se* do not raise the position of marriage. Other conditions are necessary before they can create a situation comparable to that in which the elite finds itself. Indeed, the urban experience of the elite is an intrinsically different experience from that of commoners.[3]

Church marriage[4]

Church marriage, which is gaining popularity among the urban elite, is rare in the rural town where our research was carried out (see Table 4), although 74% of the lineage, 82% of the female, and 83% of the male sample claimed to belong to a Christian church. That Christianity has had little impact on the marriage customs in Ghana is a well documented (c.f. Aryee 1967; Hulsen and Mertens n.d.). Both the Catholic and the Presbyterian church in town bless only one or two marriages per year. Church marriage is slightly more common among members of young independent churces, some of which allow polygyny, but on the whole people are little interested in acquiring this special status of 'Holy Matrimony', particulary if this entails indissolubility, as it does among the Catholics.

Table 4. *Customary marriage, church marriage, and marriage certificate in three samples (percentages in brackets)*

	Lineage	Male sample	Female sample
Customary marriage only	16 (39)	55 (55)	117 (65)
Cust. mar. plus church mar.	2 (5)	6 (6)	14* (8)
Cust. mar. certificate	3 (7)	8 (8)	4* (2)
Other	20 (49)	31 (31)	46 (26)
Total	41 (100)	100 (100)	178 (100)

Missing observations: lineage = 1; female sample = 1.
* Three have both church marriage and marriage certificate.

Marriage certificate

Marriage under the Marriage Ordinance (Cap. 127), which is becoming more common among the elite does not occur in any of the three samples. This type of marriage entitles the wife, and the children arising from that marriage, to a share of the estate of the husband when he dies intestate. This law clashes with traditional Kwahu inheritance rules, which stipulate that the entire estate belongs to the man's lineage and should be inherited by a maternal relative of his. The law further proscribes polygyny to men married under the Ordinance.

Some people (see Table 4) had their customary marriage registered at the District Council and had been given a marriage certificate. This type of registration, however, has nothing to do with marriage under Ordinance; it gives no inheritance rights to wife and children and does not preclude polygyny. The certificate is required by some employers and certain churches as a proof that one is married. Formerly, sworn affidavits from the family were accepted, but nowadays certificates from the District Council are preferred.[5]

Polygyny

Caldwell writes that 13% of his female elite respondents and 8% of his male respondents reported to be in a plural marriage union (1968:37). The corresponding figures for our female and male sample are 24% and 17% respectively, which is about twice as high (see Table 5).

Table 5. *Number of wives per husband in current or most recent marital union among respondents in three samples (percentages in brackets)*

	Lineage	Male sample	Female sample
1 wife	24 (83)	63 (83)	115 (76)
2 wives	4 (14)	9 (12)	29 (19)
3 wives	1 (3)	3 (4)	6 (4)
4/5 wives	–	1 (1)	1 (1)
Total	29 (100)	76 (100)	151 (100)

Missing observations: lineage = 13; male sample = 24, female sample = 28.

The relation of polygyny to age, urban experience, and education was tested in the male and female samples. A trend was shown in the expected direction: polygynously married respondents tended to be older, less educated, and to have less urban experience, but the relationship was significant in only one case, namely age and polygyny in the female sample (P = .02).

More detailed information about the lineage throws some light on this situation. Legal polygyny is no longer aspired to by the young who have been to school, but nevertheless it does occur among them. When it occurs it is usually because it is forced upon them or else because they find themselves in a situation where they consider a polygynous union the only way out. Such a situation exists when an extramarital affair results in a pregnancy and the man decides (or is pressed) to legalize this relationship with the woman by marrying her. Such an incident is presented in Case 1 and is only narrowly avoided in Case 3 further below. These unions, as a rule, are not destined to last for long.

Case 1

When Ntim was 21 years old and attending teacher training college he had a serious girlfriend in his home town. Unfortunately he made another girl pregnant and his friend left him. Ntim had to pay a fine to the parents of the pregnant girl and was asked to marry her 'so that the girl could become attached to me and I would not run away in future'.

During that same period Ntim met another girl in his (classificatory) brother's house. They slept together and some time later the girl reported that she was pregnant. According to Ntim she had been pregnant before but acted this way because she wanted to marry him as he was a student in training college. 'So when the child was born, I was held responsible and I had to accept it. If a woman says you are the one, there is no way to deny it.'

Ntim also married this girl legally, although he never stayed with her. It was his lineage head who insisted on marriage and paid the money because 'he did not like trouble'. Ntim divorced both wives a short time later.

If polygyny among the young is so closely linked up with unwanted – extramarital – pregnancies, it is to be expected that the one will decrease with the other. Elsewhere we have stated that birth control is practised predominantly in pre- and extramarital relations (Bleek 1974). Growing knowledge of efficient birth control will therefore certainly cut down the number of extramarital pregnancies and make unwanted polygynous unions unnecessary. Improvement of birth control methods will further establish a situation in which secret polygynous affairs can be carried on without resorting to legal polygyny.

4. DIVORCE

Another aspect of family change among the urban elite is the sharp decline of divorce. Such a development is certainly not discernible in the

Kwahu lineage. The divorce rate in the lineage has been consistently high over the past five generations. Taking as divorce rate 'the number of marriages ended in divorce, expressed as a percentage of all marriages' (see Barnes 1949), we found that the divorce rates of all marriages that had been recorded for five successive generations were remarkably high, namely: 62.50; 40.42; 60.66; and 47.06 beginning with the oldest (last two generations combined). It should be observed that these percentages apply only to strictly legalized marriages that were terminated. The percentages would have been much higher, particularly for the last two generations, if non-legalized but publicly accepted unions had been included. These unions *have* been included in Table 6, which shows the number of divorces in the three samples.

Table 6. *Number of divorces among ever-married respondents in three samples (percentages in brackets)*

		Lineage	Male sample	Female sample
Number of divorces:	0	11 (26)	32 (32)	83 (46)
	1	12 (29)	35 (35)	54 (30)
	2	10 (24)	13 (13)	17 (9)
	3	2 (5)	1 (1)	1 (1)
	4	1 (2)	4 (4)	1 (1)
	5	– –	2 (2)	– –
Never married/	6	1 (2)	– –	– –
unknown		5 (12)	13 (13)	23 (13)
Total		42 (100)	100 (100)	179 (100)
Average number of divorces per ever-married respondent:		1.30	1.03	0.61

Respondents in the female sample claim the lowest number of divorces, but the actual number is certainly higher. A later check proved that respondents had suppressed some cases of divorce.

The hypothesis, which could be made on the basis of elite studies, that the divorce rate will decline with urban experience, is not supported by our data.[6] It was noted that most respondents who had spent a considerable span of their lives in the city hardly differed from those who had never travelled. They had been totally re-integrated into their present rural environment. This remarkable phenomenon has also been observed elsewhere in Africa (see Köbben 1971:60).

Tabulation of education shows that the incidence of divorce diminishes when the educational level rises ($p < .01$), but the relationship is spurious. Most illiterate respondents are rather old and most educated ones belong to the younger generation. It would seem therefore, that the real predictor of divorce frequency is age. Those who are advanced in years have had more chance to terminate one or more marriages than the younger people who have just married. Table 7 shows that this – rather tautological – supposition is correct.

Table 7. *Number of divorces by age of respondents (male and female sample combined; percentages in brackets)*

	Age:	—29	30–39	40+	Total
Number of divorces:	0	74 (59)	31 (44)	10 (21)	115 (47)
	1*	42 (33)	29 (41)	18 (38)	89 (37)
	2+*	10 (8)	10 (14)	19 (40)	39 (16)
Total		126 (100)	70 (99)	47 (99)	243 (100)

$z = 4.26$ $p < .001$ missing observations: 34 never married.
* Combined for U-test

It is likely that those who are young will divorce in future, independent of whether they have been to school or not. The two following cases illustrate this point: both persons are 'educated', the younger has not yet divorced (he has not even married), the older has divorced twice.

Case 2
Atoubi is 22 years old. He finished middle school and attended a commercial school for two years. He is one of the six lineage members who have been educated beyond middle school. At the moment he is working in one of the ministries in the capital.

Atuobi had his first girl friend when he was about 17 years old. He and the girl attended the same school. The relationship ended because, as he said, the teacher liked the same girl. After this affair two other friendships followed which both ended because one of them moved to another place. At the moment he has his fourth friend, but he is not sure that he will keep her because he has heard some rumours that she moves with another man.

Atoubi says that he has always taken precautions to make sure that none of his girlfriends became pregnant.

Atoubi's expertise in contraception may well be the main reason that he has not yet married (read: been forced to marry) one of his girlfriends. Up to now, therefore, he has never divorced any of them either, but this is no guarantee that divorce will not come his way once he gets married. Manu's case (Case 3) could be a forecast of what may happen to Atuobi later on.

Case 3
Yaw Manu is 36 years old. After middle school he attended teacher training college for four years and he is now teaching in one of the Kwahu towns. He was divorced twice and is presently unmarried. When Manu was about 18 years old he made two girls pregnant, almost simultaneously. Both families pressed him to marry the girl. He managed to escape the first one by paying a fine, but he married the second girl. This marriage did not last long. A quarrel arose between Manu and his wife's brothers, and Manu decided to divorce her. After some time he selected a new wife with the help of his father's sister. As Manu was a catechist of the Catholic Church, he married her in church. They had two children, but after four years the woman ran away. Manu says that she did it because of family intrigues. Although the divorce ritual was never performed one may well consider it a divorce as it took place almost 10 years ago.

Manu has not married again. He seems very keen on his status as a catechist, which he would probably lose if he married another wife, because the Catholic Church does not recognize second marriages. Manu, therefore, prefers secret liaisons about which he only gives vague information.

Quantitative information of the three samples and qualitative insights from the above cases suggest that education, at the intermediate level we are dealing with, has little stabilizing effect on marriage. Those who have been to middle school and those who have attended some college beyond middle school do not have distinctly different marital attitudes and practices from those who have never been to school. They are still in a predominantly traditional environment where marriage is of secondary importance and natal ties come first. In this environment marital stability has much less to do with social repectability than among the urban elite. Only in special cases, as indicated in Case 3, can marriage have this connotation.

Fortes has suggested that '... divorce is correlated with the degree to which a person has jural status that is independent of his or her status as spouse. For a woman the significant factor is the degree to which she retains her status as daughter and sister after marriage, for this determines her claims on support as well as her jural status outside the conjugal relationship' (Fortes 1959). This certainly applies to the Kwahu lineage where kinship bonds are considered of higher value than conjugal ones. A woman derives her status form her extraction rather than from her marriage, unless her husband's status is exceptionally high. Women of the lineage tend to stick to their maternal relatives during their marriage if geographical distances permit this.[7] In such a case, divorce brings about very few changes in the life of the Kwahu woman, and indeed of the Kwahu man. It is not surprising, therefore, that marriages survive longer when they are characterized by common residence of husband and wife, than when husband and wife reside with their respective relatives (see Table 8; relation not significant). In the following tables we have tabulated all marriages in the lineage that ended in divorce and all marriages that lasted 12 years and longer. The marriages extend over five generations and cover a period of about 60 years.

Table 8. *Conjugal residence and divorce in the lineage (derived from Bleek 1975:205; percentages in brackets)*

	Common residence husband and wife	Separate residence husband and wife	Total
Marriages			
ended in divorce	35 (49)	37 (51)	72 (100)
lasting marriages	16 (70)	7 (30)	23 (100)
Total	51 (54)	4 (46)	95 (100)

df = 1 $x^2 = 3.07$ $10 > p > .05$ Missing observations: 7.

The interests of the conjugal family are sometimes diametrically opposed to those of the wife's or husband's matrilineage. A woman who attaches herself wholly to her husband can only do so by breaking away from her matrilineage. Her children are kept outside the sphere of influence of her matrikin which may have emotional and judicial consequences for them and negative feelings are likely to crop up from the side of the matrilineage. By the same token, a man who attempts to favour his own children above his sister's, particularly in financial terms, incurs his relatives' displeasure. In this situation it is clear that both matrilineages are not always eager to repair a strained conjugal relationship and may be more interested in a divorce.

Looking at the reasons for divorce that are offered we are therefore not surprised to find that one of the most frequent reasons in the lineage is is 'interference of relatives' (see Table 9). It should be noted that the responses in Table 9 were not pre-coded. Categorization of reasons took place only at the stage of analysis.

Table 9. *Reasons for divorce in the lineage (derived from Bleek 1975:212; percentages in backets)*

Bad conduct/neglect of marital duties	16 (14)
Interference of relatives	13 (12)
Infertility/low fertility	11 (10)
No love	10 (9)
Interference of other partner	10 (9)
'Partner travelled and left me behind'	9 (8)
Quarrel/beating	6 (5)
Some other reason*	18 (16)
Reason unknown	20 (18)
Total	113 (101)**

* These include: breach of exogamy rule, failure to complete marriage customs, excessive drinking, money palaver, witchcraft, sickness, spendthrift, disagreement, religion and impertinence.

** The total exceeds the total number of divorces because of multiple reasons.

As can be seen, another common reason for divorce was infertility or low fertility. This does not necessarily mean that the woman is always blamed for the failure to produce children and consequently divorced. Among the Kwahu as a matrilineal society it is the woman's lineage which is most concerned about fertility and not infrequently it is the man who is blamed for the failure to produce children and forced to let his wife go so that she has another chance. Such a situation is presented in the next case, which took place about 35 years ago.

Case 4

Informant: 'My second wife was also from A. I was about 30 and she 14. She had not menstruated yet when I married her. We stayed together in the same house and the marriage lasted about 9 years. We had one child.

'After the first child she never became pregnant again. I fought hard for it, but I was not successful. The wife's family therefore claimed her back. No payments were made.'

The relationship between marital fertility and divorce is extremely significant, as can be seen in Table 10, but the causal implications are ambiguous. Low fertility can be the cause but also the result of divorce. It is evident that a marriage which ends in divorce after a few years cannot produce many children.

Another reason that is frequently proffered is 'interference of other partner'. This reason points, amongst other things, at polygyny. The Kwahu

Table 10. *Marital fertility and divorce in the lineage (derived from Bleek 1975:210; percentages in brackets)*

	No grown children	1–2 grown children	3 or more grown children	Total
Marriages ended in divorce	38 (49)	30 (39)	9 (12)	77 (100)
lasting marriages	5 (20)	3 (12)	17 (68)	25 (100)
Total	43 (42)	33 (32)	26 (26)	102(100)

df = 2 $x^2 = 35.11$ $p < .001$

term for co-wife, *kora*, which means 'jealousy', hints at the explosive atmosphere which can surround a polygynous household, particularly when the co-wives share domestic tasks and/or reside in the same compound. Tabulation of polygynous and monogamous marriages shows a trend in the expected direction: polygynous unions are less stable, but the correlation does not reach the 5% level, due to the small size of the sample.

Table 11. *Polygyny and divorce in the lineage (derived from Bleek 1975: 204; percentages in brackets)*

	Polygynous	Monogamous	Total
Marriages ended in divorce	44 (61)	28 (39)	72 (100)
lasting marriages	9 (39)	14 (61)	23 (100)
Total	53 (56)	42 (44)	95 (100)

df = 1 $x^2 = 3.41$ $.10 > p > .05$ missing observations: = 7.

A last reason that deserves our attention is 'Partner travelled and left me behind'. In eight of the nine cases it is the husband who leaves the wife. One woman explains for example: 'He was transferred to Kanongo and never returned. That was the end of our relationship'. Similar remarks are made by others. Although most of these unions were not completely legalized, the fact that the men could terminate a conjugal relationship and leave their wife and sometimes child(ren) simply by moving to another place indicates the lightness with which they regarded the conjugal bond. No legal action was taken against them and some, who originated from outside Kwahu, completely vanished.

The list of reasons in Table 9 tallies with a list of traditional grounds for divorce that was given to us by older informants. However, one outstanding reason that was mentioned by the old is missing in the list of the lineage, namely adultery. Adultery on the part of the husband is generally condoned and not really considered as adultery. Most wives take it for granted that their husbands sleep with other women at certain times, particularly in the pre- and postpartum period. Adultery by the wife, on the other hand, is seldom overlooked and may result in domestic tiffs and eventually in divorce, but a man will not present adultery as the reason for dismissing his wife. It is felt that such a person makes himself ridiculous when he publicly admits that he has been cuckolded, and he will prefer to think of another reason. The same applies to another ground for divorce that causes embarrassment: namely witchcraft.

This brief reflection on reasons for divorce makes clear that the reasons which are brought forward are not always the real reasons and, as a consequence, one cannot draw definite conclusions from them. Furthermore, it should be taken into account that there can exist several versions of the same divorce case, depending on who is the informant; the husband, the wife or someone else.

Closely connected with this is the question: Who took the initiative? Out of 54 cases of divorce that could be reconstructed with some degree of certainty 24 had been initiated by the husband, 26 by the wife,[8] and 4 were the result of a mutual decision. Here again the information has to be handled cautiously, for it seems probable that a divorced interviewee is inclined to claim the initiative even when the opposite is true; it is more honourable to divorce than to be divorced.

As regards the legalization of conjugal separation, the divorce ritual is even simpler than the marriage ceremony, although the preceding palavers and family court sessions may be intricate. The ritual consists of the husband throwing white powder before his wife's feet, or of someone else doing this on his behalf. If the wife seeks the divorce, she usually pays back a small part of the marriage payment, the so-called *tiri nsa* or *kɛtɛ ase hyɛ*, which varies from 8 to 16 shillings (40 to 80 p.).

No substantial information was collected about the present use of this ritual, but it is our impression that some do not even perform it today. Others perform it in such a slapdash way that it leaves little doubt about the low importance they attach to it. Case 5 describes such a ritual.

Case 5

At 6:30 this morning[9] Dwamena performed the divorce ritual of his marriage. He was dressed in his farming clothes, dirty T-shirt, and tattered trousers. His wife came to his compound (she lives in her own house) with someone to represent her father. No other people had come to attend the function apart from us. Two other women and a couple of children were present only because they happened to be there. Some stopped what they were doing to listen to what was said, others quietly continued their activities.

The whole ceremony took about 5 minutes. First there was some wrangling about money and farm land, then Dwamena went to a room of one of the women and returned with some dusting powder. He invited us to throw the powder before his wife's feet, but when we pointed out that we preferred to remain observers, a young boy of about 14 years did it, laughing. Dwamena's ex-wife gave a shilling to the boy and wanted to give the divorce fee of 16 shillings to Dwamena, but he refused to accept it and the money was divided among the people present. That was the end. Dwamena went straight to his farm, the woman returned home and the people in the compound continued with their work.

In this section we have looked at some dynamics of the dissolution of conjugal unions. It has been shown that both the husband the wife can initiate divorce and that their matrilineages can play an influential role in this process, Divorce brings about no far-reaching changes in the lives of the people concerned, neither domestically nor emotionally, and little fuss is made about it. Marriage and divorce in this rural community stand in sharp contrast to what has been written about the urban elite. Among the Kwahu people divorce is frequent and there are few structural supports that uphold the status of marriage.

5. JOINTNESS OF CONJUGAL ROLE-RELATIONSHIPS

Husband-wife relationships among the urban elite are described as being more egalitarian than they used to be. Caldwell (1968) puts it in rather general terms, and Oppong (1974) has devised a scale consisting of a list of variables in order to measure jointness in the conjugal relationship more exactly and objectively.

In this section three variables will be examined as indices of jointness or segregation in conjugal roles in a more rural setting. The three variablesare presented in the form of questions.

1. Do you eat together with your wife (husband)?
2. Do you (does your husband) sometimes help with pounding *fufu?*[10]
3. Do you (does your husband) sometimes carry foodstuffs when coming back from the farm?

These three variables were chosen because they point at activities which a man was traditionally not supposed to do, except, perhaps, when he was alone with his wife in a farming settlement where nobody could see him.

We hypothesize that deference to these male dominated rules has diminished among the young, those who have been to school, and those who live or have lived in an urban centre, Application of the Chi-square test shows, however, that urban experience has no influence at all on jointness of conjugal roles. The age factor has some tendency in the expected direction, but it is not statistically significant. The only significant relation found is between education and eating together (see Table 12).

Table 12 *The practice of spouses eating together related to the education of the responding spouse (male and female sample combined; percentages in brackets).*

	Eating together	Not eating together	Total
No education	20 (20)	81 (80)	101 (100)
Primary school	15 (50)	15 (50)	30 (100)
Middle school	46 (44)	59 (56)	105 (100)
Beyond mid. school	8 (57)	6 (43)	14 (100)
Total	89 (36)	161 (64)	250 (100)

df = 3 x^2 = 19.63 p = .0002 missing observations: 29.

When we relate the three jointness variables to sex of respondent, the relationship is statistically significant in all three cases: men are more inclined to claim that they eat with their wives, help them to pound the *fufu* and carry foodstuffs from farm and women are more inclined to deny all these activities.

Although the three selected variables are inadequate for the measurement of jointness and segregation of roles, they do reveal some interesting points: 45% of the married men below 30 years of age do not eat with their wives, 23% of them never assist their wives to pound the *fufu*, and 13% of them consider it below the dignity of a man to carry home the products of the farm. According to the female respondents the male domination is even stronger: 64% of the women below 30 state that their husbands do not eat with them, 46% that they never help them with the *fufu*, and 48% that they never carry foodstuffs.

As for education, 46% of the men who have been to school state that they take their meals separately from their wives, 28% of them say that they never help to prepare the *fufu*, and 24% that they do not carry foodstuffs. Of the married women who have been to school 59% say that they have married a man who does not eat with them, 45% a man who never helps them with the *fufu*, and 43% a man who does not carry foodstuffs.

A necessary condition of shared conjugal roles seems to be common residence of the spouses. This condition, however, is not met in over 40% of all sexual unions in the male and female sample and in the lineage. Among the Kwahu a married woman is expected to continue living with her matrikin if her husband lives in the same town and has no house of his own (cf. Bleek 1972). The supposition that this custom of lineage domination will be rejected by the young and more educated and by those who have lived in the town, is not confirmed. On the contrary, separate conjugal residence shows a slight tendency to be more common among the young and those who have attended school. Once again the factor of urban experience has little impact on the issue.

6. CONCLUSION

This study of a rural community suggests that changes in marriage and family life which have been observed among the Ghanaian elite are not likely to affect the rural Kwahu, at least not in the near future. In some respects the gap between elite and commoners even seems to be widening. In the community that was studied, marriage under the Ordinance does not occur and customary marriage is subordinate to lineage interests. The marriage ceremony has little social significance, divorce has remained a common phenomenon and is easily obtainable and alternative sexual unions not infrequently replace the legal type of marriage. The hypothesis that conjugal roles will become more joint among the young, the educated, and those with urban experience is only partially substantiated. In Kwahu, marriage is certainly not gaining more importance. It is further evident that discussions on the reform of the Marriage Ordinance in Ghana bear no relevance to the members of this Kwahu Community or to many other Ghanaians except those who belong to the urban elite.

NOTES

1. Rattray (1929:9) quotes a proverb *Wo yere nko mma mmera* ('Your wife may go but the children will come to you') suggesting that the father takes the children after divorce. Actual practice does not corroborate this 'rule'.
2. Cf. Rattray (1927:76): '... the legal union of the sexes appeared to be looked upon as such a natural step from the preceding state as not to have required as many new rites as we might expect.'

3. Levine made a similar observation among the Yoruba in Nigeria: 'When one contrasts the most westernized or modernized segment of the urban Yoruba population with the least, one is also comparing people differing enormously in income and occupational prestige. From one point of view it is a comparison of new and old, but it is also that of high and low, rich and poor' (Levine 1967:224).
4. For the legal position of couples married in church, see Oppong 1974:51.
5. I am indebted to Ekow Daniels for explaining these details to me.
6. Pool even found the urban divorce rate to be twice as high as the rural one (Pool 1968:246).
7. Fortes' remark that Asante women tend to remain in the natal lineage in the early years of their marriage, then move out to live with their husbands and return to the lineage later (Fortes 1949:78), is not supported by his own data (see Bleek 1972:32). Such a 'developmental cycle' was not observed in the Kwahu lineage either.
8. Despite male domination in conjugal relationships the number of female initiatives to divorce points at the same time to a high degree of autonomy of the woman. Paradoxically, among the elite, where female emancipation has made great strides, educated woman have lost this very form of autonomy. Oppong writes : 'As regards the woman's third resource, the customary sanction of withdrawal from marriage and the possibility of entering a new and more rewarding conjugal relationship, the position has again altered to the detriment of educated wives... an educated divorcee, past her early youth, will be unlikley to re-marry a man of the same social and economic standing as the first (graduate) husband...' (Oppong 1974:118).
9. It should be noted that such an early hour for the divorce ritual is customarily prescribed.
10. *Fufu* is a staple food in Southern Ghana. It is made from yam, cocoyam, plantain, or cassave, which is boiled and then pounded into a sticky paste. The pounding is heavy and tedious work.

The emergence of the 'stranger-permit marriage' and other new forms of conjugal union in rural Sierra Leone 12

BARBARA E. HARRELL-BOND AND ULRICA RIJNSDORP
Afrika-Studiecentrum, Leiden

The trend towards the conjugally-based nuclear family in Africa, which has been interpreted as a response to the processes of urbanization and migration and the influence of western education and religion, has been well-documented.[1] That the effects of social and economic changes in African countries have not been confined to urban centres but have penetrated to the rural areas is well known.[2] However, studies of the influence of these processes on the structure of the family and on marital role behaviour in the African rural setting are relatively rare. The findings in this discussion resulted from a study of family law in Sierre Leone.[3] During the course of this research it was possible to examine the changes that are taking place in the role of women, and the new forms of conjugal unions which have developed in response to general social and economic changes in the society.

There are sixteen so-called tribes or ethnic groups indigenous to Sierra Leone, a small country where tribal groups are not, for the most part, localized. The two largest tribes are the Mende and the Temne. Intermarriage across tribal lines is very common (Harrell-Bond 1975). The *Poro* society for men and the *Bundu* society for women are closed associations which occur in nearly every part of the country, and these associations also cut across tribal lines (Turay 1971). Among the indigenous groups a considerable degree of cultural uniformity exists throughout the country, and the principles governing marriage under traditional customary law are virtually the same from place to place (Joko-Smart 1969; Harrell-Bond and Rijnsdorp 1975). The new forms of conjugal union which are discussed in this paper are most strongly institutionalized in the South.[4]

TRADITIONAL MARRIAGE PRACTICES

Before discussing our findings, we must provide a brief sketch of the organization of traditional marriage and family life. This description may be said to represent an ideal model of traditional behaviour. It is still possible to observe the practice of this pattern of family organization in rural areas, and the principles involved still form the standard for evaluating behaviour.

The traditional economic organization is based on a localized patrilineal kin group co-operating in subsistence agriculture. A man's status is bound up with the number of wives, children, and other dependants that he has. The amount of land over which he holds farming rights is associated with the size of the household for which he is responsible. Rice is the staple crop, but such supplementary crops as cassava, yams, guineacorn, cotton, benniseed, pepper, palm kernels, bananas, and several other vegetables are also grown. After a crop of rice has been harvested from one plot, the land is left to lie fallow for a period of five to seven years, although the women may plant their gardens on deserted rice farms. The heavy work of clearing and tilling the farm land is done by the men, but the women take a large share of the responsibility for planting, weeding, and harvesting the crops. A man is responsible for ensuring that the family has a sufficient supply of rice to last throughout the year. However, the day-to-day maintenance of the family depends very heavily on the dietary supplements resulting from the gardening activities of the women. Men do some hunting, but women catch the fish which provide the largest source of protein consumed.

In Sierra Leone marriage involves the transfer of rights over the sexual, domestic, and procreative services of a woman from her family of orientation to the family of her husband. Arrangements are made between the male members of both families, and the consent of both family heads is mandatory. In addition, the husband's family present marriage payments to the wife's family[5] and observe certain ceremonial obligations. Through receiving the girl in marriage, the husband assumes certain economic obligations to her relatives so long as the union remains extant. By accepting marriage payments from the husband's family (which are distributed among a large number of the girl's relatives), her family assumes the obligation to encourage the stability of the union. Should a divorce occur the girl's family will be called upon to refund the payments they have received, together with any other contributions the husband may have subsequently made to them.

Girls are marriageable after they have reached puberty and have been initiated into the *Bundu* society.[6] There are several ways of establishing a union between man and woman which is recognised as marriage. The most highly valued form is with a virgin. Infant betrothal, a practice formerly common, today rarely occurs except when families wish their daughters to be married into a chief's or other prestigious family, or when two men seek to link their families in view of their long-standing friendship.

The marriage of a woman who is a party to a prior marriage that has broken down, may take place by means of arrangements with her family and the repayment of the marriage payments to her former husband. The family which has already repaid the marriage payments to secure the divorce of their daughter may take new financial arrangements for her marriage with a prospective husband.

A widow may be remarried by a member of her deceased husband's family who assumes responsibility for her and the children. This arrangement involves the consent of the widow and some token gifts to her family as a symbol of the marriage payments and the 'remarriage', This practice is locally referred to as 'widow inheritance'. Failure on the part of the widow to accept a member of her husband's family as a new husband leads to 'divorce' proceedings, the family of the deceased claiming the recovery of the marriage payments from her relatives as well as all the contributions that the husband made to them during the marriage. The children born during the union remain with the husband's family.[7]

'Pledge marriages' have also been practised for some time. In this form of marriage a man may hand his daughter over to a creditor as security on a loan. He does not receive marriage payments, although he should be able to expect greater consideration with respect to the repayment of his loan. A marriage which is initiated by the pledge for a debt does not end when the loan is repaid. In fact, in practice, these debts are rarely repaid except in the case of divorce.

Finally, 'friendship marriages', as they are referred to locally, do occur though they are never the preferred form of marriage (Little 1962: 157). A girl's family may agree to such a union with a man without marriage payments either because he is very poor or because for some reason the family have had difficulty in arranging a more desirable marriage for their daughter. Although marriage is generally patrilocal, in these cases the husband usually remains in the wife's family's village, and he is expected to fulfill the usual obligations to them throughout the duration of the union.[8]

Under customary law a woman is not regarded as legally competent. In any dispute in which she may become involved she must be represented by her father if she is unmarried, or by her husband or a male member of his family if she is married. As a result of her legal incompetence, she may never live independent of her own natal family, or, if married, independent of her husband or his family. If problems occur between herself and her husband, it is to her family that either of them may appeal. The wife's family continue to take an interest in her well-being, and a husband who fails in his responsibilities to his wife or who is cruel to her has to answer to them for his actions. The prestige of the whole family is affected by the manner in which wives are treated. Families are hesitant to arrange for the marriage of a daughter into a family having a reputation for permitting the ill-treatment of wives. Similarly, if a wife is staying temporarily with her family (women usually return to their home villages to give birth to their children), her relatives are responsible to her husband and his family for her behaviour. A woman is under the authority of her husband and must seek his permission for all activities.

When a wife commits adultery the husband may flog her, but he also has a serious case against the man who has trespassed on his sexual rights over the woman. The lover, together with the wife, is brought by the husband before the village chief and elders. The lover is forced to pay the husband compensation. In former times he might even have been bonded to the husband as a slave to work on his farms.

Traditionally women do not have rights to personal property other than the few pots for cooking and the clothes that they bring to the marriage. Although a woman may inherit from her father's family, even this property (usually rights over land) is controlled by her brothers or other male members of her family. She is expected to allow produce from her garden to be used by the whole family. When a woman dies the husband has a duty to show her relatives the personal items, such as pots, clothing, and ornaments, that she has left. If she has borne no children he should offer these things to her family. As has been noted, although a woman is expected to be economically active during her marriage, her husband has rights over all the produce of her labours.

Children are expected to support and care for their parents in their old age. Women are especially dependent on their children for this security. The institution of widow inheritance should ensure that a woman is cared for even when her husband is deceased. In practice, however, because of the varying degrees to which the husband's family honour their obligations to the widow, women would prefer to be able to depend on their children, especially their sons.

Children born to a marriage are regarded as members of the husband's patrilineage, regardless of who is the genitor, subject to the husband's power to reject a child born to his wife as a result of an adulterous relationship. The most usual outcome of this situation is for the child to be reared by the wife's family. Such a situation usually leads to the estrangement of the husband and wife, if not divorce.[9] Rules of succession and inheritance are very flexible. Ideally, the first wife's eldest son should succeed to the father's position.[10] In practice, however, this does not always happen. A man may choose the child of a younger, more favoured wife as his successor. Since a man's successor is usually known only to the elders in the village and the name announced after his death, co-wives are involved in continuous competition to secure this position for their children.

A man may divorce his wife on a number of grounds including failure to perform domestic services, disobedience, repeated adultery, practising witchcraft, desertion, refusal to cohabit, and inability to get along with co-wives. A wife may divorce her husband on the grounds of extreme cruelty, failure to maintain her, incest, and impotence.

When a husband takes the initiative to divorce his wife, he is obliged to indicate clearly to her male relatives that he is divorcing her. He is required to prove the ground for his actions before any discussion of the recovery of his marriage payments can proceed. Recoverable marriage payments include all the expenditures from the time of betrothal to the point of divorce, including all the gifts made to the wife's family. The assessment of these amounts involves protracted discussion and dispute between the members of both families. Whatever sum is fixed upon is obtained by taking up a collection from a wide group of kin. They always attempt to reconcile the couple. The husband's case for recovering his marriage payments under these circumstances is very weak. In view of this most men tend to ignore troubles until the wife takes the initiative, usually by running away or by committing some other offence such as taking a lover. Most often the husband of a recalcitrant wife returns her to her parents' home, complains about her behaviour, and takes no further action.

On the other hand, when the wife seeks a divorce from her husband, he is in a stronger position to recover his marriage payments. It is her responsibility to prove to her family that her actions are justified, so that they will be persuaded to repay the husband and secure the divorce. However, in all but the most extreme cases of cruelty, her family try to reconcile the parties.

The maintenance responsibilities of the husband are limited to supporting the extant union. Since the custody of the children is a right of the husband, the problem of their support after a divorce does not arise. In divorce a woman may be stripped of all her possessions except those which she brought to the marriage.

SOCIAL CHANGES AFFECTING THE FAMILY

Over the past hundred years radical social and economic changes have taken place in Sierra Leone affecting even the remotest sections of the country. Trading activities encouraged some farmers to begin to plant cash crops such as coffee, cacao, oranges, and pineapple, and to sell their surplus rice. The imposition of taxes, beginning with the Hut Tax of 1898 (Fyfe 1967), made it necessary to produce surplus crops throughout the country. The increasing availability of imported manufactured goods revolutionized the definitions of minimal requirements. The subsistence economy gradually gave way to a cash economy. Today a great emphasis is laid on gaining individual wealth and many court cases arise as a result of the breakdown of family responsibility.[11]

The availability of employment in urban centres, most particularly in Freetown, the capital, encouraged large-scale migration of both men and women from the rural areas. A more dramatic motivation for migration was the discovery of diamonds which drew men and even women from the remotest sections of the country to the diamond areas.[12] The gradual extension of schools encouraged many families to send their boys away from the farm to receive an education. As a result there was a shortage of farm labour in most parts of the country. Farm production was further affected by the growing infertility of the land. As the population increased it was impossible for the land to lie fallow long enough for it to recover its former level of fertility. As a result of these factors, farm production fell until in the 1950's it became necessary to import rice. Where once the rural areas provided a surplus to sell to the towns, now even some farmers found it necessary to buy rice to supplement the family's supply. The shortage of farm labour, the need to purchase food to supplement the family supply, and the requirement of cash for purchasing imported goods and for paying tax made it increasingly necessary for people to engage in activities other than farming to earn money. Since women, through their farming and gardening activities, carried the chief responsibility for the day-to-day maintenance of the family, these economic pressures have also fallen on them. The possibilities of engaging in petty trade have encouraged women to break out of their conventional role within the household in their efforts to secure themselves and their children economically.

The development of a network of roads, the greater availability of means of transport, and the building of the railway which linked a great number of towns in the country encouraged the movement of people. Increasingly kin groups have become dispersed. Today most villages are ethnically heterogeneous. The protection and security provided by the traditional family structure have become attenuated because kin groups are increasingly dispersed. It is common for people to live far away from those relatives who would be responsible for assisting them. Just how dispersed is the extended family is illustrated by the fact that cases were encountered where the validity of a marriage was challenged because the husband was accused of 'marrying from the wrong side of the family' or 'not knowing his in-laws'. These cases were the result of a husband arranging the marriage of his wife's daughter by a former marriage. Marriages must be arranged by the male members of the girl's family, not by her mother or new husband. In most of these cases it appeared that the plaintiff was unaware that he had negotiated his marriage with the 'wrong' relatives. Such a problem could not arise if people were living amongst their kinsmen.[13]

Other influences have also come to bear upon the traditional family system. During their colonial rule, the British imposed the English-type court and legal system. Although they allowed customary law to continue to be practised in the Provinces, influences from the English system began to filter down to the local level very quickly. In the 1950's the judicial function was transferred from the traditional rulers, the Paramount Chiefs, to court presidents who were appointed by the government (Brooke 1954). Local Courts were established to replace the former native courts. These Local Courts are under the supervision of the Ministry of the Interior. Recently their jurisdiction has been extended to include some statute law which is based on English law (Harrell-Bond and Rijnsdorp 1975). Although customary cases are supposed to be decided according to customary law, these Local Courts do not, for the most part, admit that women are legally incompetent under customary law, but allow them to represent themselves in their own disputes. These courts are also beginning to recognize the rights of women to own their own property (particularly when they pay property tax and register houses which they build in their own names). They are even beginning to recognize in divorce cases the rights of women to property which was obtained through the joint efforts of the husband and wife.[14]

The official registration of births provides extra-familial evidence of paternity, and, by implication, of legitimacy. Such institutions as the Magistrate's Court (which administers English-based statutory law) and the Department of Social Welfare have now become arenas for settling family disputes. These do not advise or decide cases only on the basis of customary law, and they do not recognize the legal incompetence of women or the sole right of a father to his children. Most important, they do not question the right of a woman to reside separately from her husband or her family. They provide a means for a woman to secure maintenance for her children from their father when she is separated from her husband and not living in the care of her family.[15]

THE PERSISTENCE OF SOME TRADITIONAL VALUES

However, three important principles of traditional family organization persist and must be considered in order for us to understand the new forms of conjugal union and the changes in recognition of the right of the legal husband to sue for compensation for the loss of his wife's sexual and domestic services. Firstly, the husband retains the right to claim custody of the children whom his wife bears, regardless of who is their genitor. Secondly, the right of a husband in the case of divorce to recover the marriage payments that he made to the wife's family is still recognized by the courts applying customary law. Finally, it is still considered improper for a woman to live without the care and protection of a man. It is regarded as a threat to the community's moral standards for a single woman to be moving about on her own, and certainly as unbecoming to the woman. Because of the high incidence of women living apart from their families or their husbands, it has even been written into some chiefdom regulations that no woman is allowed to reside on her own without the care and protection of a man. Formerly, this 'man' had to be either her father, another male relative, or her husband. Today this rule has been altered in practice to include *any* man.

In the traditional family the married woman's security is heavily dependent upon the goodwill of her husband and his family. Their willingness to fulfill their obligations to her rests on her good performance of her domestic duties, her obedience to her husband and respectfulness towards his relatives, her ability to get along with her co-wives, the fact that she bears children who survive, the force of community opinion, and the continued concern of her family for her welfare. Failure on any one of these counts will erode her position. Once her relationship within her husband's family begins to deteriorate, her only refuge is with her own family. Their willingness to support her case will depend on their own ability to repay the marriage payments and their assessment of her chances for remarriage. They will not welcome the idea of her continuing indefinitely as their dependant.

If her husband dies, the woman's situation is precarious. Although she may be 'inherited' as a wife of one of her husband's male relations, who is obliged to provide for her, she will be subordinate to his other wives and her children will take a second place in the family to those children whose father is alive.

The relationship which has always afforded a woman the greatest amount of security is that which exists between herself and her children, particularly her sons. Early in life children are taught their obligations to their mother. Even if they have been deprived of a mother's presence and care during their childhood, men and women have a highly developed sense of loyalty and a strong attachment to her. Part of their relationship with her includes the expectation that they will support her in her old age.[16] Hence, women are strongly motivated to work for the advancement of their own children. Competition between co-wives for the betterment of their own children is a source of considerable friction within the household.[17]

WOMEN'S ECONOMIC ACTIVITIES

It is understandable, given the transformation of the rural society and the economic possibilities which lie outside the household, that wives find the requirements of their traditional role burdensome and confining. Today women in the rural areas may be involved in all kinds of economic activities. They engage in petty trade, selling vegetables, fruit, or cooked food along the roadside. Others have more extensive business interests such as selling rice, cement, or firewood, or owning transport vehicles. Some build houses in larger towns and rent them. Many have stalls selling a variety of imported goods or small bars which serve drinks. Women are often involved in the *gara* trade,[18] some even employing several men. Many of these business activities require that women travel a great deal and spend long periods away from the household.

Because the cash requirements of the household are usually greater than most men can afford, many husbands may even encourage their wives' trading activities by providing them with the initial capital.[19] Other women are able to secure loans to start their trading from members of their family. There is a considerable variation in the attitudes of husbands towards their wives' business activities and the necessary separations that they entail.

SEPARATION OF SPOUSES

Under customary law the husband retains certain privileges even when he is separated from his wife, no matter how long this separation may last. He continues to have sexual rights over his wife and so may sue for compensation any man involved in an adulterous relationship with her. He may also sue her family for 'giving his wife to another man' since if she is not residing with her husband, her family should be answerable for her actions. Furthermore, in principle, a husband has control over all the economic gains of his wife. If he has loaned her money to trade, he can at any time sue her for his initial investment, and in many cases he will include, as interest, any money that he believes she has earned in profits. He continues to have a right to claim any children born to his wife. Moreover, during a separation, a husband may exercise the right to suspend his economic obligations to her family. If a wife has left without his consent, he is also relieved of any responsibility to maintain her. Finally, and most important, he always has the right to seek a divorce and sue his wife's family for the return of his marriage payments and all the other contributions made to them. The strength of his case for recovering these monies is only increased by her prolonged failure to co-habit and perform domestic duties, not to mention the increasing possibility of her committing further marital offences.

Furthermore, the practice has grown up of suing a wife and/or her family for compensation for the offence of 'self detention' or 'detention of wife' (i.e., the refusal by the wife, or the unwillingness of her parents to force her, to return to the marital home). At the same time, since customary law allows for plural marriage, it may be assumed that the husband is not suffering a total loss of domestic services since they are probably being provided by a co-wife.

THE 'STRANGER-PERMIT MARRIAGE'

While separation may not disadvantage a husband, it does put the wife in a highly ambiguous position. If she involves herself in a relationship with another man, she puts her family and the man in legal jeopardy vis-à-vis her husband. At the same time, given the geographical dispersion of the extended family, her own economic activities, and the general acceptance of the importance of bearing children, it is highly unlikely, even if it were possible, that a woman would be content to remain simply under the authority, care, and protection of her own family. Moreover, as we have seen, she is often allowed to reside on her own when her business activities may necessitate long periods of residence in a different community from that of her husband or her family. Either as a result of the local regulation or her own inclinations to live with a man of her choice, a woman is often found cohabiting with an unrelated man. Because of the commonness of this practice (and the attending excess of court cases in which husbands are suing for compensation for adultery), an informal conjugal union having the limited sanction of the local authorities has grown up in some parts of the country. It has been dubbed the 'stranger-permit marriage'.[20] Some background information must be provided if this new institution is to be understood.

When a stranger enters a village he must present himself (or be presented by his host) to the chief of the village. A small gift or 'shake-hand' is given to the chief, who, by receiving it, accepts the responsibility for providing hospitality to the stranger. It is improper for a stranger to remain in a village even overnight without all of the inhabitants being informed of his presence. In this way they all assume responsibility for the stranger, for both his and their protection.

When migration into the Southern Province (particularly into the Bo area) for diamonds became a large-scale matter in the 1950's the chiefdom authorities passed a bye-law requiring every stranger to pay a fee of Le. 8.00 for a 'stranger permit'.[21] As the rush for diamonds subsided, the imposition of this fee generally fell into disuse, and although it is still regarded as mandatory for strangers to be presented to the chief, the 'stranger-permit' fee is applied only to *women.* Today a man who wishes to co-habit with a woman who is not a resident presents her to the Chiefdom Administration and pays Le. 8.00 for a 'stranger permit'. Should her husband appear, threatening to sue for compensation for adultery, he is informed that the 'stranger-permit' fee has been paid and the Local Court does not recognize his right to compensation for adultery. Of course, the husband retains his other legal rights over his wife. He may sue her family for the recovery of the marriage payments and other contributions he has made, and he may sue his wife for compensation for her failure to perform domestic duties and for any money he has loaned her. However, his rights to claim the children she has borne may also have been placed in jeopardy.

BIRTH REGISTRATION

The provision for the registration of birth has been extended throughout the country. It frequently happens that the genitor takes the initiative in registering the birth of his children.[22] For example, a young woman, estranged from her husband who was a paramount chief, gave birth to three children fathered by a lover. The father of the children registered their births. When the children were old enough to leave their mother, he took them to his own mother who reared them. The paramount chief did not attempt to contest the lover's claim to the children. In another case, where the legality of a customary marriage was challenged, the man produced the birth certificates of his children to prove that the marriage was legal. The authority of central government institutions over customary legal practices is widely accepted and in the minds of illiterate people the possession of a printed birth certificate is taken as ultimate proof of paternity, in flagrant disregard of recognized customary rights.

THE 'CARETAKER MARRIAGE'

Another type of conjugal union is practised by married women. The family of the woman separated from her husband may agree to what has come to be called a 'caretaker marriage'. The man involved in this arrangement pays a token fee to the woman's relatives. Often the relatives also take a larger sum from him and hold this money in reserve. If the husband appears they show this money to him as proof that they have attempted to protect his rights as husband by informing the caretaker that the woman was married. Sometimes this money is paid by them to the husband in lieu of compensation for adultery. While the husband may sue the wife's family for 'giving his wife to another man', the family hopes that the caretaker will eventually answer any legal claims and refund the marriage payments if they are demanded.

CHANGING DIVORCE PRACTICES

Clearly, the woman who separates herself from her husband is in a better situation if she can actually divorce her husband but there is always the problem of the refunding of the marriage payments. The Native Marriage and Divorce (Registration) Bye-Law (Chiefdom Council Act, Cap. 61, sec. 16 *Laws of Sierra Leone*) first adopted in 1960, provided for the registration and regulation of divorces under customary law. This bye-law specifies that a divorce may not be granted until the case has been heard in open court, with the decision given following the representations of *both* spouses. One of the implications of the law is that decisions about the monies recoverable by the husband and the terms for their repayment will be made as part of the divorce judgement. In practice something quite different occurs. In most areas a woman may go to the office of the Chiefdom Administration accompanied by one of her male relatives and state her intention to divorce. The court official asks only who is going to be responsible for the refund of the marriage payments. The woman pays the local charges for a 'divorce permit' and is given a receipt for the amount. This 'divorce permit' is strictly an invention since no bye-law has ever prescribed such a procedure. The court clerk then addresses a letter to her husband informing him that his wife has, as of the date of the letter, divorced him with the permission of her relatives. The husband is informed that he no longer has the right to claim anything against his wife. He is advised that he may sue for the recovery of his marriage payments if he should so desire. All this takes place despite the specific provisions of the law requiring the presence of *both* parties in a court hearing of a divorce case.

Of course, most men do desire to recover their marriage expenses and eventually (although they may wait for several years) take the necessary steps to sue the wife's family in court. These cases involve long disputes over the amounts the husband has contributed to the wife's family and, since the family may be unwilling or unable to pay, settlement may be very protracted. Often the family have to borrow money which eventually leads them into further litigation with their creditors when they cannot repay them.[23] Very often the burden for these expenses falls on the unlucky relatives who by chance are accessible, since most of the other relatives who should also be responsible live in distant parts of the country. Although, in principle, by taking out the 'divorce permit' a wife has relieved herself of any obligation to her husband, she has involved her relatives in unpleasant and expensive litigation. Clearly it would be more desirable if she could find this money herself. Her own family may well instruct her to do exactly that.

THE 'DEBTOR-CREDITOR MARRIAGE'

As a result of these financial burdens, another form of conjugal union has arisen. This is referred to locally as the 'debtor-creditor marriage'. This type of union results when a woman approaches a wealthy man for a loan to repay her husband the monies for which her family would be sued upon her divorce. He, in turn, will require that she pledge her sexual and usually her domestic services to him until the debt is paid. These cases often end up in court disputes over the repayment of the debts and custody of the children which have resulted from the union. Sometimes the creditor will regularize the union by paying a fee to the parents as a token marriage payment in order to gain rights over the children. However, in many cases he will attempt to claim them simply as 'interest' on his loan.

IMPLICATIONS OF NEW TYPES OF CONJUGAL UNIONS

These various types of conjugal union give rise to several problems in determining who is entitled to the children born under them. Under customary law children may be claimed by the legal husband regardless of who has fathered them. If he refuses to accept them as his, it is usually the mother's family who has the right to claim them. Formerly, in traditional society, every child was of unquestioned value since every man's prestige and status were strongly associated with the number of his dependants. Questions regarding legitimacy became a matter of concern only when candidates were being chosen to contest an election for chieftaincy or when decisions were being made about the appointment of the head of the family. Inheritance, in a subsistence economy, is, for the most part, limited to the inheritance of the rights over farming land and the responsibility for dependants. These rights and responsibilites are vested in the head of the family, whose status is measured in terms of the numbers of persons dependent upon him. Formerly, when there was no land shortage (and still today in those areas where there is sufficient land) family size was associated with the amount of land which was allocated to the family head, so all new recruits were welcomed.

However, in most parts of the country there is today a shortage of land and farm produce.[24] More important, there is the possibility of an individual amassing personal wealth and possessions. As a result, many people realize that it is in the interest of their heirs to limit the number of their dependants. So, although some men continue to welcome additions to the family and are prepared to claim their rights to custody of the children born to their legal wives, often others are loath to incur the financial burdens that children represent. After all, today it is expected that a father attempts to provide school fees for his own children in addition to the cash that will be required simply to feed them. A woman, on the other hand, realizes that her future security is best assured through bearing children, supporting them, and, if possible, educating them so that they will be able to enter the wage-earning economy successfully. If these children are fathered by a man who is not her legal husband, her rights over them are less likely to be challenged. After all, in view of the financial costs involved, her family are unlikely to insist on custody, and unless the putative father is clever enough to register their births, his chances of winning custody under customary law are relatively weak.

Apart from the problems of finding the money to repay the marriage payments and the disputes which may arise regarding the rights over children, it is clear that being divorced and remaining unmarried, entering into only informal conjugal unions, holds for a woman certain advantages over a legal marriage under customary law. As a divorced woman, she is no longer subject to the authority of a husband, and no one can press claims for compensation for her failure to perform domestic duties. The profits she may earn through her own economic activities are her own. She is free to acquire property in her own name and there is an increasing tendency for Local Courts to acknowledge her rights to her own property. Because of the dispersal of her kin group, she is more or less freed from its authority, although she may, in times of need, activate kinship obligations and press her relatives to provide for her. She is free to move about the country, and those conjugal unions that she establishes (even if required by local legislation) are based upon her own individual preference and volition. Such institutions as the Magistrate's Court and Department of Social Welfare will support her rights to independent action and may even assist her in securing maintenance from those who father her children. Most important, there is a greater chance that the children she bears will be solely under her care and authority and she will have an opportunity to devote herself to their interests and thereby invest in the relationship most likely to ensure her own future security.

Traditionally there was only one possible role to be allocated to a physically mature woman, that of wife. Although we cannot make any statements about the relative stability of marriage in any earlier period, stability was formerly encouraged by the force of community opinion and the continued and involved interest of the wife's relatives. The latter benefited from the relationship with the husband's family established by the marriage, and stood to lose considerably in the event of its dissolution. If a marriage did fail, the only alternative for a woman was another marriage, even if only the least desirable 'friendship marriage'. On the other hand, conforming to the requirements of the role of a wife provided a woman with considerable security.

Today, however, economic and social changes which include the dispersion of her kin group, who served to protect her interests, have considerably reduced this security. Moreover, new possibilities for economic independence have become available to women, but to exercise them requires behaviour not permitted within the ideal role of a wife. As a result women endure considerable hardship.

Several innovations have begun to alter the character of the traditional rights of a husband. The development of the 'stranger-permit marriage' has successfully challenged the idea of a husband's continued sexual rights once separated from his wife. The utilization of the provision for the registration of births has, in many cases, eroded his rights over the children she bears. Departments of Social Welfare and the Magistrate's Courts assist women in claiming maintenance support from fathers even when they are living independently from their husbands or their families. The introduction of the 'divorce receipt', which many courts issue to women who are able to pay the fee, has eliminated the husband's rights to sue for compensation for the loss of his wife's domestic, sexual, and procreative services.

However, the husband's right to reclaim his marriage payments continues to involve a woman's relatives in enormous legal difficulties and expense. Their unwillingness to assume these costs has forced women who are eager to divorce to pay them by their own efforts. Although many a woman finds it necessary to accept another man who is willing to repay the husband by marrying her, other women have secured their own release from marital ties by pledging themselves as security for a loan. Perhaps even the institution of marriage payments, which is such a continued source of litigation and expense, will gradually disappear. Certainly this is the direction of change being taken in urban areas in Sierra Leone, where the commonest form of conjugal union is that which occurs between young people without the consent of parents. Only after a baby is expected are the formal customary procedures begun. The actual marriage payments are made over a protracted period, and often a girl's family is loath to accept them until there is considerable assurance that the union will continue.

However, today in rural areas it would appear that in many cases a woman's best interests are served through informal conjugal unions. We have seen how these informal unions, which fulfill the local requirement that a woman reside with some man, allow women the independence they require in their attempts to make themselves financially secure. This development of informal conjugal unions based upon individual volition is similar to the findings of many investigations which have been described as studies of the 'culture of property'.[25] As Riviera has pointed out:

> a formal marriage may well prove a handicap in such an economic environment, and the ability to change one's partner or even to have several of them may offer a real safeguard against the pressures of the economy – especially if the women are earning (1971:72ff.).

These findings also relate to the questions raised by Rodman (1971) as to whether the conjugal behaviour he found among lower class persons in Trinidad is to be interpreted as 'situational' or 'subcultural'. Today in Sierra Leone the values of traditional marriage continue to be idealized but economic necessities have compelled men to allow their wives to earn money outside the household. Women are not able to confine their behaviour to the conventions of the role of the traditional wife and at the same time make themselves financially secure in the contemporary economic situation. Families are no longer localized and thus are unable to enforce their authority. As a result both the role of the wife and the rights of a husband have altered and some of these changes have been partially recognized and institutionalized by the community. As Rodman observed, man is both an 'adaptive creature' as well as 'a creature of some coherence'; if situations require adaptive behaviour which is not in accord with his values it is likely that he will subsequently modify his values. In Sierra Leone, among the western-educated elite, the preferred form of marriage is monogamous and based on the individual's choice rather than a family decision. Idealized marital roles are patterned on the 'companionate model' (Harrell-Bond 1975). Since this model is available it may well happen that some aspects of such values will also be incorporated into the culture of lower socio-economic groups in Sierra Leone in order to rationalize partially the adaptive behaviour we have observed.

The informal unions that we have described and the associated disruptions of the customary standards of family life can best be understood as solutions to the problems of adjusting to a rapidly changing social and economic milieu. Of course, these new family arrangements do not solve all the problems, and they bring many others in their wake.

NOTES

1. See Gutkind 1962, Little 1973, and Little and Price 1974 for references to most studies of family life in urban Africa.
2. For some discussions of the inadequacies of the rural/urban dichotomy and the importance of considering changes occurring in the rural environment, see Little 1969, Southall 1961, Hoselitz 1955, Chin 1959, and Mair 1969.
3. This paper results from a team study of customary family law in Sierra Leone with particular emphasis on data gathered in the rural areas of the Southern Province. The methods used for collecting data included: analysis of court records; observing and recording court cases; intensive interviews with the participants involved in cases; interviews with lawyers, court presidents, paramount chiefs, tribal headmen, and other elders regarded as 'experts' in customary law; observation of informal settings of dispute settlements; interviews and observations of individuals not involved in disputes; collection of official records; observation of social welfare cases; and the results of a questionnaire filled in by clerks of local courts throughout the whole country. The research was supported by the Afrika-Studiecentrum, Leiden, Netherlands, and the Netherlands Foundation for the Advancement of Tropical Research (WOTRO), The Hague, Netherlands.
4. Our research findings suggest that the new forms of conjugal union are recognized in communities along the railway. The railway was built around the turn of the century and extended the trading possibilities of both men and women. These towns along the railway have also had long contact with the larger urban centres.
5. It does sometimes happen, as a result of poverty, that the volunteer labour of the husband-to-be on the farm of his wife's family will be accepted in lieu of marriage payments.
6. The *Bundu* Society is a closed association for women which initiates girls into membership who have reached the age of puberty. Girls are secluded for a period of time and given instruction in domestic work, medicine, and the songs, dances, and secrets of the society. During their seclusion girls have an opportunity to indicate their acceptance of the man who has been selected for their husband. Shortly after 'graduating' from the society, girls are handed over to their husbands.
7. Such marriages differ from a levirate union in that any children born are treated as those of the new husband.
8. These obligations include making financial contributions to the wife's family and providing other kinds of assistance such as hospitality when it is required.
9. If the genitor wishes to claim his child it will be necessary for him to secure the woman as his wife through arrangements with her family. A child's umbilical cord is buried beneath a tree in his home village. Children who have been rejected as the legitimate children of their mother's husband will usually identify their mother's family as their kin group, and their umbilical cord will be buried in her village.
10. In reality the situation is much more complicated. Traditionally the role of the head of the extended family is the only position to succeed to, and usually the successor to this role is a brother of the deceased or some other elderly male member of the family. He assumes the responsibility of the family, and property rights are vested in him. A father who is not head of the extended family would have his own personal rights over land to pass on to his successor, but competition for the position of head of the family is spread over a wider group than one man's household. Today, however, with the possibility of acquiring personal wealth, there is a tendency to follow the 'English-type' pattern of inheritance of giving preference to one's own sons and by-passing the family head whenever possible.
11. The breakdown in family responsibility can be seen in a number of cases which appear before the Local Court. For example, one man found himself forced by the court

to repay the marriage payments of a female relative. He sued his other relatives who had refused to assist for 'disassociating themselves from the family'. It is becoming more common for heads of families to be sued in court for appropriating family land or monies for their own personal use. The association between economic change and breakdown of family responsibility has been observed by many other researchers. For example, see Nukynya 1964, Azu 1974, and Caldwell 1966.

12. Diamonds were actually discovered and mined by the British during the 1930's, but an awareness of their value and a massive exploitation by Sierra Leoneans did not begin until the 1950's (see van der Laan 1965).
13. To begin with, the man's relatives would have negotiated the marriage and would have investigated the family background of the girl. Part of the trend towards individualism in Sierra Leone is expressed not only in economic terms but also in the tendency for individuals to act on their own behalf, ignoring the role, authority, and functions of the family.
14. Although it was necessary for the wife to take the initiative to sue for these properties, we observed that when she did, she usually won.
15. She must, however, sue under the Bastardy Act (Bastardy Laws Amendement Act, 1872 [35 & 36 Vict c. 65]) and the Bastardy (Increase of Payments) Act, 1961. The Married Woman's Maintenance Act. (Cap. 100, *Laws of Sierra Leone*) does not recognize a customary marriage.
16. Many a professional today has the efforts of his illiterate mother to thank for his education. The obligation to support one's mother is a strong motive among persons in all levels of the society. It is upheld by such supernatural sanctions as the fear of the mother's curse (Harrell-Bond 1975).
17. Co-wives are believed to be capable of poisoning another's child. If it is known that a father favours one of his children it is often thought advisable for that child to be reared in another village away from its own household for its own safety.
18. *Gara* is the local name for the craft of tie-dyeing. Sierra Leone women are famous for their beautifully designed cloth.
19. Some men give their wives a lump sum of money for trading and expect them to maintain themselves and their children from then on with the profits.
20. While this union and the other new forms of conjugal union described here are locally referred to as 'marriage', the new 'husband' does not, in fact, have all the rights of a husband under customary law. For example, in this case as long as the woman chooses to remain with him he can sue any man who has sexual relations with her. However, he cannot sue in court for compensation for any other marital offences and has no claims on her family.
21. Le. 2.00 equals one pound sterling.
22. This is despite the instructions to the registrar that the legal husband, *not* the lover, is to be registered as the father of the child ('The Births and Deaths (Provinces) Registrations Act' (Cap. 93)).
23. Intensive study of many court cases indicated that people rarely have sufficient money to repay marriage payments when a woman in the family is seeking a divorce.
24. The shortage of land is indicated by the growing number of court cases which arise over disputes about land boundaries and questions of ownership.
25. For example, Lewis 1959, 1961, and 1964, and Roman 1971.

Nullity of marriage and divorce: relevance of a western distinction to modern African law

13

JOHAN M. PAUWELS
Catholic University at Louvain

1. INTRODUCTION

Various circumstances and juristic acts may put an end to a marriage: negotiated or arbitrated separation of persons or of groups, death, divorce, disappearance, annulment; legal systems considerably differ on this point. We intend to examine a particular form of termination of marriage, annulment, in order to draw attention to an essential difference between the traditional African law and the modern law of Western Europe, and to contribute to the study of the influence exercised by the legal systems of colonial powers on the systems of African law.

We shall study the annulment of marriage, a form of termination of marriage peculiar to Europe, but which has solidly settled in African law. We shall attempt to prove that African law does not need this technique, as its form of dissolution of marriage in cases of breakdown of marriage suffices to cope as well with conflicts arising after the marriage has taken place as with those caused by circumstances which already were present at the moment of the celebration of the marriage.

In the field of termination of marriage the difference between Western law and African traditional law as far as nullity is concerned is not the only significant one. In particular, the breaking up of marriage following the death of one of the spouses seems to be quite different in both legal traditions: the death of a spouse (in particular of the husband) does not automatically terminate the marriage according to many African customary legal systems.[1]

Faced with restrictions of space, we shall not enter into the latter subject as it seems to be of purely historical and theoretical interest: indeed, the eminently personal character of marriage is universally stressed so firmly today that it is hardly likely that a concept of 'divorce after death' would be retained by an African legislator.[2] On the contrary, it is submitted that the choice between annulment and divorce raises only technical questions, so that the African traditional solution, simple and adequate as well, can be retained without hesitation.

Nothing would be more preposterous than to formulate imprudent generalisations about African customary law. Therefore we stress the fact that when we quote an example of dissolution of a marriage for violation of the conditions of the marriage, taken from a Tio court in Zaïre,[3] we do not pretend it is representative of the whole of African customary law, although we think it is fairly representative of the Zaïrese situation. Likewise our statement of legislative and judicial intervention during the colonial period only concerns Zaïre. The law we state is the law which has been elaborated during the colonial period in the Belgian Congo and which up to now is upheld in Zaïre, at least provisionally.[4] However, to the extent that we consider the impact of western conceptions on African law, we shall examine the modern family legislation of Ethiopia, Mali, Madagascar, Ivory Coast, Tanzania, and Senegal.

As we intend to study a concept which, in our opinion, has been introduced into African law through colonial influence, we shall explain the European concept of nullity before analysing its influence in Africa.

2. NULLITY OF MARRIAGE IN EUROPEAN LAW

2.1 *The need for a doctrine of nullity of marriage in Canon law*

European legal systems make a clear distinction between nullity of marriage and dissolution of marriage (either by divorce or by death). Whereas dissolution puts an end to a valid marriage which will have produced effects during its existence, annulment implies that there has never been a marriage. As an element important to the formation of the marriage was missing or imperfect at the moment the marriage took place, the latter is considered as having never existed. The grounds of nullity are circumstances which are contemporaneous with the celebration of the marriage, whereas the grounds of divorce are facts which have occurred thereafter. Dissolution works in the future *(ex nunc)*, the effect of nullity is also retrospective *(ex tunc)*.

As the annulment takes place a long time after the marriage, the retrospective effect of nullity often implies a fiction. If there has been cohabitation, this fiction assimilates reality to nothingness. Sometimes logic is invoked to justify this fiction, but this is a fallacy: indeed nullity implies retrospectivity (although in law annulment does not always work retrospectively). But who pretends that nullity has to be the sanction?

The clear-cut division between nullity and dissolution originated in Canon law, the most important source of inspiration of the family law of Western Europe. In Canon law, nullity of marriage is a most useful device. As a matter of principle, the law of the Roman Catholic Church ignores divorce, i.e., dissolution of a marriage during the lifetime of both spouses. However, even in this system there is no objection to admitting the separation of spouses who never were linked to each other by marriage. Would it be incorrect to think that human feelings and the need to solve some practical problems urged the practitioners of Canon law to take advantage of the possibilities offered by the concept of nullity if applied to the indissoluble marriage? Be that as it may, Canon law developed a highly complicated law of nullity, multiplying its grounds; in order to prevent annulment from working too much hardship, the doctrine of putative marriage – operation *ex nunc* of annulment if at least one of the spouses is in good faith, in favor of the children and of the *bona fide* spouse(s) – was elaborated. To a variable extent, these techniques have been introduced into the European law systems.[5]

2.2 *France and Belgium*

France and Belgium are countries whose marriage laws are very close to Canon law rules. In addition to the basic concept of annulment, which they took over from Canon law, they have adopted the distinction between absolute nullity and relative nullity. Grounds of absolute nullity are: spouses of the same sex, total lack of consent, incest, bigamy, clandestinity. In these cases, any person proving an interest may petition for annulment; generally spraking, these grounds are subject neither to confirmation, nor to limitation. Grounds of relative nullity are error, duress and lack of consent of parents of a minor spouse. In these cases, only a few persons may ask for annulment, confirmation is possible and the law provides for limitations.

Nowadays, most lawyers agree that any nullity has to be pronounced by the courts, and they reject the doctrine of nonexistence of marriage according to which in essential matters annulment is not needed. Both absolute and relative nullity have retrospective effect.

If at least one of the spouses was in *good faith*, i.e., was not aware of the nullity of the marriage at the moment it took place the doctrine of putative marriage will be applied; as such, the marriage will be considered as bringing about the effects of a valid marriage until the annulment becomes effective. This favor of the law may not be invoked by a spouse in bad faith. Moreover, according to French law (since the Act of January 3, 1972), children of the marriage are considered legitimate, even if neither spouse was in good faith (new ss. 201–202 C.C.).

The assimilation of annulment to divorce is far from being reached in French and Belgian law; legal writers refer favourably to the germanic legal systems (cf. *infra*, n° 2.4).[6]

2.3 *English law*

In English law, nullity of marriage has also developed to a highly elaborate doctrine, although considerably different from its French equivalent. The English law on nullity of marriage has recently been 'restated, with certain alterations', by the Nullity of Marriage Act 1971 (now consolidated in the Matrimonial Causes Act 1973).

Common law systems make a distinction between void and voidable marriages.[7] According to English law the following unions are void: marriages of persons not being male and female, of persons under the age of 16, bigamous marriages, marriages between persons within the prohibited degrees of relationship, and marriages celebrated in disregard of certain requirements as to the formation of marriage. A marriage is voidable if it has not been consummated owing to the incapacity of either party to consummate it or owing to the wilful refusal of the respondent to consummate it; if either party to the marriage did not validly consent to it, whatever the cause of the lack of consent be; if at the time of the marriage either party was suffering from mental disorder so as to be unfitted for marriage, or was suffering from a communicable venereal disease; or if at the time of the marriage the respondent was pregnant by some person other than the petitioner.[8]

Void marriages do not have to be annulled: the nullity exists even without judicial intervention and may be relied on by every person showing an interest. On the contrary, voidable marriages are not void *ab initio;* they have to be annulled by the court, and the annulment may only be applied for by the spouses or by one of them. Voidable marriages may be confirmed,[9] and there are a number of circumstances which prevent an application for annulment from being successful.

Void marriages are void *ab initio*; their nullity is retrospective. Until 1971, voidable marriages produced full effect as long as they were not annuled by a court, but the annulment operated retrospectively. Since the Nullity of Marriage Act 1971,[10] a decree of nullity granted in respect of a voidable marriage will operate only prospectivley and the marriage will be treated as if it existed up to the time of annulment: 'A decree of nullity granted after the commencement of this Act on the ground that a marriage is voidable shall operate to annul the marriage only as respects any time after the decree has been made absolute, and the marriage shall, notwithstanding the decree, be treated as if it had existed up to that time.'

This certainly forms an important step towards the complete abolition of the retrospective effect of annulment. It is only the most recent move in an evolution which started many years ago. Although English law seems to ignore the doctrine of putative marriage (except to a limited extent with respect to children), the English courts have reduced the retrospective effect of annulment by holding that any transaction concluded at the time of the annulment cannot be undone or reopened (cf. Bromley 1971:71). Moreover, since 1959, children of a void marriage are considered legitimate if at least one of the spouses was in good faith at the moment the marriage took place. Children born of voidable marriages have been considered as legitimate since 1937, by provisions extended in 1965. (cf. Bromley 1971:237–39). The concept of voidable marriage may well be rejected completely: unwillingness to depart from canonical rules seems to be the only obstacle (Cretney 1974:69–71).

2.4 *Germany, Switzerland, and Sweden*

The Germanic law systems (particularly the law of Germany and Switzerland) have opted much earlier in favor of *ex nunc* dissolution. These law systems departed entirely from the Canon law tradition, in an attempt to assimilate nullity of marriage to divorce. They distinguish *Nichtigkeit* (void marriages) and *Aufhebung* (Germany) or *Anfechtbarkeit* (Switzerland) (voidable marriages). Moreover, the authorities recognize *Nichtehe* conexistent marriage) if no celebration whatever has taken place. Except for *Nichtehe*, any annulment has to be pronounced by the court.

The Germanic law systems ignore the institution of the putative marriage, but more than any other European law system, they succeeded in minimizing the retrospective effect of annulment. The Swiss civil code abolished it altoghether: if the marriage is annuled, it produces the effects of a divorce (s. 132 ZGB). The German civil code provides that children born of a void or voidable marriage are legitimate; moreover, voidable marriages have the effect of a divorce (Ehegesetz, 37).

Sweden went even further, by abolishing in 1973 the institution of annulment of marriage altogether.[11] The law of nullity was formally incorporated in the divorce law.[12] At present, one of the grounds of divorce is the fact that a marriage has been celebrated in violation of the rules regarding the conditions of marriage.[13] There are some significant differences between the law on this ground of divorce and other grounds: (a) in case of violation of the provisions on the conditions of marriage there is no 'reconsideration period' (six months), required otherwise if there are children or if the divorce is sought only by one of the spouses; (b) the Public Prosecutor may apply for divorce.

2.5 *Nonexistence and no-marriage*

As our purpose is to show that for historical reasons, the concept of nullity complicates the dissolution of marriages which effectively took place, we did not deal with the situation where the parties claim to enjoy the effects of a legal marriage (a situation which could be qualified as 'no-marriage'), although no ceremony whatsoever took place.

In systems which consider marriage as the only lawful form of union between a man and a woman, concubinage is logically denied every effect of marriage. We would only like to stress that in the European systems which distinguish between *nonexistence* and *nullité* (France and Belgium) or *Nicht-Ehe* and *Nichtigerklärung/Aufhebung* (Germany),[14] this distinction only partially tends to cope with the problem of 'no-marriage': the concepts of *nonexistence* and *Nicht-Ehe* also apply to some situations where a marriage ceremony took place.

2.6 *Conclusion*

The situation of the law of Western Europe on annulment of the marriage can be summarized as follows: on the one hand, up to now almost all Western legal systems are searching for the means to alleviate the retrospective effects of nullity; on the other, some of them, notably Sweden, have achieved complete assimilation of the effects of annulment and divorce.

3. NULLITY IN THE LEGAL SYSTEMS OF AFRICA

3.1 *Conditions of marriage and their sanctions*

Conditions of marriage are of course not absent from African customary law; for example, quite important conditions in Tio law are the consent of certain relatives of the spouses, the monogamy of the wife, the abstention from incest, and marriage payments.[15]

In all law systems, the conditions of marriage are upheld by the strength of certain sanctions, but these sanctions are not identical everywhere. Whereas European law stresses the importance of the sanction of nullity of marriage (at least in theory, for it seems that in fact annulment proceedings occur only exceptionally), this technique seems to be quite generally ignored by African law. In the latter, preventive sanctions (refusal to celebrate the marriage, fear of magic sanctions and of public opinion) undoubtedly form the most important sanctions. This does not mean, however, that the violation of a condition cannot lead to legal reactions after the marriage has taken place. There are penal sanctions and other techniques, such as the splitting of lineages or expiatory rites in order to divert harmful effects of incest. Finally, a marriage may be dissolved for reasons related to the violation of rules regarding the formation of the marriage. However, in this case the dissolution is achieved in the same way as an ordinary 'divorce'. As such, dissolution may be a sanction of the conditions of the marriage, but this dissolution is not different from dissolution by divorce.

This does not mean that African law ignores 'no-marriages'. Obviously a relationship between a man and a woman living in concubinage would not produce effects of a marriage if their pretentions force a court to decide that indeed they are not married. As such, in a sense, African law recognizes 'nonexistence of marriage', especially in cases where the formal requirements of the law of marriage are not complied with. This means only that individuals are not able to pretend that they are married if no marriage has taken place.

3.2 *A Tio example*

Cases tried by courts, in which a marriage is dissolved because of the violation of marriage conditions, appear to be very exceptional in Tio case law. This is easily understandable. On the one hand legal and other devices prevent most marriages violating essential conditions from taking place. On the other hand, the parties seldom look for dissolution at the very beginning of the marriage. Only after some time has passed and when conflicts between the spouses or their families accumulate, one of the parties may seek relief in court. At the moment, the older complaints (non compliance with marriage conditions) will not be stressed: they often will yield to more recent causes of conflict and complaint, i.e., the grounds of divorce in the proper sense.

Yet we are able to relate a case, decided by a Tio customary court near Kinshasa in 1970: *Court of the 'Commune' of Maluku, chamber of Kinshi, Judgment no. 1/70 of May 20, 1970, Im.–Nk. v. Ng.*

In this case two fathers were opposed to each other. The father of the boy, petitioner, had approached the defendant in order to persuade him to marry his daughter to the petitioner's son. The petitioner refunded the expenses a former suitor of the girl had paid to her father. Afterwards, he paid money and gave various articles in order to complete the marriage payments for his son. Despite all these efforts, the girl was not handed over to her husband (her 'fiancé', as the decision puts it)[16], and the boy's father went to court in order to claim her.

During the session, it appeared that the defendant's daughter refused to join her fiancé, because on a first meeting she had experienced his sexual impotence. Owing to these circumstances, the boy's family proposed to marry a younger brother of her fiancé, but the girl declined this offer on the grounds of incest regulations of the Tio. Another circumstance had hampered the marriage: the family of the girl from mother's side objected to the marriage of their 'niece' because her father had omitted to consult them; yet it appeared that the opposition of the maternal relatives to the marriage would not be irretrievable.

The court did not find nor make any allusion to any 'ground for annulment' of the marriage, this institution being ignored by Tio Law. On the contrary, it 'broke the betrothal' and 'pronounced the divorce'. The future wife's father was ordered to refund the marriage payments.

It is quite clear that the court was not aware of any distinction between annulment and divorce, and looked upon the facts as grounds for dissolution of the marriage. And thus a judgment of 'divorce' was pronounced. The French word divorce stands for the larger expression 'to break up the marriage' (*koboma libala* in Lingala).

3.3 *The concept of nullity introduced into Zaïre customary law*

Many customary courts in the Belgian Congo (a sovereign state since 1960, known as Zaïre since 1971) went on dissolving marriages, without making any distinction between nullity and divorce, in conformity with the customary tradition. Thus, several published cases reveal that divorce was pronounced on grounds such as sexual impotence,[17] sterility[18] failure to fulfil marriage payments,[19] and contagious disease contracted prior to marriage.[20]

But the influence of western concepts has been notable in this field. During the colonial period, some customary courts started annulling customary marriages for a number of reasons. To these courts, imperfections which in European law are grounds of nullity became grounds of nullity according to customary law: e.g., incest,[21] a woman's bigamy.[22] Customary imperfections also became grounds on which a marriage was considered void: e.g., lack of consent of the wife's family.[23]

Finally, 'modern' imperfections became grounds on which annulment was pronounced: e.g., lack of consent of the wife herself,[24] contracting of customary marriage by a man married already according to statutory law[25] or married religiously.[26]

No doubt, this evolution was stimulated by the authority of Antoine Sohier, who taught that the distinction between nullity and divorce, although unknown by traditional law, compelled recognition in customary law for elementary reasons of logic.[27] He drew up a long list of grounds for annulment: incest, impotence, sterility, certain diseases, sorcery,[28] and affirmed that procedure and effects of nullity and divorce are different, but he did not explain the latter affirmation. Writing since then, Jean Sohier still insisted on the distinction between divorce and nullity, but he admitted that the courts hardly make this distinction.[29]

Although the customary courts of Leopoldville (at present Kinshasa) took over the concept of nullity, they refused to adopt the correlative concept of putative marriage.[30]

Legislative interventions in the field of customary marriage had a contradictory effect. On the one hand, the (colonial) ordinance of May 21, 1958, on the recording of civil status *(état civil)* of the population ruled by customary law, has provided for the separate registration of decrees of annulment of customary marriages (s. 42–44); this measure no doubt stressed the distinction between divorce and annulment. On the other hand, on the only occasion on which the colonial legislature had the opportunity to take a decision about the retrospective effect of nullity, it provided an important exception to retrospectivity: when by decree of April 4, 1950, polygamous marriages contracted after January 1, 1951, were declared void, it was stipulated that children of such marriages would nevertheless be legitimate (s. 3).

3.4 *Recent African legislation*

Almost without exception, recent statutes on the law of marriage have introduced or confirmed the concept of nullity in the uniform or general law of marriage. This happened as well in the French speaking countries which generally speaking stick to the conception of 'divorce-sanction' according to which divorce is viewed as a sanction of marital misconduct, as in English speaking countries, which are rather inclined to adhere to the breakdown principle, which is so close to the African traditional divorce law. One exception: Ethiopia, which has replaced annulment of marriage by dissolution as a sanction of the conditions of marriage.

The *Code de la famille* of Mali (Act of February 3, 1962, ss. 25–31) adopts rules about the nullity of marriage which are very close to the French example, with the exception of an original solution as far as the non-compliance with the rules on the celebration of marriage is concerned (s. 28).

The Malagasy Marriage Act of October 1, 1962, provides for more cases of absolute nullity than French law (s. 21–25) and for a doctrine of putative marriage (ss. 48, 50, 51), which is original in some respects. An identical formulation of the doctrine is found in the legislation of Ivory Coast and Senegal.

The Ivorian Marriage Act no. 64–375 of October 7, 1964, has provisions on the nullity of marriage (ss. 31–44) which are very similar to contemporary French law. Likewise, the Senegalese Family Code (Act of June 12, 1972) retains the distinction between grounds of absolute and relative nullity (ss. 137–145).

The modern African doctrine on the effect of nullity, as adopted by the Malagasy, Ivorian, and Senegalese legislation, may be summarized as follows. (a) The void (or voidable) marriage produces full effect, as if it were valid, until the decree of annulment becomes absolute. The marriage is considered dissolved from that moment; (b) only the spouse (or spouses) in good faith may invoke this disposition; indeed, as far as the *mala fide* spouse is concerned, the void(able) marriage is considered never to have existed; (c) retrospective effect has been squarely rejected with regard to the position of the children, at least as far as their *rights* are concerned: in respect of their parents and third persons, the children born of the marriage, or legitimated, keep the quality conferred to them by the marriage, without the spouse in bad faith being entitled to take advantage of it against them (Senegal, s. 145, 4th al.).

In the same way, the Tanzanian Marriage Act (1971)[31] confirms the concepts of nullity and annulment, the distinction between void and voidable marriages, and the principle that annulment has retrospective effect. As far as children are concerned, their legitimate status is not affected by the annulment (s. 98[1]).

We hesitate to include in our statement the very similar provisions of the Nigerian Matrimonial Causes decree (1970) and the Ghanaian Matrimonial Causes Act (1971)[32] because they do not affect, as a matter of principle, customary law.[33]

3.5 *Ethiopian law*

The Ethiopian Civil Code adopts the classical doctrine about nullity in the field of contracts and wills (ss. 1808 sq., 973 sq. C.C.). But as far as marriage is concerned, it has preferred the concept of dissolution of marriage as a sanction of the conditions of marriage (ss. 607–618: age, incest, bigamy, marriage of uncapable persons, vitiated consent).

This type of dissolution is dealt with together with other causes of dissolution (death and divorce, cf. s. 663). The assimilation to the latter types of dissolution is particularly relevant with respect to the effects of dissolution. Section 696 C.C. provides that the judges shall determine the effect of dissolution because of the violation of conditions of the marriage according to equity, and that they shall draw inspiration from the rules governing divorce. They shall take into consideration the good or bad faith of the spouses, the question whether the marriage has been consummated or not, the interests of the children of the marriage and the interests of third parties in good faith. This means that Ethiopian judges normally will dissolve *ex nunc* marriages contracted in violation of the conditions of marriage. According to O'Donovan, '(g)ood faith is relevant to Ethiopian law not in determining when the dissolution will have effect but only in determining the consequences of dissolution' (O'Donovan 1972:442). We submit that, in exceptional cases at least, dissolution as a sanction could have more than prospective effect, according to the text of s .696 (3) C.C.

As such, Ethiopian law surely takes an eminent position in modern

African family law. At present, its solution of the problem of sanctioning violations of the rules on conditions of the marriage is unique in its closeness to African tradition.[34] Moreover, its recourse to rules of equity prevents injustice or scandal in the rare cases were annulment *ex nunc* would not be justified.

Recently, O'Donovan (1972:349–455) proposed to introduce the concept of a marriage void *ab initio* into the Ethiopian Code, in order to cope with evident causes of nullity not dealt with by the Code. The effect of annulment here would be retrospective. However, the author stresses the exceptional nature retrospectivity would retain in this field: '(t)he concept must be limited to cases where the nature and purpose of marriage are frustated, for example where there is no consent to marry or no appearance of marriage. (...) The law, in regulating defective marriages, must limit itself to these two cases. There is no reason to introduce the notion of voidable marriages which can be retroactively declared void. Such a concept puts personal rights in jeopardy and is undesirable for this reason' (pp. 454–55).

We cannot but approve these last words. We even wonder if it is wise to reintroduce retrosprectivity, be it under exceptional circumstances, in the only African legislation which wisely rejected this dubious product of Western jurisprudence. There are cases in which there is no marriage whatsover, a 'nonexistent marriage', as we pointed out above; there are also cases in which giving purely prospective effect to the annulment would hurt deep feelings of justice. Do these rare cases justify reconsidering the technique of equitable departure from the rule of prospective annulment?

4. CONCLUSION

4.1 *Nullity to be distinguished from non-existence*

In discussions about nullity of marriage, a clear distinction should be made between purely technical 'nullity' and non-existence. It is clear that there are 'no-marriages': a man and a woman who cohabit without being married are in a situation of no-marriage. If they pretend to be married or if third persons consider them as married, a court will pronounce the 'non-existence' of the marriage. But this is quite different from nullity cases as known in European law, although in some countries (France, e.g.), subtle distinctions were drawn between non-existence and absolute nullity. In fact, even cases considered by some authors as 'non-existence' are situations in which a marriage has taken place; criticism against the unrealistic nature of the technique of annulment is valid in respect of these.

In fact, the problem of 'no-marriages', not examined here, may well appear to be a question of practical impact considering the intricacy of the formal requirements of the traditional African marriage (e.g., several distinct marriage payments).

4.2 *Annulment of marriage not an appropriate technique*

Although the annulment of marriage has been adopted by most of the recent African family law acts, we persist in thinking that it would have been possible to work out solutions which are much closer to the traditional views.

Should logic be invoked in favour of nullity? We agree that it is possible to defend the view that the dissolution of a marriage may be imposed as a sanction when essential conditions of marriage are not complied with. But as we see it, this sanction does not necessarily have to work retrospectively. Retroactivity is often inconsistent with the real facts. And as *sanction*, dissolution *ex nunc* is not less logical than nullity *ab initio*. Moreover, in most cases it works less hardship to *bona fide* spouses and, in any case, to the children. Annulment has to be retrospective in the system of Canon law, according to which marriage is indissoluble. But as African marriages may be dissolved during the lifetime of both spouses, no fundamental argument in favour of retrospectivity seems to us to be available. In our opinion, African law does not need the concept of nullity of marriage anymore than French law needs the concept of nonexistence of marriage.

At a time when European legislators are looking for various devices in order to assimilate annulment to divorce, it is rather frustrating to see how African legislators take over the out-of-date European solutions, without adapting them substantially.

Rather than mitigating the retrospective effect of nullity by exceptional provisions in favour of the spouses in good faith or in favour of the offspring it would be useful to draw inspiration from the traditional African law, i.e., to integrate nullity into divorce. In our view, the Ethiopian solution – close to tradition, realistic, and flexible – is excellent.

Yet, the assimilation of annulment to divorce is hard to achieve in a divorce system based on guilt. It is much easier in legal systems which adopt the breakdown principle as the basis of divorce law. The English example (Divorce Reform Act 1969) clearly might favour assimilation in countries with a Common Law tradition. Although the French speaking states of Africa are rather hesitant on this point, it is gratifying to find that some recent legislative measures recognize grounds of divorce which indicate that a too strict application of the 'divorce-sanction' principle is being abandoned.[35] Maybe the example of French law, in which guiltless divorce has just been introduced[36] may well speed up this evolution. A more radical adhesion to the breakdown principle (which seems to have been the basis of traditional African divorce law) might favour the assimilation of nullity cases to divorce.

NOTES

1. Cf. the questions about the status of widows: is a levirate marriage a 're-marriage' or a continuation of a subsisting marriage? – In the Tio (Bateke) region of Zaïre (see note 3), many cases tried in 1970–1971 and collected by the author reveal that widows may go to court and apply for divorce, either if they feel that the family of their deceased husband does not take care of them and does not provide for a man able to replace the deceased, or if they refuse any marriage within the family of their deceased husband. In the latter case, the family of the deceased also may apply for divorce. Confronted with problems of this type, the courts pronounce the divorce of the widow and her deceased husband and take into account any rules which apply in case of an ordinary divorce (e.g., attempts of conciliation, penalizing of the spouse who brings about the divorce, restitution of marriage payments).
2. As a general rule, the recent marriage acts of African states decide that marriage is dissolved by the death of either of the spouses: Ethiopian C.C., s. 663; Mali, s. 57; Madagascar, s. 9 and 69 (implied); Ivory Coast, s. 99; Tanzania, 12; Senegal, s. 100.
3. The Tio or Bateke live in the People's Republic of Congo and in Zaïre, east and north-east of Kinshasa. They number under a hundred thousand.
4. A *Commission de Réforme et d'Unification du Droit Civil Zaïrois* has been created in 1971; it is preparing a uniform civil code.
5. Codex Iuris Canonici, Can. 1036, 1067 sq., 1971 sq.
6. Cf. Rigaux, F., 1971, *Les Personnes*, I., *Les relations familiales*, Brussels, Larcier, nos 1509 sq.; Carbonnier, J., 1972, *Droit civil*, Paris, P.U.F., 9th ed., II, nos 36 and 38.
7. On the origin of the distinction, see: Goda, P.J., 1967, The Historical Evolution of the Concepts of Void and Voidable Marriages, *Journal of Family Law*, 7 (2): 297–308.
8. Matrimonial Causes Act, ss. 11–12.
9. The English concept of confirmation seems to be far wider than the French *ratification;* cf. Matrimonial Causes Act 1973, s. 13 (1); Bromley, P., 1971, *Family Law*, London, Butterworth's, 4th ed., 61–69; 1974, *Supplement*, A8–A9. On knowledge of the defect and approbation under the new law, see Cretney, S., 1974, *Principles of Family Law*, London, Sweet & Maxwell, 62–64.
10. Now Matrimonial Causes Act 1973, s. 16.
11. Act no 645 of July 4, 1973, which came into force on January 1, 1974, modifying the Marriage Act of June 11, 1920; chapter 10, Annulment of Marriage, of the latter act was abolished.

12. Since 1920 annulment had no retrospective effect.
13. Marriage Act as amended, chap. 11, s. 5.
14. On 'no-marriage' in English law, see Cretney, 1974: 67–68.
15. Vansina, J., 1973, *The Tio Kingdom of the Middle Congo 1880–1892*, London, 84–93; Pauwels, J.M., 1968, *Mécanisme et fonction de la dot chez les Tyo (Teke) du Kongo Central*, in: *Colloque sur la dot*, Lubumbashi, C.E.P.S.I., 123–149; Idem. L'alliance en coutume tio-droit et magie, 1971 *Revue Juridique du Zaïre* 47 (2): 200–13.
16. According to Tio law (as well as according to many African legal systems) what is called *fiançailles* (betrothal) forms the first phase of the customary marriage; as such, betrothal is to be considered as part of marriage, not as a status preceeding the matrimonial status.
17. Sohier, Jean, 1957, *Répertoire général de la jurisprudence et de la doctrine coutumières du Congo Belge et du Ruanda-Urundi*, Brussels, Larcier, V° Divorce, nos 181–183; Pauwels, J., 1970, *Répertoire de droit coutumier congolais*, Kinshasa, O.N.R.D., V° Divorce, no. 18.
18. Sohier, J., 1957, V° *Divorce*, nos 184–190; Pauwels, J., 1970, V° *Divorce*, nos 14 and 19.
19. Sohier, J., 1957, V° Divorce, nos 260–265.
20. Pauwels, J., 1970, V° Divorce, no. 16.
21. Sohier, J., 1957, V° Divorce, nos 144–146.
22. Sohier, J., 1957, V° Divorce, nos 147–152; Territory Court Mitwaba, June 6, 1953, *Journal des Tribunaux d'Outre-Mer*, 1954, 27, note Jean S. – See also note 32.
23. Sohier, J., 1957, V° Divorce, nos 164–170.
24. Sohier, J., 1957, V° Divorce, nos 153–163.
25. Sohier, J., 1957, V° Divorce, no 178.
26. Sohier, J., 1957, V° Divorce, nos 175–177.
27. Sohier, A., 1954, *Traité élémentaire de droit coutumier du Congo belge*, Brussels, Larcier, 2d ed., no. 269, p. 182.
28. Sohier, A., 1954, nos 170–173, pp. 182–183.
29. Sohier, J., 1964, *Institutes coutumières katangaises*, Elisabethville, C.E.P.S.I., 190–197.
30. Territory Court of Leopoldville, no. 5.010, January 25, 1955, *Bulletin des Juridictions Indigènes*, 1956, 358, note M. Petit; Territory Court of Leopoldville, February 2, 1956, *Journal des Tribunaux d'Outre-Mer*, 1958, 76, summary, note.
31. The Law of Marriage Act, 1971, ss. 38–40, 96–98.
32. Nigeria: 1970, ss. 3–6 and 34–38; Ghana: 1971, s. 13–14.
33. Yet see Ghanaian Act, s. 41 (2).
34. Yet it is more likely that R. David, the draftsman of the Ethiopian Civil Code, drew his inspiration from Swiss and German law rather than from Ethiopian traditions.
35. The Ethiopian Civil Code considers as grounds for divorce: mental illness, absence (s. 670) and any causes (s. 673). The Senegalese Family Code authorizes divorce by mutual consent (s. 158) and divorce on the ground of sterility, incurable disease, incompatibility of characters (s. 166).
36. Act of July 11, 1975. (*Journal Officiel de la République Française*, July 12, 1975, 7171).

The Kgatla marriage: concepts of validity* 14

SIMON ROBERTS
London School of Economics

Ceremonies and formalities associated with the formation of marriage have been closely studied by both anthropologists and lawyers whose research has yielded richly detailed descriptions and full inventories of associated normative statements.[1] On one level, due largely to the insights of van Gennep (1908), these ceremonies and formalities are widely understood. But more questionably they are sometimes also taken to have specific jural significance, as operating *to confer validity* on marriage. Schapera adopts this interpretation of the formalities associated with marriage in his reports on the Kgatla (1938; 1940). The purpose of this paper is to reconsider his interpretation, as it will be argued here that in the Kgatla case any attempt to isolate essential formalities associated with formation conflicts with the way in which Kgatla see marriage and its formation and leads to a misunderstanding of the way in which norms related to the process of formation operate in the context of a dispute.

* I first did fieldwork in the Kgatleng between November 1968 and March 1970 while acting as Adviser on Customary Law to the Government of Botswana. This appointment was arranged under the United Kingdom Government Special Commonwealth African Assistance Plan, leave of absence being granted from the London School of Economics. Further field trips to Mochudi were made during the summer of 1971 and the early months of 1973. Dr. J. L. Comaroff, of Manchester University, kindly read and commented upon an earlier draft of this paper; many of the suggestions he made are incorporated in this version.

I

Schapera's approach to formalities associated with the formation of marriage is widely followed in reports, particularly those of lawyers, from other preliterate societies.[2] Cotran, for example, in his Kenya restatements (1968) treats what he considers to be the most important formalities associated with marriage, presumably those most stressed by informants, as providing an essential element of validity. Thus in respect of the Kikuyu he states (1968: 16):

(c) NGURARIO. No marriage is valid under Kikuyu law unless the *ngurario* ram is slaughtered.
(d) RURACIO. There can be no valid marriage under Kikuyu law unless a part of the *ruracio* has been paid.

Such a jural approach to these formalities involves two assumptions: that the validity of a marriage lies ultimately in compliance with these formalities, and that the norms associated with them operate in the same way as rules of law are seen to operate in a western legal system. Consider, for example, the most important procedural requirements associated with the formation of marriage in English law.[3] There, visits to civil or religious specialists, in the course of which prescribed formalities are undertaken, are essential to validity. Without going into the field to check reports like those of Cotran, it is impossible to say whether they correctly treat ceremonial features as conferring validity upon the marriage-type relationship in question. However, it is now well established that in many small-scale societies stated norms are not treated like legal rules, and there must be the suspicion that the jural approach to formalities outlined above can result from preconceptions acquired by the fieldworker in his own society, particularly in the course of legal training, rather than from anything suggested in the data themselves.[4]

II

As seems to be the case in many African societies (e.g., the Nuer, Evans-Pritchard 1951: 97; the Kgalagari, Kuper 1970: 468-577), the Kgatla marriage is not formed on a single identifiable occasion, but comes to maturity slowly over time, progressively attracting different incidents as this process continues. The process of formation has been described in detail elsewhere (Schapera 1938; 1940; Roberts 1972) and needs only be summarized here. Traditionally, the initiative in choosing a wife and commencing negotiations towards marriage lie with the man's guardian.[5] When an initial choice has been made, an informal approach is made to the woman's guardian. This overture is accompanied by widespread consultation within the two groups of kin involved, by no means confined to the members of the descent groups principally involved but extending to the maternal kinsmen on both sides. The respective paternal and maternal uncles play an important part in these consultations, and their agreement with the initial choice manifests itself in the fact that it is through them as intermediaries that subsequent formal negotiations are conducted. Provided the initial consultations prove favourable, formal negotiations are then conducted in the course of a series of public visits paid to the *kgotla* of the woman's guardian by representatives of the man's guardian. The conclusion of these negotiations is marked by the acceptance of gifts *(dilo tsa patlo)*[6] by the woman's guardian, who thus signifies his agreement to the marriage. Thereafter, as soon as the young couple are (in the opinion of the respective guardians) sufficiently mature, the man is allowed to spend nights at the woman's homestead. This stage may continue for months and even years, with children being born to the couple, before further formal steps are taken. The next stage involves the woman being taken over to a homestead prepared for her in the *kgotla* to which the man belongs. Her removal is preceded by further formal visits to the *kgotla* of her guardian by male and female kin of the man, in the course of which ceremonial requests for the woman are made and granted. These visits are traditionally accompanied by extensive feasting and celebration, and are followed immediately by the woman's departure to live among the members of the man's descent group. At this stage, or at some time later, bridewealth cattle *(bogadi)* are driven to the *kgotla* of the woman's guardian and presented to him.

Among these procedures, Kgatla informants tend to place most importance upon the initial process of request and acceptance concluded by *dilo tsa patlo*, and upon the presentation of *bogadi*. They associate the acquisition of the initial right of sexual access with *dilo tsa patlo*, the transfer of guardianship over the woman (and the correlative responsibility for maintaining her) with her removal to the man's home, and the man's paternal rights over children born to the union with the presentation of *bogadi*. However, I have never heard a Kgatla informant spontaneously suggest that the validity of a marriage depends upon compliance with the formal procedures described. It is certainly true that such firm evidence as is available suggests that in respect of Kgatla marriage-type relationships the formal requests are typically carried out and *bogadi* presented,[7] but an essential link between these formalities and validity is not suggested in the data. If the essence of validity is sought, this seems rather to lie in the reception and acceptance of the woman by the members of the man's descent group.

This view of validity is, however, in conflict with that taken by Schapera (1938; 1940). He adopts the jural approach to formalities. already discussed, treating some of the formalities associated with formation as operating to confer validity. He isolates two essential elements. First, the initial process of request and acceptance 'without which (he asserts) no marriage is regarded as proper' (1938: 131-32). Secondly, he refers to the presentation of *bogadi:* 'No matter what other ceremonies may have been observed, no form of cohabitation between the couple is ever considered a true marriage until these animals have been given... If it (*bogadi*) is still outstanding, the couple are held to be living in concubinage' (1940: 73).

In order to understand the Kgatla view of validity, and to assess these different approaches, it is necessary to look to the instance of dispute in which a relationship is in a state of breakdown, the woman claims her right to be supported, and the man denies that she is his wife. The following case history, investigated in the course of my field work among the Kgatla, is illustrative:[8]

Case 1: A dispute between Molefe and Madubu

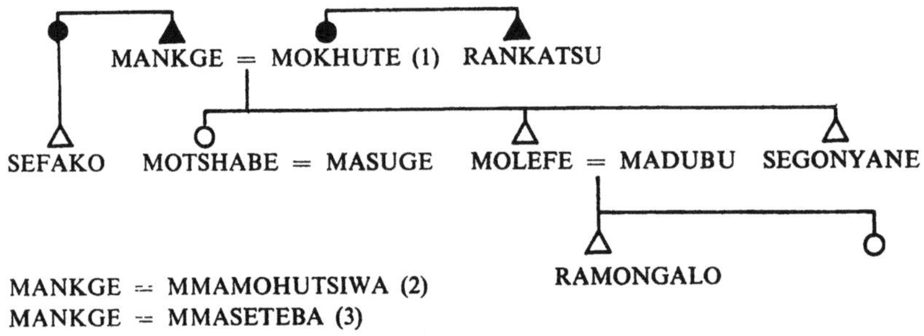

Figure 1

Molefe belongs to the Masiana *kgotla*, a small sub-division of the main Kgatla village of Mochudi; he is the eldest son of Mankge by the latter's first wife, Mokhute (see genealogical diagram). Madubu comes from Mookane, a small settlement in the adjoining territory occupied by the Ngwato tribe. They met while Molefe was working at his father's cattle post in the extreme north of the Kgatleng; perhaps when Molefe went to buy stores at Mookane, or it may have been at one of the cattle posts, as those of the Kgatla and Ngwato are close together at this point. Molefe soon decided that he wanted to marry Madubu, but there were difficulties in the way of this. Mankge had already chosen a prospective wife for Molefe, and would not agree to the match with Madubu. Mankge's choice was Thothome, a girl from the Monneng *kgotla*, and a member of the descent group from which Molefe's own mother had come.[9]

Despite his father's disapproval, Molefe went ahead and himself conducted negotiations with members of Madubu's kin through a Mongwato friend of his, Lekula Mannaesi. Although accounts of these negotiations differ, it is clear that they broke down, and that Molefe took Madubu away without her parents' permission in about 1945. He took her first to the Kgatla cattle posts and then to live in the ward at Mochudi into which his elder sister, Motshabi, had married. He kept her away from the Masiana *kgotla* because of Mankge's disapproval. But after a while, Mankge seems to have become reconciled to the fact that Molefe would never marry Thothome and began to treat Madubu as a daughter-in-law. She and Molefe were received together at Mankge's homestead by Mmamohutsiwa (Mankge's second wife; Molefe's mother was long dead); Mankge gave her a present of some cloth, and eventually approached Motshegare Ramalepa, headman of the Tlagadi ward, and asked for an allotment of residential land for Molefe and Madubu to build on. This allotment was made and a homestead built. Some say at this stage further steps were taken to obtain the agreement to the marriage of Madubu's kinsmen, and that Rankatsu Monametsi, Molefe's maternal uncle, sent representatives to Mookane to attempt this. When the dispute later arose between Molefe and Madubu surviving senior relations of Madubu strongly denied before the Chief that these later overtures had ever been made, let alone that they had been successful. Certainly no *bogadi* passed between the two sets of kin. Nonetheless it is clear that Molefe and Madubu were allowed to set up house together in the Masiana *kgotla*.

Molefe and Madubu seem to have lived peacefully for a while, but Madubu bore no children, and in about 1953 Molefe persuaded her to allow him to enter a sororate relationship with one of her younger sisters.[10] But when Molefe approached Madubu's kinsmen to ask permission to do this, it was refused. Madubu's maternal uncle stated that such a relationship must await a proper marriage between Molefe and Madubu. Despite this, Molefe took the younger sister home with him to Mochudi where she bore him a daughter and later a son, Ramongalo. Although Madubu initially agreed to this sororate relationship, it led to disagreements and quarrels between the two sisters and between Molefe and Madubu. These initial difficulties were added to when, after Mankge's death in about 1956, Molefe went off to live with the former's third wife, Mmaseteba. This was a potentially permissible levirate arrangement, but no members of Molefe's descent group ever assigned him to undertake it. Certainly Molefe's relationship with Mmaseteba further strained matters between him and Madubu and, by 1959 he had wholly ceased to maintain her and the younger sister. During that year Madubu complained of neglect to members of Molefe's descent group and to Motshegare Ramalepa, and the latter ordered Molefe to sell a beast to clothe and feed her. At first Molefe failed to carry out this order and Madubu took the matter to the Chief's *kgotla.* There Molefe agreed that Madubu was his wife and promised to sell a beast as Motshegare had required. Following the hearing in the Chief's *kgotla* Molefe did sell a beast for Madubu, but he made no sustained effort to maintain her.

In response to this neglect Madubu approached a Kgatla medico-religious specialist *(ngaka)* called Radisoa, hoping to be given herbs that would dampen down Molefe's desire for Mmaseteba and return his attentions to Madubu. This magician refused to help Madubu, however, and reported her visit to Molefe.[11]

Following the failure of this approach Madubu made a further claim of neglect to Molefe's kinsmen while he was living away at the cattle post with Mmaseteba. She went first to Molefe's younger brother, Segonyane, who took her to a senior surviving member of the descent group, Letsebe (Letsebe was a descendant of an older brother of Mankge's grandfather, Dithare). Segonyane urged Letsebe to provide direct material support for Madubu by opening an account in Molefe's name at the local trading store. But Letsebe was reluctant to act in Molefe's absence, and sent Segonyane to fetch him back from the cattle post.

When Molefe returned, a few members of the descent group, and some other kin and affines, met at the Masiana *kgotla* to discuss the dispute. Letsebe was the senior member of the group present at this meeting, and among those also present (besides Molefe and Madubu) were Segonyane, Molefe's sister Motshabi, and her husband Masuge. Letsebe began the discussion by confronting Molefe with Madubu's claim of neglect. Molefe answered him by saying that he had left her with six bags of corn when he set off for the cattle post. Talk then turned to the general state of the relationship between Molefe and Madubu, and the former asserted that the relationship had completely broken down, citing Madubu's solo approach to Radisoa, and suggested that the best thing to do was to take her back to the kinsmen at Mookane. It seems that all the male members of the descent group present were in agreement with this plan, and that it would have been carried out, had not Madubu protested to Motshegare Ramalepa at the Tlagadi *kgotla.*

Motshegare agreed to hear Madubu's complaint, and what took place in the Tlagadi *kgotla* on that occasion was recorded as follows:

Madubu: Molefe has left me in our home and is staying with his mother.[12] Now he has turned her into his wife. It is because of her that I will have to leave his house. Molefe has built a house for me but he has taken all the household goods to his mother's place. He does not support me. He eats, sleeps and washes his clothes at his mother's place.

Molefe sleeps with his mother in the same house. Three years have passed since he deserted me. I do not deny Molefe the right to marry two women, but I do not like my rival to be his mother. He can rather marry another wife, I am Molefe's wife. My marriage was arranged with Lekula Mannaesi. Lekula said he would pay *bogadi* on behalf of Molefe, he was sent by Rankatsu Monametsi.[13] After my marriage arrangements were completed, Molefe took me to his cattle post. This was in 1944.

Mmamohutsiwa: I know Madubu to be my daughter-in-law because Molefe once came to his father and told him he had seen a wife he wanted at Mookane. Mankge replied that he (Mankge) had already found Molefe a wife. Mankge then went to tell Rankatsu that Molefe did not want the wife he had found for him, and Molefe confirmed that he had found one at Mookane.

Molefe then went away and when he came back he brought this woman with him. Rankatsu had refused to undertake the marriage negotiations because Molefe had disappointed him by refusing the wife Mankge had found. Molefe brought her and put her into Motshabi's yard.

Molefe: Madubu is only a woman who lives with me in the yard. I do not love her any more. I have had many troubles with her. The first quarrel we had was about the children she had chased away from my home.[14]

Lekula is my friend. I asked him to find me a wife but the woman's father refused. This woman I am with at present was not formally negotiated for. I once fell in love with her and took her away with me. I told them to make the negotiations for our marriage in 1942.

Mmasteba: Molefe is my son and Madubu my daughter-in-law. I have not drawn Molefe away from Madubu. Molefe has no belongings in my home. Molefe brought his belongings and even Motshabi's money to my house and told me he had fought with his wife. Later he came and took all these things away. There is nothing in my house belonging to Molefe.

Letsebe (Mankge's FFOBSSS): In May Segonyane and Madubu came to me and told me that she was not being supported. I sent Segonyane to go and call Molefe. On the third day Madubu came again with Masuge,[15] and told me that Molefe did not support her. I told her that I had sent for him. She answered that she could not wait for the time Molefe would take before coming here. I told her I could not do anything about it while Molefe and Segonyane were absent. I told her to wait.

Masuge: When Molefe came, he told us that when he went to the cattle post he left six and a half bags of corn for her and he was surprised that she claimed he did not support her. Madubu answered that she had opened the sixth bag when Molefe went away. Molefe said even then there would still be a lot because the pot she was using was very small.

Letsebe: I told them that I wanted to hear their opinions. Molefe answered he had nothing to say except that he wanted to take Madubu back to her people. I agreed with Molefe, because I did not know her. She was only brought to me by Segonyane who told him she was his brother's wife.

Molefe Matlhage (a senior member of the Masiana *kgotla*): I say that he knew the woman. All he wanted was to be rid of her. He overlooked the authority of the Masiana *kgotla* and thus has made the case more serious.[16]

Motshabi: Letsebe said he wanted Molefe to send her away. He asked someone to accompany them so that Molefe should not beat her on the way home. Those who were present when they took this decision were Letsebe, Monametse,[17] Masuge, Segonyane, and myself. Madubu said that she understood she was to be taken back home but she first wanted a case because Mmaseteba had taken her husband.

Mathibedi (a senior member of the Tlagadi *kgotla*): Was it right of you Letsebe to grant a divorce in your *kgotla* like you did?

Letsebe: I just agreed to be a witness.

Mathibedi (questioning Segonyane and Motshabi): What relationship has Madubu to you?

Segonyane: I know her to be my brother Molefe's wife.

Motshabi: I know her to be my brother Molefe's wife.

[Some discussion of Molefe's property then follows]

Headman Motshegare Ramalepa: I am glad to listen to your case but I want to draw your attention to the fact that men in this *kgotla* have been cheating women.

Molefe you lied to us and said that you would go back and stay with your wife but you did not do that.[18] I fine you four head of cattle for having stolen this woman. I direct you to give a big ox to be used for buying the woman's clothing. Your divorce will be heard and judged by the big *kgotla*, not me.

You Letsebe, because the children are yours, I fine you £ 2 for not controlling your children, and for granting a divorce in your *kgotla*.

[The following account was then recorded when the dispute came before the Chief:]

Madubu: I am bringing an action against Molefe. I am bringing an action against him because he deserted me. My witness is headman Motshegare Ramalepa. Molefe deserted me in our home. He went away with his father's third wife. She is the one who separated us. I am appealing to the *kgotla* to help me by preventing Molefe from enjoying all the fruits of our wealth without giving me a share. I also wish to find out whether it is proper of Molefe to desert me and go away with his father's third wife. Molefe has taken his father's wife; that is why he has deserted me.

I am starving, I have nothing to eat. It is the sixth year since Molefe deserted me. Even when I am ill he does not care to see that I get medical treatment. He does not even care about our children.[19] Eventually, I was forced to report to his *kgotla* at Masiana, that he had deserted me and was living with his father's third wife.

Molefe is my husband. He got married to me in the Ngwato area. Our marriage was according to Tswana law (*ka lenyalo la Setswana*). He married me but he did not pay *bogadi.* He promised my parents that he would pay during the course of our marriage. Molefe was with Lekula when he negotiated with my parents. Lekula is a Mongwato. There was no Mokgatla save for Molefe himself. My parents agreed that Molefe should marry me all the same.

[Madubu speaks of the livestock held by Molefe. She then continues:]

Lekula negotiated my marriage with Molefe. Lekula is a Mongwato. He is not related to Molefe. Probably he is a friend of Molefe's. Lekula said he had been sent by Molefe to ask my parents to allow me to marry him. No Mokgatla came to negotiate for our marriage. Molefe pointed out that according to Kgatla custom people married first before paying *bogadi.* While I was still at my home no relative of Molefe came to confirm that they wanted us to marry, or that *bogadi* would be paid after marriage.

The Bakgatla people did not go to fetch me as their daughter-in-law. Rankatsu never came to my home. When I still lived happily with Molefe, Mankge used to call me his daughter-in-law.

On my arrival I found Mmamohutsiwa, my mother-in-law. I was introduced to her as her daughter-in-law. We lived together peacefully for 12 years. For the last 8 years we have been living in separation. I gave birth to our youngest child in Mmamohutsiwa's home. When Molefe deserted me I was living in our marriage home, i.e., the home we built together. When we were allotted the plot on which we built our home Mathibedi and Mogotsi were present.[20] In fact they are the ones who allotted the plot to us. I am quite convinced that I am married into the Masiana ward. We got married in 1944 and were separated in 1955.

Molefe: I did not get Madubu from her parents. I got her from her home and her parents did not know about it. I disagree with Madubu when she says that Lekula negotiated on my behalf. I fell in love with Madubu while parents were still alive. I stole her in 1945. I never said anything about *bogadi* to Madubu's parents. I did not tell my father anything when I came with Madubu. We went to the cattle post instead of coming home. I told my sister Motshabi that I had brought a wife with me. I did not tell Mmamohutsiwa. I disagree with the statement made by Madubu when she says that we lived in my parent's home when we came from the cattle post.

[Molefe speaks of property accumulated while he was living with Madubu. He then continues:]

The misunderstanding between us started in 1953. Madubu went to her home to work on the lands so that she could be given some corn. She left me at our lands and I was with her sister. She spent the remainder of 1953 at her parents home, only to come back at the beginning of winter in 1955. She found us harvesting. When she came in 1955 she said she had come to fetch the children. She said she had been sent to collect them. When Madubu came, she found that her sister had a baby boy by me. She expelled her sister and the baby without asking my opinion.

I look after my father's third wife. I started doing so after Mankge's death. I look after her by ploughing for her. I disagree with Madubu when she alleges that I do not look after her. I also disagree with her when she says that I am distracted by the fact that I look after my father's third wife. It is true I do not plough my father's fields.

Madubu is not telling the truth when she says Lekula was the man who acted as a link in our marriage negotiations. I actually stole Madubu away. I was quite aware of the law *(molao)* when I stole her. I did not tell my father when I came with Madubu. When we came on the first occastion, we went to my father's home. I did not introduce my father to her after my arrival. When I arrived home with Madubu I found Mankge, Mmamohutsiwa, and Segonyane. I did not introduce Madubu to Mmamohutsiwa. I hesitated to introduce them because Mmamohutsiwa did not like Madubu. I did not introduce Madubu to other members of Masiana *kgotla*. I did not tell my father's elder brother either. I was afraid of members of our *kgotla* so I did not introduce Madubu.

I have a baby whose mother is Madubu's sister. I love this baby as well as its mother. Madubu sent away both the baby and its mother and I went and fetched it. I went to fetch the child so that it could come and live with its father. The baby that Madubu's sister had by me is a boy. His name is Ramongalo. Ramongalo is a name that is common among my people, i.e., the Bakgatla. My other child who is a girl was born before the boy. I have not yet asked

Madubu's parents if I can marry Madubu's sister. I have paid several visits to the Ngwato area to see Madubu's sister. I have already mentioned that the dispute between me and Madubu started after she sent away her sister and the baby.

Motshabi: Molefe told me about Madubu while she was still at her home. He asked me to go and see her. I declined to go and see Madubu because Molefe had already promised to marry another woman here in the Bakgatla area. I feared that it might appear that I was encouraging him to turn down the woman that our parents had arranged he should marry. One day Molefe came to my home to introduce Madubu to me. After Molefe had introduced Madubu to me, I went to tell my father about the fact that Molefe had come with a wife. They were staying with me.

Mmamohutsiwa came to see Madubu but our father did not come because he did not like the marriage. Later, my father came with a present for his daughter-in-law. Molefe and his wife went back to the cattle post only to return later. They indicated that they had come to stay. This time they stayed at my father's home. Molefe and Madubu were entertained by my father as his own children and they were using the same cooking facilities. Later they went to the lands.

Segonyane: I was not told anything about Madubu's arrival. Molefe introduced me to her when I found them together at the cattle post.

Molefe did not tell me anything about the child which Madubu's sister had by him. I gathered that from the last words said by my father before he died. He said that Molefe's son should be given some cattle.

Odireleng Mabua (a paternal kinsman of Madubu): I heard a rumour that Molefe was proposing to marry Madubu, but before I confirmed this rumour Madubu had disappeared. I did not know where she had gone to. Lekula is the one who negotiated on behalf of Molefe. When I returned from military service at the end of the World War II, I met Molefe. After that I was told that my daughter had been stolen. I was made to understand that she was at Mochudi in the Kgatla area.

Balekanye Makgoeng (Madubu's mother's brother): I do not know anything about the marriage between Madubu and Molefe. I only heard by the way that Madubu was married to a Mokgatla. I was told this when I arrived from Johannesburg. In 1953 Madubu and Molefe visited my home. Madubu told me that as she did not have children she had decided to take her sister so that the younger sister could bear children for her. I asked Molefe whether her was married to Madubu and he denied it. I asked him how he could marry Madubu's sister before he married her. I told Madubu that I would have to discuss it with Madubu's parents before any decision could be reached.

We met and discussed the matter and we told Molefe that he could not marry Madubu's sister before he married Madubu. Molefe agreed with us and he returned to his home, promising to come back later to arrange to marry Madubu. Up to the present day we are still waiting for Molefe to fulfill his promise. We told Molefe that we wanted the children sent to their maternal grandparents because Molefe had not married their mother. We sent Molefe back to his home to urge his parents to initiate proper negotiations for marriage between him and Madubu.

We were surprised later to see Madubu come to fetch the children. When Madubu came to fetch the children, she did not consult with us. We are also surprised to find ourselves gathered here for what is alleged to be a divorce case. Molefe has not acted according to our custom by stealing both Madubu and her younger sister. Molefe lived with Madubu for several years. He stole her and lived with her as husband and wife.

Sefako Pilane: Molefe, your father Mankge is my mother's younger brother. I regard Madubu as my daughter-in-law and also as my grandmother because she is married to my uncle's son. Though we do not know how the marriage started, Mankge ultimately accepted Madubu as his daughter-in-law. I even had to give a sheep to Molefe and his wife Madubu as I was expected to do when my uncle's son got married. I was doing so in my capacity as the nephew. I did not help in the building of their home because they lived in the Masiana *kgotla*.

The Chief: Molefe and Madubu, I have listened to your case attentively. Molefe you have stolen Madubu and lived with her for eight years. You point out that at the beginning your father was not keen on Madubu but ultimately he accepted her as your wife. I gather from your relatives that Madubu is known to be your wife. Motshabi, your sister, Segonyane, your younger brother Sefako Pilane your father's nephew and Mmamohutsiwa, your father's wife, all speak to this. For those reasons there is no doubt in my mind that Madubu is your wife.

You are now declaring before this *kgotla* that you wish to divorce her. You must divide everything that you acquired in the last 18 years between yourself and Madubu. You must share your 36 head of cattle. You Molefe will get 26 head while Madubu gets the remaining 10. Out of the 7 sheep you will give Madubu 3 and you will take the remaining 4. As for the donkeys each of you get half of them.

In this case history several successive attempts at settlement are made prior to adjudication by the Chief. First, by taking the children back to Mookane, Madubu puts pressure on Molefe to return to her and formalize their relationship. Later, she attempts to strengthen the relationship through sorcery, and lastly she tries to enlist the support of Molefe's kinsmen by taking her complaints of neglect to them. For the present purposes these attempts at settlement are important both because they help us to locate the later stages of adjudication in the overall process of dispute settlement, and because they have crucial repercussions for the way in which the case subsequently unfolds. The involvement of one spouse in sorcery affecting the other is almost always an enduring source of trouble in a Kgatla marriage, so Madubu's clandestine approach to Radisoa must have strongly influenced members of Molefe's descent group in wanting to be rid of her quickly. Related to this, the agreement within the descent group that she should be treated as a concubine strongly influenced the strategy which Molefe followed when the dispute went on to higher levels. Among the Kgatla it has long been an accepted rule that a marriage, once formed, may only be dissolved by the Chief.[21] Consequently, once the members of Molefe's descent group had resolved to send Madubu back to Mookane without resort to any higher agency, they were virtually committed to the position in subsequent proceedings that the union was of an informal nature. Any contrary argument would have involved a tacit admission that they had flouted an accepted procedural norm; one which touched directly upon the Chief's authority.

At descent group level, and subsequently, these efforts to settle the dispute follow the orthodox Kgatla procedures.[22] Within the descent group, there is no one with power to adjudicate and a successful outcome at this level is thus dependent upon agreement; at the two subsequent levels the headman and the Chief are in a position to impose a decision from a third party standpoint. The manner of argument is also characteristic. Clear-cut issues in dispute (whether Madubu has been neglected, and whether she is a 'wife') are isolated early on, and argument is subsequently directed towards these issues. Further, although few norms are explicitly invoked, reliance upon norms (and the identity of the norms relied on) is implicit in the manner in which the facts adduced are selected and organised.[23]

The issue before Motshegare Ramalepa and the Chief was, therefore, clear-cut: were Molefe and Madubu to be recognised as married? The arguments which they respectively formulated around this issue, and the reaction of the Chief towards them, require close examination as they reveal clearly the Kgatla approach towards validity. Madubu directed her arguments towards three matters: the negotiations carried out with her kinsmen; the promise of *bogadi;* and the issue of her acceptance by members of the Masiana *kgotla*. With respect to the negotiations, she described these to the *kgotla*, suggesting that they had been concluded successfully, and tried to lend legitimacy to them by stating that they had been undertaken at the request of Molefe's maternal uncle, Rankatsu. Similarly, with the *bogadi*, she asserted that this had been promised, justifying a promise rather than the deed by reference to Kgatla custom. Lastly, she referred to Mankge's ultimate acceptance of her as a daughter-in-law, her introduction to Mmamohutsiwa, and the allocation of a residential plot within the ward to which members of Molefe's descent group belonged.

Molefe did not challenge the framework of Madubu's argument: he simply offered a conflicting interpretation of the facts to which it had been directed. Seeking to neutralize any effect she had achieved, he stressed that the negotiations carried out were of an unauthorised character and had ended without success. He emphatically denied the promise of *bogadi.* He then went on to say he had not introduced Madubu to Mankge and Mmamohutsiwa, or to other members of the Masiana *kgotla.* On this question of recognition and acceptance Madubu enjoyed the general support of Segonyane, Motshabi and Sefako. Molefe was understandably supported by Letsebe,[24] and his account of the negotiations was strengthened by the speeches of Madubu's kinsmen from Mookane.

The relative weight of these different arguments, as they must have appeared to the Chief, is not difficult to assess. On the question of the formalities – the negotiations and the promise of *bogadi* – Molefe had much the stronger case; note how Madubu's kinsmen even did not feel able to support her assertion that these had been properly concluded. But on the matter of Madubu's recognition and acceptance in the Masiana *kgotla,* all the weight was on the other side: Madubu's yard was there in the Masiana *kgotla* for everybody to see, and Molefe and Letsebe's arguments on this point were weak and blatantly self-seeking.

In judgement, the Chief found that Molefe and Madubu were married, even though Madubu had been 'stolen', and expressly justified his decision on the ground of Madubu's acceptance by Molefe's kinsmen.

In this case history the indigenous view of formation comes across plainly. If the Kgatla followed the jural approach suggested by Schapera, Molefe *must* have succeeded: the stated norms associated with the formation procedures had not been complied with. In this respect it is particularly significant that Molefe felt it necessary to counteract Madubu's argument directed at the issue of recognition and acceptance; if the essence of validity lay in the formalities associated with formation any such rebuttal would have been quite superfluous. Validity is here seen to lie in the recognition and acceptance of the union by the kinsmen with whom the parties live, and it is thus misleading to treat the stated norms associated with formation procedures as rules, compliance or non-compliance with which determines validity.

III

One consequence of the fact that validity lies in recognition and acceptance, rather than in compliance with a given set of formalities, is that the nature of a particular relationship, in the eyes of the parties and their kinsmen, is liable to change over time. So long as a relationship succeeds it remains 'marriage', but where things begin to go wrong and a state of breakdown develops there is a tendency to dismiss the union as mere concubinage. It follows that a person may revise and up-date his version of a particular relationship to suit contemporary interests; and this freedom is seen as particularly valuable when strategies are developed in the context of a dispute. The history of the relationship between Molefe and Madubu provides an illustration of this process. When Madubu initially complained in 1959 that Molefe was neglecting her, he made no attempt to meet her complaint with the reply that she was not his 'wife'. When he came before the Chief for failing to sell an ox as Motshegare had ordered, he began his speech in the *kgotla* by saying that Madubu was his wife *(Madubu ke mosadi wa me)* and that they had been married for fourteen years. And yet, two years later he was trying to justify his treatment of Madubu on the ground that they had never been married. Kgatla see nothing incongruous in such revisions, which constitute a frequent feature of the management of marital conflict. Nor are they limited to the duration of the relationship concerned, but may be resorted to years after the immediate parties are dead, as the following case history shows.

Case 2: A dispute between Modise and Lesoka

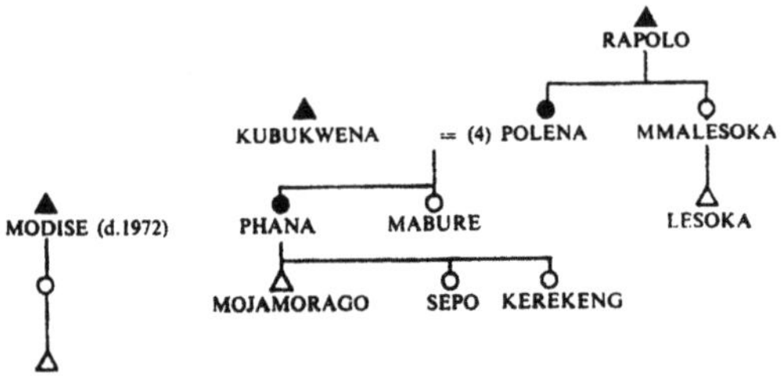

Figure 2

Kubukwena, an immigrant from the nearby Kwena tribe, asked Rapolo (a member of the Phuteng *kgotla*) for his daughter Polena as a fourth wife (See Figure 2 above). It seems that this request was granted as Polena went to live in a homestead prepared by Kubukwena; but no *bogadi* was presented. Polena bore two daughters Phana and Mabure. Phana never married, but she gave birth to a son, Mojamorago, and two daughters, Sepo and Kerekeng (see Figure 2) Mabure did marry, after both Kubukwena and Rapolo were dead. *Bogadi* cattle were presented for her, but these were claimed by Lesoka, the son of Polena's younger unmarried sister. Lesoka also took four beasts which were paid as compensation when Sepo was later made pregnant by Teko, one of Sefako Pilane's sons. He justified this action on the grounds that Kubukwena had failed to present *bogadi* for Polena and his claims were not at the time resisted by surviving male descendants of Kubukwena.

Some years after these events, when Mojamorago was a young man, he made one of Modise's daughters pregnant. When this pregnancy was noticed, and the girl had named Mojamorago as being responsible, Modise visited Lesoka to inform him of what had happened. Before the birth, Lesoka returned this visit, told Modise that Mojamorago accepted responsibility and would marry the girl. Modise put up no objection to this proposal. Later when the baby was born, Modise reported the birth to Lesoka. Some months later, seeing that Mojamorago showed no sign of marrying the girl, Modise again visited Lesoka and demanded instead the four head of cattle payable as compensation for pregnancy of an unmarried women. But Lesoka repeated his promise that Mojamorago would marry. Still, no marriage took place. Modise made further informal requests to Lesoka for the payment of compensation, but without success. Eventually, Lesoka told Modise that as Mojamorago was a member of Kubukwena's lineage, Kubukwena's sons should pay for the pregnancy. Modise then approached members of this group, but they too refused to take responsibility for the pregnancy.

Having failed to settle his claim through these informal approaches, Modise then took his complaint to Sekapa Mariri, headman of the Phuteng *kgotla* to which Lesoka belonged. Sekapa also tried informally to persuade Lesoka to pay the compensation demands but his efforts were unsuccessful. Lesoka again denied responsibility on the ground that Mojamorago was a member of Kubukwena's descent group. He also said that because of this the dispute was not one which could not be properly handled formally by his own ward *kgotla*. Accordingly, Sekapa reported the matter to the Chief.

The following speeches were recorded when the dispute was heard by the Chief:

Modise: I am suing Lesoka for seduction. Lesoka's child impregnated my daughter. She had a child by him. After my daughter told me that Lesoka's son had impregnated her, I went to Lesoka and told him about the pregnancy. After the baby was born, I went and told Lesoka that the baby had been born.

Lesoka came to me before the birth of the child and told me that he had asked his son about the matter. He said his son admitted paternity, and Lesoka told me that his son intended to marry my daughter. I told him that if his son intended to marry my daughter then I had no objection. I waited for a very long time but there was no sign of preparations for marriage being made. Eventually, I decided that it was wise for me to ask Lesoka to pay damages for seduction if his son no longer wished to marry my daughter. I repeatedly went to Lesoka's place to ask him to pay the damages but each demand was met with a promise to marry. The promise to marry was never fulfilled.

For a very long time I tried to persuade Lesoka to pay me but he failed. Eventually I was forced to hand the matter to his headman, Sekapa, so that he could deal with it. When the matter was supposed to be heard by the headman, the headman told me that Lesoka had said that he did not want the matter to be heard in Photeng *kgotla* nor indeed in the Mabodisa *kgotla*. Rather, he wanted the matter to be decided by the Chief's *kgotla*.

Lesoka now repudiates liability in damages for seduction. He says the child is Kubukwena's and therefore it is only fair that Kubukwena should pay.

The matter was reported to Kubukwena's children, that is to say Rasekhurutshe Shadi, Samotho, and Rasekei.

They refused to pay as well, on the ground that the illegitimate child was not their responsibility.

When I realised that Lesoka was reluctant to pay and also unwilling to pay, I resolved to bring the matter to the Chief's *kgotla.*

Sekapa Mariri (headman, Phuteng *kgotla*): Modise reported the matter to me. He told me that Lesoka was refusing to pay damages for seduction. I talked to Lesoka, trying to persuade him to pay damages to Modise. He told me that the boy who had impregnated Modise's daughter was not his son but Kubukwena's son. Lesoka told me that his case was such that could not be properly handled by the Phuteng *kgotla* or the Mabodisa. Only the Chief's *kgotla* could manage it.

Johanah Moremi (daughter of Kubukwena, by his first wife): The boy who impregnated Modise's daughter is Lesoka's son and not Kubukwena's son. The reason why I say that is because I took part in the arrangement of the marriage of Mabure, i.e. Kubukwena's daughter. *Bogadi* was paid for her. Lesoka took the *bogadi* cattle paid for Mabure. Lesoka argued that Kubukwena had not been formally married to his aunt, (i.e., his mother's sister). After that incident Lesoka went to my father's enclosure and took the cattle belonging to Mojamorago (that is to say the boy who impregnated Modise's daughter). He took those cattle without consulting anybody. Lesoka also took the cattle paid for the seduction of Mojamorago's sister. He took them from Sefako Pilane. Mojamorago is Lesoka's son on the following grounds; Lesoka took the cattle paid for Mojamorago's sister as *bogadi*; when Mabure got married he took Mojamorago's cattle: he got seduction damages from Sefako. They were damages for the seduction of Mojamorago's sister. Lesoka took all the cattle mentioned above in his capacity as father, now he is faced with a responsibility which he has to shoulder in the same capacity as father, and he wants to avoid it.

Samotho Molwane (daughter of Kubukwena, by his second wife): Mojamorago is my younger sister's son. Her name is Phana. After Mojamorago impregnated Modise's daughter, Lesoka was informed of the matter. He was made aware that Mojamorago had impregnated Modise's daughter but Lesoka did not tell anybody.

Lesoka took the cattle paid for the *bogadi* of Mabure who is Mojamorago's mother's sister. Lesoka also took the cattle for the seduction of the other sister of Mojamorago's from Sefako. All the time Lesoka treated Mojamorago as his son but now Mojamorago is in trouble he (Lesoka) no longer wants to continue as a father. Lesoka should pay Modise the damages on behalf of Mojamorago because all the cattle are with him.

Rasekhurutshe Lesejane (an agnate of Kubukwena): I can testify that Mojamorago's cattle are with Lesoka. Even the cattle paid for Mabure's *bogadi* are with Lesoka. Mabure is Mojamorago's mother's sister. Further, Lesoka took the cattle for the seduction of Mojamorago's younger sister from Sefako. Lesoka should be held responsible for what Mojamorago has done because he has always acted as the latter's father as he is keeping Mojamorago's cattle. Lesoka was not supposed to take Mojamorago's cattle.

Lesoka: Modise came to me and told me that Mojamorago had impregnated his daughter. I asked the boy and he admitted responsibility. I then told Modise that Mojamorago had admitted responsibility and he had indicated that he wanted to marry the girl.

I am quite aware that Modise wants me to pay damages on behalf of Mojamorago and I refuse to be held liable on behalf of Mojamorago. In 1963, Mojamorago's mother, that is to say Phana, came to me in the company of Modise. Modise then told us that Mojamorago had impregnated his daughter. I received his complaint and promised to ask the boy in question (Mojamorago). After Mojamorago came, I told him that Modise had lodged a complaint to the effect that he had impregnated Modise's daughter. Mojamorgo replied that Modise's complaint was true. Mojamorago explained that he intended to marry the girl. I relayed this story to Mojamorago's mother and she pointed out that Mojamorago had already told her the same story.

Some time later, Modise came to me and demanded that I should pay seduction damages on behalf of Mojamorago. I refused to pay damages on behalf of Mojamorago because he is not my son. He was not even to be my charge. I had to pay seduction damages for him. Mojamorago is my aunt's son (that is my mother's sister's son).

After Mojamorago impregnated Modise's daughter, I did not tell anyone of Kubukwena's children, i.e., Johanah and Samotho. It was only Phana who knew about it.

It is true that I took the *bogadi* cattle paid for Mabure and I also took Mojamorago's cattle as well as cattle paid as seduction damages for the younger sister of Mojamorago.

I was given the cattle paid for Mabure's *bogadi* by Phana so that I could look after them. Those cattle rightfully belong to Mojamorago. He should use them for paying seduction damages after consulting his sister Mabure.

The cattle which were paid by Sefako as seduction damages for Mojamorago's younger sister are also in my possession. They are among my cattle but I never told any of Kubukwena's children that I had received any seduction damages for Mojamorago's younger sister called Sepo.

Chief (Linchwe Kgafela): Modise, I have listened carefully to the case between you and Lesoka, concerning seduction damages. Lesoka, you must admit that Modise came to you and told you that Mojamorago had impregnated his daughter. You do not deny his allegations. Above all, you promised Modise that Mojamorago would marry his daughter. You failed to fulfil your promise about marriage. You refused to meet the demand by Modise for the payment of seduction damages. You have made schemes by which you can disclaim liability on behalf of Mojamorago on the alleged ground that he is not your son. Clearly, the evidence that has been adduced from this *kgotla* is consistent with one fact, that Mojamorago is your son because you took the *bogadi* cattle paid for his sister. You also took the cattle paid for the seduction of his younger sister. This *kgotla* believes that Mojamorago is your charge and you are therefore liable on his behalf.

Lesoka, this *kgotla* finds against you. You must pay Modise four head of cattle since you have Mojamorago's cattle. You will also pay an extra beast for wasting Modise's daughter's time by promising marriage and then breaking your promise. She probably would have been offered marriage by somebody else had she not pinned her hopes on you. In all you will have to pay five head of cattle. This *kgotla* orders that you should by the 14th October, 1965, have paid the five head of cattle.

This case history shows the time scale over which attempts to exploit ambiguities in a marriage-type relationship may take place, and some of the hazards inherent in such attempts over the longer term.[25] Because no *bogadi* cattle were given for Polena when Kubukwena took her, Lesoka was able to assert that the children and remoter issue did not belong to Kubukwena's lineage, but to his own. Initially, this strategy was successful as it enabled Lesoka to gain control of Mabure's *bogadi* and the *marebana* cattle paid in respect of Sepo's pregnancy, but it failed when he was ultimately forced to accept less pleasant implications of Mojamorago's membership of his group. Having consistently placed one interpretation upon Kubukwena's relationship with Polena prior to the incident involving Mojamorago, Lesoka revises this when confronted with Modise's demands for compensation. By asserting that Mojamorago is Kubukwena's child, i.e., a member of Kubukwena's lineage, he implies that Kubukwena and Polena were really married after all. But as the hearing in the Chief's *kgotla* proceeded, this version was strongly and effectively contested by members of Kubukwena's lineage. Just before the Chief speaks, Lesoka implicity admits that he has failed when he offers a final re-interpretation of his own conduct. When he speaks for the last time he says: 'I was given the cattle paid for Mabure's *bogadi* by Phana *so that I could look after them*' (my italics). Here he is trying to place in a more favourable light his original control over these cattle by saying that he took them in a fiduciary capacity as a good mother's brother. An inescapable implication of this re-interpretation is that he had assumed Kubukwena and Polena to be married all along.

IV

Both of the case histories related here show how unhelpful western legal concepts and categories are in trying to understand the Kgatla marriage. The first case illustrates how failure to comply with well established socially approved norms relating to formation procedure does not necessarily mean that a marriage is 'invalid'. The second case spells out further implications of the fact that validity is not tied exclusively to compliance with formal procedures; notably the extent to which the interpretation of a particular relationship may change over time and be subject to manipulation in the context of a dispute. All of these elements are quite foreign to the marriage law of modern western societies. In conclusion it must be noted that 'jural' approaches to marriage, derived explicitly or by implication from western jurisprudence, have been widely invoked in the study of marriage in small scale societies. While we should be wary of trying to generalize on the basis of experience in a single society, the Kgatla case suggests that the dangers inherent in this type of borrowing may not have been fully appreciated.

NOTES

1. In most of these accounts, the description has centred upon ceremonial visitations, resort to religious specialists, the slaughter of livestock, feasting, and transfers of property.
2. See, for example, Cotran 1968; Ibik 1970; Rubin 1970.
3. Marriage Act, 1949, ss 25, 49.
4. Bohannan has warned of the danger of giving a 'folk system' of one society wider application than its merit and usefulness allow (1957:5), and despite the controversy that has surrounded his elaboration of his views on this topic, the general tenor of his warning seems uncontroversial; nonetheless, lawyers have been slow to heed it.
5. A man's natural guardian is his father or, when he is dead, some other member of his patrilineage. Among the Tswana, the prohibited degrees of marriage are relatively narrowly drawn, and marriage with a child born to a sibling of either parent is generally permitted (and in many cases encouraged): see, Schapera 1957.
6. Schapera (1938; 1940) describes the relationship established at this point as 'betrothal', and I have previously followed his usage in distinguishing between betrothal and marriage (1970; 1972). However, this dichotomy is suggestive of a clear cut transition from the stage at which an agreement to marry has been reached to the stage of marriage itself. This is not present in the Kgatla case, where the process of formation seems most accurately depicted as continuing smoothly to maturity over time.
7. In February, 1973, I carried out a detailed survey of one Kgatla ward, Rampedi, in the village of Mochudi. In that ward there were at that time 31 couples living together in apparently open, continuous cohabitation. I found that in 21 cases (68%) both *dilo tsa patlo* and *bogadi* had been presented and that in a further six cases (19%) *dilo tsa patlo* had been forthcoming. In the remaining four cases (13%) the agreement of the two groups of kin had not been obtained and neither type of prestation had passed.
8. This case history is compiled from accounts of the dispute given to me by Motshegare Ramalepa, Segonyane Dithare, Amos Kgamanyane Pilane and other Kgatla tribesmen, and from the written record kept when the dispute was heard before the Tlagadi *kgotla* (unnumbered record) and the Chief's *kgotla* (case 51 of 1962). The records are translated by Mr. Passevil Phumaphi.
9. Such a match enjoys particular approval among the Kgatla who consider that a man should look first for a wife among the young females of the descent group to which his mother's brother belongs.
10. This would have been a perfectly acceptable form of the sororate, had Madubu's senior kinsmen agreed to it; see Schapera 1938.
11. Kgatla husbands and wives should not approach these magicians without letting

each other know; a solo approach carries a presumption of intended harm to the other spouse. Radisoa evidently judged it in his best professional and personal interests to steer clear of this quarrel.

12. I.e., Mmaseteba, Mankge's third wife.
13. Rankatsu was a brother of Molefe's mother. It ideally falls to a man's mother's brother to supervise the negotiation of his marriage.
14. He refers here to a dispute which arose following the birth of children to Madubu's younger sister.
15. Masuge is the husband of Molefe's elder sister, Motshabi.
16. The speaker refers to the fact that Sebopelo, the headman, and other senior members of the Masiana *kgotla* were absent from the initial discussion of Madubu's future. The implication is that this meeting was improperly conducted.
17. One of Rankatsu's sons.
18. Motshegare refers to an undertaking which Molefe had given when he had previously been ordered to maintain Madubu.
19. That is, the children which Madubu's younger sister had born for her under the sororate relationship.
20. Two senior members of the Tlagadi ward who had been delegated by Motshegare to make the allotment.
21. The origin of this custom is obscure; it has been followed as long as the oldest men now living in the Kgatleng can remember. Some say that the rule was introduced as a direct legislative measure by Lentswe I (1875–1924).
22. These procedures are discussed fully in Schapera 1938; Comaroff and Roberts 1977.
23. The use of norms in the Tswana processes of dispute settlement is considered in detail in Comaroff and Roberts 1977.
24. Letsebe could hardly have argued otherwise as he had been the senior man at the meeting of the Masiana *kgotla* at which it has been decided to send Madubu back to Mookane without further formality.
25. The case history also shows how these 'uncertain' marriage-type relationships are nothing new in the Kgatleng but have been a feature of the society over a long period of time. Kubukwena and Polena must have established their relationship at least 50 years ago. This point is important, as Kgatla themselves (as well as observers) tend to see marriage-type relationships in respect of which the traditional formalities are not precisely complied with as a product of recent 'changes' in Kgatla society.

Bibliography

Abel, R. 'A comparative theory of dispute institutions in society', *Law and Society Review* 8(2), pp. 250–347.
Achike, O. 'Some aspects of African customary law of contract', unpublished paper delivered at Workshop on African Law, Nsukka, Nigeria, 6–9 August, 1974.
Allott, A. N. *Essays in African Law*, London, 1960.
—. *New Essays in African Law*, London, 1970.
Aryee, A. F. 'Christianity and polygyny in Ghana: the role of the church as an instrument of social change', *Ghana Journal of Sociology* 3, 1967, pp. 98–105.
Asmis, R. Die Stammesrechte der Boxiske Sandanne Mangu, *Zeitschrift für vergleichende Rechtswissenschaft*, 1912, pp. 78–89.
Azu, D. G. *The Ga Family and Social Change*, *African Research Document Series*, Leiden and Cambridge, 1974.
Barnes, J. *Politics in a changing society*, Manchester, 1954.
—. 'Measures of divorce frequency in simple societies', *Journal of the Royal African Institute* 79, 1949, pp. 37–62.
Beckford, George L. *Persistent Poverty: Underdevelopment in Plantation Economies of the Third World*, New York, 1972.
Beefried, Freiherr von. 'Beiträge zur Geschichte des Manguvolkes in Togo', Zeitschrift für Ethnologie, 1913, pp. 421–435.
Bennion, F. A. R. *Constitutional Law of Ghana*, London, 1962.
Bleek, W. 'Geographical Mobility and Conjugal residence in a Kwahu lineage', *Research Review* 8(3), pp. 47–55.
—. 'Young parents and children in a Kwahu lineage', forthcoming in: *Legon Family Research Papers No. 4*, ed. by L. Engberg, I. A. S. University of Ghana.
—. 'Perception and practice of birthcontrol in a Ghanaian matrilineage', in: *The Neglected factor: Family Planning, Perception and Reaction at the Base*, ed. by D. G. Jongmans and H. J. M. Claessen, Assen, 1974.
—. 'Marriage, inheritance and witchcraft; a case study of a rural Ghanaian family', forthcoming in: *Research papers*, Afrika-Studiecentrum, Leiden 1975.
Bohannan, P. *Justice and Judgment among the Tiv*, 1957.
Brelsford, V. W. *The Tribes of Zambia*, Lusaka, n. d. (1965).
Bromley, P. *Family Law*, 4th ed., London, 1971.
—. *Family Law, Supplement to the 4th ed.*, London, 1974.
Brooke, N. J. *Report on the Native Court System*, Freetown, 1954.

Caldwell, J.C. 'Extended family obligations and education: a study of an aspect of demographic transition amongst Ghanaian university students', *Population Studies* 22, 1965, pp. 361–77.

—. 'The erosion of the family: a study of the family in Ghana', *Population Studies* 20, 1966.

—. *Population Growth and Family Change in Africa: The New Urban Elite in Ghana*, Canberra, 1968.

Cameron, D. *My Tanganyika Service and Some Nigeria*, London, 1939.

Caplan, G.L. *The Elites of Barotseland, 1878–1969*, London, 1970.

Carbonnier, J. *Droit civil* II, 9th ed., Paris, 1972.

Chin, W.H. 'The family in areas of rapid urbanization', Proceedings of the Conference of Social Development through the Family and Home, Oxford, Colonial Office Document 5406/59 (mimeographed), 1969.

Clay, G.C.R. *History of Mankoya District*, Lusaka, 1945.

Collier, J. *Law and Social Change in Zinacantan*, Stanford, Calif., 1973.

Colson, E. *Marriage and the Family among the Plateau Tonga of Northern Rhodesia*, Manchester, 1958.

—. *The Plateau Tonga*, Manchester, 1962.

Comaroff, J.L. and Roberts, S.A. 'The invocation of norms in processes of dispute settlement among the Tswana', in *Anthropology and Law*, ed. by Hamnett, 1977.

Contini, P. 'Integration of Legal Systems in the Somali Republic', 16 I.C.L.Q., 1088 (1967).

Cotran, E. *Kenya I: Marriage and Divorce*, No. 1 in the Restatement of African Law Series, London, 1968.

Cretney, S. *Principles of Family Law*, London, 1974.

Cunnison, I.G. *The Luapula Peoples of Northern Rhodesia*, Manchester, 1959.

Date-Bah, Eugenia. 'Some features of marriage patterns among the members of one elite group in Ghana', *Legon Family Research Papers No. 3*, I.A.S. University of Ghana, (forthcoming).

Delafosse, M. *La langue mandingue*, 2e vol., Paris, 1955.

Driberg, J.H. 'The African conception of law', *Journal of Comparative Legislation and International Law* (3rd series), 1934, pp. 230–50.

Duncan, P. *Sotho Laws and Customs*, Capetown, 1960.

Dundas, C. 'Native law of some Bantu Tribes of East Africa', 51 J.R.A.I., 1921.

Elias, T.O. *The Nature of African Customary Law*, Manchester, 1956.

—. *The Nigerian Legal System*, 1963.

Epstein, A.L. 'Some aspects of the conflict of law and urban courts in Northern Rhodesia', *Rhodes-Livingstone Journal*, 1951.

—. *The Administration of Justice and the Urban African*, London, 1953.

—. 'Divorce law and the stability of marriage among the Lunda of Kazembe', *Rhodes-Livingstone Journal*, 1954a.

—. *Juridical Techniques and Judicial Process*, Manchester, 1954b.

Evans-Pritchard, E.E. *Kinship and Marriage among the Nuer*, O.U.P., 1951.

Frank, A.G. *Capitalism and Underdevelopment in Latin America, Historical Studies of Chile and Brazil*, New York, 1967.

Fisch, R. *Nord-Togo und seine Westliche Nachbarschaft*, Basel, 1911.

Fortes, M. 'Time and social structure', in *Social Structure*, ed. by M. Fortes, Oxford, 1949.

—. 'Descent, filiation and affinity', *Man* 59, No. 339, 1959.

Fyfe, A. *A Short History of Sierra Leone*, London, 1967.

Gennep, A. van. *Les rites de passage*, Paris, 1908.

Gibbs, J.L. 'Marital instability among the Kpelle', *American Anthropologist* 65, 1963, pp. 552–73.

Gluckman, M. *Economy of the Central Barotse Plain*, Manchester, 1941.
—. *Essays on Lozi Land and Royal Property*, Livingstone, 1943.
—. *The Judicial Process among the Barotse of Northern Rhodesia*, 2nd ed., Manchester, 1967a.
—. Introduction, in: Epstein, A.L., ed. *The Craft of Social Anthropology*, London, 1967b.
—, ed. *Ideas and Procedures in African Customary Law*, London, 1969.
—. *The Ideas in Barotse Jurisprudence*, 2nd ed., Manchester, 1972.
—. 'Limitation of the case method in the study of tribal law', *Law and Society Review* 1973(7), p. 611.
Goda, P.J. 'The historical evolution of the concepts of void and voidable marriages', *Journal of Family Law* 7(2), 1967, pp. 297–308.
Gulliver, P.H. *Social Control in an African Society*, London, 1963.
—. 'Dispute settlement without courts: the Ndendeuli of Southern Tanzania', in *Law in Culture and Society*, ed. by L. Nader, Chicago, 1969.
Gutkind, P.C. *African Urban Family Life*, *Cahiers d'études Africaines*, vol. 3, no. 2, 1962.
Guttman, E. 'The Reception of Common Law in the Sudan', 6 I. C. L. Q., 401 (1957).
Harrell-Bond, B.E. *Modern Marriage in Sierra Leone: A Study of the Professional Group*, The Hague, 1975.
—. and Rijnsdorp, U. *Family Law in Sierra Leone*, Afrika-Studiecentrum, Leiden, 1975.
Hintze, U. 'Die sprachliche Stellung des Anufo (Chokosi), ein Beitrag zur Gliederung der Akansprachen', *Mitteilungen Institut für Orientforschung*, Vol. 1, 1953, p. 151.
Holleman, J.F. 'Trouble-cases and Troubleless cases in the study of customary law and legal reform', *Law and Society Review* 1973(7), p. 585.
Hoselitz, B.F. 'The city, the factory, and economic growth', *American Economic Review* (supplement) 45, 1955, pp. 166–84.
Hulsen, C., and Mertens, F. 'Chapter eight: Marriage and family', in *Survey of the Church in Ghana*, Pro Mundi Vita, n.d.
Ibik, J. *Malawi I: Marriage and Divorce*, No. 3 in the Restatement of African Law Series, London, 1970.
Jackson, J. *Matrimonial Finance and Taxation*, London, 1972.
Johnstone, H. 'The importance of Africa', 17 *Journal of Africa Society* 179, 1918.
Joko-Smart, H.M. 'Inheritance to property in Sierra Leone', *Sierra Leone Studies, New Series No. 24*, January 1969.
Kasunmu, A.B. 'The Matrimonial Causes Decree', *The Nigerian Journal of Contemporary Law*, 1970, Vol. 2 102.
—, and Salacuse, J. *Nigerian Family Law*, 1968.
Kludze, A.P.K. *Ewe Law of Property*, London, 1973.
Köbben, A.J.F. *Van primitieven tot medeburgers*, Tweede gewijzigde en uitgebreide druk, Assen, 1971.
Kritzeck, J., and Lewis, W.H. (eds.), *Islam in Africa*, New York, 1969.
Kumekpor, T. 'Marriage and the family in a changing society', *Legon Research Papers No. 3*, I.A.S., University of Ghana, (forthcoming).
Kuper, A. 'The Kgalagari and the jural consequences of marriage', *Man* 5(3), 1970, pp. 466–82.
Kwame, A., ed. *The papers of George Ekem Ferguson, a Fanti official of the Government of the Gold Coast, 1890–1897*, African Social Research Documents No. 7, Cambridge, 1974.
Laloum, J.D. *Manuel du juge de paix*, Lome, 1963.
Leach, E.R. 'Polyandry, inheritance and the definition of marriage', *Man* 182, 1955.
Levtzion, N. *Muslim Chiefs in West Africa: A Study of Islam in the Middle Volta Basin in the Pre-colonial Period*, Oxford, 1968.

Lewis, O. *Five Families: Mexican Case Studies in the Culture of Poverty*, New York 1959.
—. *The Children of Sanchez*, New York, 1961.
—. *Pedro Martinez*, New York, 1964.
Laws of Sierra Leone, 1960 edition.
Levine, R. A. 'Father-child relationships and changing life-styles in Ibadan', in *The City in Modern Africa*, ed. by H. Miner, London, 1967.
Liebenow, J. G. *Colonial Rule and Political Development in Tanzania: The Case of the Makonde*, Evanston, Ill., 1971.
Little, K. *The Mende of Sierra Leone*, London, 1967 (1st ed. 1951).
—. *African Women in Towns: An Aspect of Africa's Social Revolution*, Cambridge, 1973.
—., and Price, A. 'Urbanization, migration and the African family', Addison-Wesley Module in Anthropology, No. 51, 1974.
Llewellyn, K. N., and Hoebel, E. A. *The Cheyenne Way*, Norman, 1941.
Lloyd, P. C. (ed.). 'The new elites in tropical Africa', Studies presented and discussed at the Sixth International African Seminar, O.U.P., London, 1966.
Lowy, M. 'The ethnography of law in a changing Ghanaian town', unpublished Ph. D. dissertation, University of California at Berkeley, 1971.
—. 'Me Ko Court: The impact of urbanization on conflict resolution in a Ghanaian town', in *Anthropologists in Cities*, ed., by G. Foster and R. Kemper, 1974, pp. 153–77.
—. 'A good name is worth more than money: strategies of court ase in urban Ghana', in: *The Disputing Process: Law in 12 Societies*, ed. by L. Nader and H. Todd (forthcoming), n.d.
Lugard, F. *The Dual Mandate in British Tropical Africa*, London.
Lystad, R. *Ashanti, A Proud People*, Princetown, 1958.
Mainga, M. *Bulozi under the Luyana Kings*, London, 1973.
Mair, L. *African Marriage and Social Change*, London, 1969.
Marwick, M. *Sorcery in its Social Setting*, Manchester, 1965.
McCall, D. 'The effect on family structure of changing economic activities of women in a Gold Coast town', unpublished Ph. D. dissertation, Columbia University, 1965.
McCulloch, M. 'The Nkoya-Mbwela peoples', in: McCulloch, M. *The Southern Lunda and Related Peoples*, London, 1951.
Memo No. 2, Local Government Memoranda, No. 2 (Local Courts), Dar es Salaam, Government Printer, 1957.
Mitchell, J. C. *The Yao Village*, Manchester, 1956.
Nader, L., and Yngvesson, B. 'On studying the ethnography of law and its consequences', in: Honigmann, ed. *Handbook of Social and Cultural Anthropology*, 1973.
Nukynya, G. K. 'Kinship, marriage and family: a study of the influences of contemporary social changes on an Ewe tribe', unpublished Ph. D. thesis, London, 1964.
Nwabueze, B. O. *The Machinery of Justice in Nigeria*, London, 1963.
Nwogugu, E. I. *Family Law in Nigeria*, 1974.
O'Donovan, K. 'Void and voidable marriages', *Journal of Ethiopian Law* 7(2), 1972, p. 439–55.
Ollennu, N. A. *Principles of Customary Land Law in Ghana*, London, 1962.
Oppong, C. *Marriage among a Matrilineal Elite*, Cambridge, 1974.
—. 'Chains of change in family systems and family size', I.A.S. University of Ghana, mimeographed, 1974a.
—. 'Attitudes to jointness, segregation and family size: a study of norms among Ghanaian students', I.A.S. University of Ghana, mimeographed, 1974b.
—. 'Marriage among a matrilineal elite: a family study of Ghanaian senior civil servants', *Cambridge Studies in Social Anthropology* 8, London, 1974c.
Palmer, V. V., and Poulter, S. M. *The Legal System of Lesotho*, Charlotteville, 1972.

Parker, I. 'Ideological and economic development in Tanzania', Paper presented at 14th Annual Meeting of African Studies Association, Denver, November 1971.
Parkin, D.J. 'Medicines and men of influence', *Man*, 1969.
Paulsen, M.G. 'Support rights and duties between husband and wife', *Vanderbilt Law Review*, Vol. 9 (1956), No. 4, 709.
Pauwels, J.M. 'Mécanisme et fonctions de la dot chez les Tyo, (Teke) du Kongo Central', in: *Colloque sur la dot*, Lubumbashi, 1968, pp. 123–49.
—. *Répertoire de droit coutumier congolais*, 1954–1967, Kinshasa, 1970.
—. 'L'alliance en coutume tio-droit et magie', *Revue Juridique du Zaïre* 47(2), 1971.
Peil, M. 'Ghanaian university students. The broadening base', *British Journal of Sociology* 16 (1965), pp. 19–28.
Petit, M. 'Territory Court of Leopoldville, February 2, 1956', *Journal des Tribunaux d'Outre-Mer*, 1958, 76, summary, note.
Phillips, A. *Survey of African Marriage and Family Life*, London, 1953.
Pool, D.I. 'Conjugal patterns in Ghana', *Canadian Review of Sociology and Anthropology* 5, 1968, pp. 241–53.
Prost, R.P.A. *La langue des Anufom de Sansanne-Mango*, Documents Linguistiques No. 3, Université de Dakar, Senegal, 1958(?).
Radcliffe Brown, A.R. and C.D. Forde (eds.). *African Systems of Kinship and Marriage* London, 1950.
Rattray, R.S. *Religion and Art in Ashanti*, Oxford, 1927.
—. *Ashanti Law and Constitution*, Oxford, 1929.
Rey-Hulman, Diana. 'Les dépendants des maîtres Tyokossi pendant la période précoloniale', in: Cl. Meillassoux (éd.). *L'esclavage en Afrique précoloniale*, Paris, 1975, pp. 297–320.
Rivière, P.G. 'Marriage: a reassessment', in: *Rethinking Kinship and Marriage*, Association of Social Anthropologists Monograph No. 11, London, 1971.
Richards, A.I. *Land, Labour and Diet in Northern Rhodesia*, London, 1939.
Rigaux, F. *Les personnes, I, les relations familiales*, Brussels, 1971.
Roberts, S.A. *Tswana Family Law*, No. 5 in the Restatement of African Law Series, London, 1972.
Rodman, H. *Lower-Class Families*, New York, 1971.
Rodney, Walter. *How Europe Underdeveloped Africa*, London and Dar es Salaam, 1972.
Rouveroy, E.A.B. van Nieuwaal van. *The Tyokossi or Anufom*, The Yearbook of the Foundation for Scientific Research for the Tropics, The Hague, 1971.
—. *Essai sur quelques aspects du droit matrimonial chez les Anufòm, Mededelingen No. 10* (Afrika-Studiecentrum, Leiden, 1973).
—. *Mbambim, un chef de famille d'Ayikpèrè* (Afrika-Studiecentrum, Leiden, 1973). *Musulmans à Mango* (Afrika-Studiecentrum, Leiden, 1974).
—. *Sherea, la justice coutumière à la cour du chef supérieur à N'zara*, (Afrika-Studiecentrum, Leiden, 1975); forthcoming in: *Recueil Penant*, vol. 752, 1975.
—. The Plot of the Sophisticated Son-in-Law, Disparity between Old and New Ways of Establishing Rights over Land in N'zara, North Togo', *Kroniek van Afrika*, (1) 1973: 47-60.
Rubin, N.N. 'Matrimonial law among the Bali of West Cameroon: a restatement', *Journal of African Law* 14 (1970), pp. 69–97.
Salisbury, R., and Salisbury, M. 'The rural oriented strategy of urban adaptation: Siane migrants in Port Moresby', in: *The Anthropology of Urban Environments*, ed. by T. Weaver and D. White, 1972, pp. 59–68.
Sanjek, R. 'Pat-Pat, Pat-mat, Mat-pat, Mat-Mat: mixed marriages and ethnic identity in Adabraka', unpublished ms., n.d.
Sawyerr, Akilagpa. 'The internal conflict of laws in Ghana', unpublished dissertation for degree of Master of Laws, University of London, 1965.

—. 'Internal conflict of laws in East Africa', in: A. Sawyerr (ed.). *East African Law and Social Change*, Nairobi, 1967, pp. 110 f.
—. 'Reflections on the internal conflict of laws in Tanzania: an outline', *Afrika Spectrum* 3/69, 23, 1969.
—. 'Interpersonal conflict of laws in Tanzania', unpublished dissertation for the degree of Doctor of the Science of Law, University of California at Berkeley, 1971.
—. 'Customary law in the High Court of Tanzania', *Eastern Africa Law Review*, Vol 6. (1973), pp. 265–284.
—. 'Application of law in Tanganyika: a proper remedy approach to some problems of legal pluralism', *Eastern Africa Law Review*, Vol. 7 (1974), pp. 223–246.
Schapera, I. *A Handbook of Tswana Law and Custom*, London, 1938.
—. *Married Life in an African Tribe*, London, 1940.
—. 'Marriage of near kin among Tswana', *Africa* 7, 1957, pp. 139–59.
Schneider, H.K. *The Wahi Wanyaturu: Economics in an African Society*, Chicago, 1970.
Seers, D. *The Meaning of Development*, Agricultural Development Council Reprint, 1972, pp. 1–11.
Seidman, A. 'The inherited dual economics of East Africa', in *Socialism in Tanzania*, Vol. 2, ed. by Lionel Cliffe and John Saul, Nairobi, 1972, pp. 41–64.
Simons, H.J. *African Women: Their Legal Status in South Africa*, London, 1968.
Smith, M.G., and Kuper, L. *Pluralism in Africa*, 1969.
Sohier, J. *Traité élémentaire de droit coutumier du Congo belge*, Brussels, 1954 (2e édition).
—. *Répertoire genéral de la jurisprudence et de la doctrine coutumière du Congo belge et du Ruanda-Urundi jusqu'au 31 décembre 1953*, Brussels, 1957.
—. *Institutes coutumières katangaises*, Elizabethville, 1964.
Southall, A.W. (ed.). *Social Change in Modern Afriea*, London, 1961.
Stefanisyn, B. *Social and Ritual Life of the Ambo in North Rhodesia*, London, 1964.
Stephens, H.W. *The Political Transformation of Tanganyika, 1920–1967*, New York, Washington and London, 1968.
Stewart, J.M. 'Akan history: some linguistic evidence', *Ghana Notes and Queries*, No. 8, 1966.
Stokes, E. 'Barotseland: the survival of an African state', in: *The Zambesian Past*, ed. by E. Stokes and R. Brown, Manchester, 1966.
Sutton, J.E.G. 'The peopling of Tanzania', in: *A History of Tanzania*, ed. by I.N. Kimambo and A.J. Temu, Dar es Salaam, 1969.
Szentes, Tamás. *The Political Economy of Underdevelopment*, Budapest, 1971.
Tanner, R.E.S. *The Selective Use of Legal Systems in East Africa*, Uppsala, 1970.
Tanner, N. 'Disputing and the genesis of legal principles: example from Minangkabua', *Southwestern Journal of Anthropology* 26, 1970, pp. 375–401.
Taylor, J.C. *The Political Development of Tanganyika*, Stanford, Calif. and London, 1963.
Thierry, von. *Deutsches Kolonial Blatt*, Bond 1899, No. 10.
Turay, A.K. 'Loan words in Temne', unpublished Ph.D thesis, School of Oriental and African Studies, University of London, 1971.
Turner, V.W. *Schism and Continuity in an African Society*, Manchester, 1957.
—. *Ndembu Divination: Its Symbols and Techniques*, Manchester, 1961.
—. *Chihamba: The White Spirit*, Manchester, 1962.
—. *The Drums of Affliction*, London, 1968.
Van Binsbergen, W.M.J. 'Bituma: Preliminary notes on a healing cult among the Nkoya', paper read at the Conference on the History of Central-African Religious Systems, Lusaka, 1972.
—. 'Kinship, marriage and urban-rural relations', paper read at the Seminar on New Directions in African Family Law, Leiden, 1974 (partly included in the present volume, Chapter 3).

—. 'Ethnicity as a dependent variable: The 'Nkoya' ethnic identity and inter-ethnic relations in Zambia', paper read at the 34th Annual Meeting, Society for Applied Anthropology, Amsterdam, 1975; revised version forthcoming in *African Social Research*.

—. 'Ritual, class, and urban-rural relations: elements for a Zambian case study', *Cultures et Développement* 8, 1976a, 2.

—, and Van Velsen, J. 'Labour migration and the generation conflict: an essay on social change in Western Zambia, *Cultures et Développement* 8, 1976b, 4.

—. 'The dynamics of religious change in Western Zambia', *Ufahamu* 7, 1976c.

—. 'Explorations into the history and sociology of territorial cults in Zambia', in: J. M. Schoffeleers (ed.). *Guardians of the Land: Essays on Central-African Territorial Cults*, Gwelo (in press).

Van der Laan, H. L. *The Sierra Leone Diamonds*, London, 1965.

Vansina, J. *The Tio Kingdom of the Middle Congo, 1880–1892*, London, 1973.

Van Velsen, J. *The Politics of Kinship*, Manchester, 1964.

Van de Walle, E. 'The relation of marriage to fertility in African demographic inquiries', *Demography* 2, 1965, pp. 302–08.

Watson, W. *Tribal Cohesian in a Money Economy*, Manchester, 1958.

Werbner, R. 'Constitutional ambiguities and the British administration of royal careers among the Bemba of Zambia', in: *Law in Culture and Society*, ed. by Nader, Chicago, 1969.

Wilks, I. 'A note on the chronology and origins of the Gonja Kings', *Ghana Notes and Queries*, No. 8, 1966.

Zech, Graf von. 'Land und Leute an der Nordwest Grenze von Togo', *Mitteilungen des deutschen Schutzgebietes*, 1904, Heft 17: 107–135.